# SAIL PLAN OF A FULLY RIGGED SKIPJACK

Rosie Parks, a two-sail bateau (skipjack) built in Wingate, Maryland, in 1955 by Bronza Parks. Drawing by Leavenworth Holden based on an earlier drawing by J. G. Lord. (Courtesy of Chesapeake Bay Maritime Museum)

# Chesapeake Bay Skipjacks

Happy Birthday
from

Mom + Dad

# Chesapeake Bay
# Skipjacks

*Text and Photographs by Pat Vojtech*

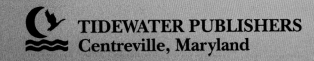

**TIDEWATER PUBLISHERS**
**Centreville, Maryland**

Library of Congress Cataloging-in-Publication Data

Vojtech, Pat.
    Chesapeake Bay skipjacks / by Pat Vojtech. — 1st ed.
       p.   cm.
    Includes bibliographical references and index.
    ISBN 0-87033-451-4
    1. Skipjacks.    2. Oyster fisheries — Chesapeake Bay.    I. Title.
VM431.V65    1993
387.2′8 — dc20

                                              93–29666
                                                CIP

*Photos*

*Facing page i*—The *Virginia W,* one of the last working sailboats in the United States, sails home to Tilghman Island after a day harvesting oysters in the Choptank River.

*Title page spread*—The *Kathryn,* with Captain Russell Dize, dredging at dawn in the upper Chesapeake Bay.

*Page v*—Skipjacks dredge off Howell Point in the Choptank River.

*Page vi*—The *Thomas Clyde,* captained by Lawrence Murphy, hauls up two dredges after a lick across the oyster bar in the lower Choptank River.

*Page 1*—Continuing a dying art, a skipjack captain works an oyster bar in the Choptank River under sail power alone. Of the hundreds of skipjacks built to dredge in the Chesapeake since just before the turn of the century, only twenty vessels were still working the bars in 1992.

Manufactured in China
First edition, 1993; second printing, 2000

# CONTENTS

*To the Chesapeake Bay
skipjack captains*

# PREFACE

*One day planting, I run up there on the top of the cabin to help knock some [oysters] off. That boom come in and switches me right overboard in forty feet of water. I had this big, heavy rig on and rubber coat on top of all my other clothes. It hit me right back behind the neck and I went overboard head first. I went right on down to the bottom. I like to lost all my breath before I come up to the top. My brother-in-law, Little John, wanted to turn the yawl boat loose and let me swim to it, but Skiggs got a rowboat and come and got me.*

—Captain Jesse Thomas about the day when he nearly drowned

ON A WARM autumn day in 1991, I walked into Scott's Cove Marina in Chance, across the Thorofare from Deal Island, looking for a retired skipjack captain. I had just started work on a book about skipjacks and somebody had directed me to Eldon Willing, Jr., who owned the marina. Willing's father had owned the *Robert L. Webster*, the longest skipjack ever built, and Willing had owned the *Amy Mister.*

At the front of the store, two old men were seated in armchairs, whiling away the afternoon with small talk. Captain Willing was behind the counter, in a swivel chair at his desk. I introduced myself, explained my plan to write a book, and he invited me to have a seat.

I learned that he started working on the water at age nine, as did most sons of watermen years ago, and quit school at age fifteen to work full-time on the water.

"We didn't make much money, but I loved it out on the water. It isn't too bad of a life. You've got a lot of independence," he said.

After a while, I asked him if anyone had ever fallen overboard, a common danger in the business and a standard question in my interviews. Up until now, I had gotten all "no's" to this particular question, and I expected the same from Captain Willing. But as soon as the question was out, I knew I had touched on a sensitive issue. Captain Willing's eyes clouded over and he looked away. Then he began the story, what little of it he knew.

They were dredging near Sharp's Island Light in 1966 when a storm blew up on the Chesapeake Bay.

They had hauled in their dredges and were running for a safe harbor when Willing noticed that his uncle, who worked the middle deck on his skipjack, had disappeared. He looked back and saw him in the rough seas; he had fallen overboard.

Willing got in the rowboat, which skipjacks commonly hauled behind so that the crew could get back and forth to shore from an anchorage, and went after him.

"We thought he was going to get drowned in that little rowboat in that big sea," said Captain Norman Benton, who was dredging nearby with Captain Jesse Thomas.

Willing rowed as hard as he could through the big seas, but couldn't reach his uncle who, undoubtedly, was pulled under by his oilskins.

As Captain Willing talked softly in the back of the room, the old men at the front of the store must have gotten up and left. I didn't notice. Somewhere a clock ticked loudly. It was near quitting time, five o'clock. Captain Willing talked on for a while about how he quit dredging and sold his boat in 1973 when the government made captains pay unemployment tax on their men, but it was obvious to me that he no longer wanted to talk about skipjacks. As I got up to leave, thanking him for his time, Eldon Willing seemed lost in another world. I walked out with the unsettling feeling of having pried open a door on a memory he had long ago tried to put to rest.

Outside the sun was setting over Deal Island. I turned my car east toward home and watched in the

The *Wilma Lee*, with
Captain Robbie
Wilson at the helm,
dredges under sail.

rearview mirror as a blood red sun sank until it was absorbed by the sea of scarlet clouds on the horizon. During all the years I was growing up on the Eastern Shore and even during the half-dozen years I plied the Bay in a pleasure boat, I had never witnessed such a dramatic sunset. Perhaps it was the place, this island, so long home to the largest skipjack fleet on the Chesapeake, that made the difference—even in the brilliance of a sunset.

All day long, while interviewing captains on Deal, I had been amazed by the beauty and peace of this island in the Chesapeake. Maybe it was the autumn coolness that kept away the mosquitoes, or the breeze gently rustling the fields of untamed marsh grass consuming most of the island that made me fall in love with the place. Or maybe it was the handful of beautiful old homes that spoke of a long-ago era of prosperity, mixed in with a raggedy, unkempt waterfront of crooked wharves and shanty outbuildings that I found so naturally attractive. Even the wooden boat graveyard which stretched across hundreds and hundreds of yards of marsh was a picture of beauty. I had often heard people refer to these islands on the lower Shore as little pieces of paradise dropped into the Chesapeake. I didn't believe it until that day.

Over the next eighteen months, I interviewed some thirty men whose memories of captaining dredge boats went back as few as two years and as many

as seventy-five. Most of them had fond memories of their dredging days. Even when they spoke of their battles with nature and their fights to survive hurricanes, floods, sinkings, ice floes, and falls overboard, the captains reminisced with a certain sparkle in their eyes. They obviously treasured these memories, spiced with the challenge, struggle, and triumph that makes a lifetime worth looking back upon with satisfaction.

That they were all willing to take the time to share their stories with me is something for which I will always be grateful. Having lived on the Eastern Shore all my life, with the skipjacks a constant part of the colorful background here, and having written about them from time to time during my career as a newspaper reporter, I was particularly interested in learning the full story of the skipjack and photographing the remaining boats. I never expected to get this opportunity nor, if I finally did, to receive such cooperation from the men and women whose lives were so intimately tied to the history of dredging.

My only regret is that I entered Captain Willing's store that day—not that I didn't want to hear another story of struggle and death over an oyster bar; I have heard quite a few over the year and a half I worked on this book. But that story had a price. That warm autumn afternoon, I walked uninvited into a man's life and with a single, rather insensitive, question ruined his day.

# Chesapeake Bay Skipjacks

The last sloop hull working the oyster bars under sail, the *Rebecca T. Ruark* has carried a skipjack rig for most of her years. Built in 1886, she is the oldest dredge boat in the fleet and was refurbished by Captain Wade Murphy, Jr., in 1986.

# RESCUE ABOARD *REBECCA*

*When in cold and freezing weather we sit by a cheerful open grate, and take in its genial warmth, and enjoy a delicious stew taken from the bars on Great Rock or the Middles, we little imagine the suffering and danger to which the dredger has been exposed to supply this part of our comfort, yet in part of both discomfort and danger he has been much more exposed than the miner who procured the coal.*
—Joseph B. Seth, Commander of the Maryland State Fishery Force, February 1, 1892

EVEN BEFORE the man fell overboard, it had been a bad day.

At dawn, a slit in the dark cloud bank let a spray of red sunlight shoot heavenward. The light lasted long enough for the tall, raked mast of the *Hilda M. Willing* to slide across the morning sun, silhouetted in the red dawn. Then the sun climbed behind the clouds to stay.

Off and on in the last hour, the gray sky had rained over the three skipjacks working the oyster bars in the lower Choptank River. It was a teasing sort of drizzle from a sky that promised worse.

Rain meant drudgery. It meant the skipjack crews, already working down on their knees to pick healthy oysters out of a pile of shell, mud, and debris dredged from the river bottom and dumped on deck, had to wear heavy oilskins. The decks were slick. The men were constantly leaning over the rail to dip up buckets full of seawater and slosh it on deck to wash away the mud that ran in streams from the dredge piles.

The rain caused problems with equipment, too. Downriver from the *Hilda M. Willing* and the *Thomas Clyde*, the crew of the *Rebecca T. Ruark* was having problems with the winder engine that hauls in the dredges. Now, as the two dredges clattered on deck, it sputtered one last time and failed for good.

Six crewmen leaned over the steaming engine. After the deafening roar of the winders, the silence was eerie. Now the only noise was the rhythmic thumping of *Rebecca*'s hull against the waves as, free of the dredges, she gained momentum. One of the men retrieved a belt that had spun loose. Seconds ticked away as they studied the problem inside the engine box.

Captain Wade Murphy could wait no longer. "Throw the dredges over," he yelled to them.

Several of them turned to stare at him.

"Throw 'em over," Murphy repeated.

No one moved.

Suddenly Murphy leaped on deck and grabbed a dredge.

"The winder's broke," a crewman shouted at him. For a moment, it looked like a fight would erupt as the men exchanged words. Then the captain, ignoring the crewman, threw one dredge overboard, and someone threw the other. The steel cable rattled out as the dredges sunk to the river bottom. Murphy turned abruptly and went back to the wheel.

*Rebecca* slowed against the weight of the two dredges as they filled with mud, oysters, and shell. Finally, she shuddered and ground to a halt. Now there was no sound at all but an occasional crackle of canvas as *Rebecca,* sails puffed full of wind as if sailing before a stiff breeze, lay dead in the water, anchored to the bottom by her dredges.

Murphy popped a Pepsi top and descended into the cabin to find a sandwich. He often played tough in front of his crew, but it bothered him when they second-guessed him. He knew how quickly things went wrong on a skipjack. Two men had died falling off *Rebecca* in years past, when she belonged to another captain. And just the year before, a crewman had taken a wrong step while working the middle deck on *Rebecca* and had fallen overboard. Fortunately, the man had grabbed hold of the winder cable and the crew was able to haul him back on deck.

"I worry about the crew getting hurt," Murphy confided while recounting another close call. He had been "spatting," moving seed oysters in the Choptank River during the early seventies in his old boat, the *Sigsbee*. Like all skipjacks, then and now, the *Sigsbee*'s only source of power was a little yawl boat equipped with an automobile engine. Whenever the skipjack dredges under sail, the yawl, also called a push boat, hangs from davits at the stern of the workboat. To use the engine, a skipjack crew must lower the yawl into the water and position its bow against an old tire or a V-shaped chock of wood at the stern of the skipjack. Then the yawl pushes the big boat like a tugboat pushes a barge.

They had been pushing ahead of a strong nor'-wester, the engine running at three-quarters throttle, when the weather began to moderate. Murphy decided to slow the engine. Today, a skipjack captain would simply reach for the throttle lever rigged forward from the engine to the skipjack. But back in the seventies, the controls were still located on the engine itself. A man had to climb back into the push boat to increase or reduce the throttle.

Since his crew was inexperienced with handling the push boat, Murphy jumped in the yawl himself. He was reaching for the throttle lever when a gas line broke, spraying fuel all over him. When the gas hit the hot engine, it burst into flames, setting both the engine and the captain on fire. Murphy leaped out of the push boat into the river to douse his burning skin and clothes. With one hand, he held onto the yawl. If he had let go, he might have sunk to the bottom in his heavy oilskins before anyone could have reached him. The intense heat imprinted his watch on the wrist of the hand he used to grip the boat. Finally, he grabbed the boat with the other hand, doused his burning arm, and hauled himself back into the yawl. The engine was still on fire. He had to put it out before the engine blew up or set the skipjack ablaze.

The crew threw him a fire extinguisher, but Murphy couldn't get it to work. He tossed it overboard and

Captain Lawrence Murphy looks on anxiously as the crew of the *Rebecca T. Ruark* try to rescue Mike Irwin, who had just fallen off the *Thomas Clyde* into the Choptank River.

*Left,* the crew of the *Rebecca T. Ruark* haul Mike Irwin aboard. Mike, *center photo and at far right,* recovered quickly, thanks in part to the mild December weather.

they threw him another. This one worked and the fire went out as soon as the chemical foam hit it.

Fifteen years later, the captain still feels certain that if he'd sent his sixteen-year-old crew into the yawl that day, the boy would have died.

These concerns often played on his mind as he watched the water for signs of shifts in the wind and current, and watched his crew for signs of careless-ness or playful behavior. When the men moved slug-gishly or failed to do a job right, Murphy was likely to get angry with them. And if they played, throwing shells at each other until someone got mad enough to throw a fist, Wade Murphy had been known to drop his sails, head to port, and fire the culprits on the spot.

But while the crew on *Rebecca* occasionally balked at his orders, they respected Murphy's judgment. A third-generation skipjack captain with thirty-five years of experience on a dredge boat, Wade Murphy knew as much as anyone about the dying art of dredging oysters under sail. In earlier years, he had dredged with nothing to guide him but a knowledge of the oyster bars, handed down to him by his father and grand-father, and by the feel of the dredge; crewmen would sit on the cables to feel—literally through the seat of their pants—whether the dredges were hitting good oysters or mud and debris.

In recent years, however, Murphy and other skip-jack captains had gone high-tech, equipping their old

wooden vessels with modern lorans that plotted lati-tude and longitude, and video depth-sounders that clearly showed changes in the river bottom.

The day the winder engines failed, he was work-ing an "edge," the outer fringes of an oyster bar often left unharvested when dredgers work a bar. Even with the modern equipment, however, it took time to find these narrow clumps of shellfish, and with oysters scarce in 1991, Murphy knew that if *Rebecca* sailed off this edge, he might waste the rest of the day trying to find as good a lick of oysters as the one he was on now.

Murphy knew how badly the young men on his boat needed the money. While a life of following the water has its rewards, there are many weeks in the year when watermen are forced to stay in port due to bad weather. Occasionally, a skipjack will hit a good "lick," the weather will hold out, and the crew will harvest enough oysters to have money left over after they pay their bills. But in recent years, as disease and parasites snuffed life out of the Chesa-peake's once-bountiful shellfish population, good licks had become scarce. Dredging oysters had be-come more often a life of drudgery: long days, start-ing before dawn and ending after sunset, working in bitter cold far away from home and families. When they weren't hauling the dredges aboard or culling oysters, the crew often would huddle around the winder engine, warming their hands on the engine heat and drying their gloves over the exhaust pipe.

No one makes money on a skipjack unless oysters pile up on deck, including the crew which gets a cut of the harvest docked each day. One-third of the total goes directly to the boat to pay for upkeep, which can run upwards from $3,000 a year. The remainder is split between the crew and captain, after expenses such as fuel and food are taken out.

In the winter of 1991-92, crews aboard a skipjack could still make between $100 and $150 apiece per day on push days, if they could only keep the winder engine running and hit a decent lick. But whether you made money or not, "drudgin'," as watermen call it, has always been hard, cold, dirty work.

Unlike in other jobs, dredgers can't make up lost time at the end of a day. The oyster industry in Maryland waters on the Chesapeake is highly regulated to prevent overharvesting the dwindling delicacy. At three o'clock on sail days, dredgers have to quit—wind or no wind, oysters on deck or not. This was on the mind of all the men aboard *Rebecca* as they raced against an invisible clock that ticked away lost time and lost wages.

It was just starting to breeze up when the winder engine roared into life and the dredges clattered aboard. *Rebecca,* as if roused from a midday nap, moved sluggishly at first, then rapidly gathered speed. Whitecaps were breaking the surface of the water as the wind picked up to twelve, maybe fifteen, knots. Captain Murphy yelled, "Hey," and the crew grabbed the dredges on either side of the boat and, with a long-practiced dip-and-rise motion, shoved them overboard. A few seconds later, *Rebecca* shuddered as the iron teeth dug into the oyster bar. Then she bore down into the water and pulled ahead, powered only by the wind in her sails. For several long minutes she pulled and pulled against the increasingly heavy load of the dredges until, just as it seemed she could pull no more, Captain Murphy tugged on the engine throttle. Two men pushed down the steel clutch handles on the winders, which began to spin in cable. One dredge, then the other, broke the surface of the water at mid-deck, leaking mud and dirty water back into the river as the crew jerked the dredges up and down in the river, washing away mud before hauling the new harvest of oysters aboard.

*Rebecca,* free again, leaped ahead. For a minute or two or three, she gathered her speed on a fast broad reach, slicing easily through the light chop until, finally, the captain reached for the big wooden-spoked wheel finished in brass that is as old as *Rebecca*—104.

He grabbed hold of one spoke, and putting all his weight behind it, spun the wheel round. Then he spun it again. *Rebecca* balked, then reluctantly she started to turn, first into the wind until her sails fluttered and her big boom shifted from starboard to port, then off the wind until her dirty white Dacron sails filled again on a new tack. She had made a U-turn and was again on a path that would carry her past the black-and-white plastic bottles anchored with old engine parts that Murphy used to mark their best "lick," or harvest, of the day.

The captain made it look easy: just sail back and forth across the same strip of oyster bar on a comfortable broad reach, making sharp U-turns every quarter-mile or so. On the two days a week when dredgers are allowed to harvest oysters under power, with the yawl boat pushing the dredge boat across the bars, it is a fairly easy job.

Sail dredging was a whole different ball game, however, especially when oysters were scarce and a good lick might only be a few yards wide. Without an engine to power her, the skipjack could easily be pushed off course by a strong current or a gust of wind. A captain was constantly compensating for these fluctuations with a spin of the wheel. Occasionally, wind and current were equal in strength, canceling each other's effect on the vessel, then dredgers would have near-perfect sailing conditions. But it never lasted long; the tide is always rising or falling; the wind is seldom steady and dependable.

Murphy kept one eye out for his buoys, one eye on the depth-sounder. As the bottom line on the depth-sounder rose, noting a hill or, perhaps, a clump of oysters, he yelled, "Hey, windward, hey, lu'ward," and the dredges smacked the water.

*Rebecca,* who had just regained her speed, shuddered as if in irritation, slowed abruptly, then started to pull again. While it appeared to be the dredges that slowed her down, the captain was regulating the speed of the boat by turning slightly into the wind to slow her as the dredges were hauled aboard, off the wind to let her gain momentum for the turn.

Even on a rainy day, the constant motion of a skipjack under sail, the feel of its tremendous power as it drags its dredges, and the sight of its sails aloft, even though they may be patched and splattered in mud, is a captivating scene. Particularly on *Rebecca*.

Built in 1886, just before the advent of the skipjack on the dredging scene, *Rebecca* had the gently rounded lines of a sloop, unlike most of the skipjacks in the fleet which have boxy hulls. But while her rounded hull is more pleasing to the eye and more seaworthy than the V-bottom of a skipjack, it's also much more expensive to rebuild. *Rebecca* should have suffered the fate of the other round-bottomed sloops and bugeyes which, one by one, were sailed up a gut to die. But in 1984, Wade Murphy bought her from Emerson Todd at Cambridge and sailed her leaking hull back to Tilghman Island, and later down to Deltaville, Virginia, to have her rebuilt. Over the next two years, the price of *Rebecca's* restoration grew and grew until it had cost Murphy all his savings and a mortgage on his home. She was still unfinished when Murphy finally sailed her out of the boatyard, and brought her home to Tilghman where a friend helped complete the topside work.

For her hundredth birthday, *Rebecca* had a new lease on life, but the price tag for her salvation had been staggering: close to $100,000.

In time, *Rebecca* proved a powerful enough workhorse to pay back her owner with good harvests, despite a scarcity of oysters in the late eighties. In the meantime, financing an expensive lady like *Rebecca* was something else to worry the captain. Despite her cost, however, Murphy obviously enjoyed sailing her.

"The *Sigsbee*, she would rip my guts out," said Murphy, referring to the effort it took to keep his old, flat-bottomed skipjack sailing a straight course. "*Rebecca* can sail herself." When Murphy speaks of *Rebecca*, it is with a reverence one usually reserves for someone who deserves respect, and that's exactly how Murphy treats the old boat. A race—whether an organized event or an impromptu run from the oyster bar to market—was a challenge to her honor. If he lost, it made him miserable and he blamed it on himself. "I let the ole lady down," he said once, after running aground in a race off Tilghman Island.

"Wadie, he loves that boat," one captain noted.

Unlike some of the present-day skipjack captains who got into dredging for the money when oysters were plentiful in the seventies, Wade Murphy comes from a long line of dredgers who passed on to their sons their intense love of sailing.

Murphy was only sixteen when he quit school to work the middle deck on his father's skipjack, the *George W. Collier*. "It blowed a gale, nor'west and rain, solid rain, for three days. I thought, 'God almighty, I'll go back to school and to hell with this,'" he remembers. Then, the skies finally cleared, the weather moderated, and Murphy decided to stay aboard after all.

Captain Wade Murphy, Jr., at the helm of the *Rebecca T. Ruark*, may not have reached Mike in time if the crew of the *Thomas Clyde* hadn't moved quickly to throw him a life jacket.

That was 1957, when more than eighty skipjacks plied the waters of the Chesapeake. Back then, captaining a skipjack was still largely a skill passed down from father to son. But in the 1990s, with about twenty dredgers left working, many new captains didn't have the benefit of a long apprenticeship under a father's watchful eye. They bought a boat and learned it the hard way: by trial and error and by talking with other captains.

Then, some new captains, like Lawrence Murphy, dredging north of his cousin, Wade, in the Choptank, had grown up with dredge boat captains in their family and had worked on skipjacks in their youth before going on to do other things on the water. Lawrence Murphy had hand tonged, patent tonged, and clammed, but he had always wanted a dredge boat.

"They make good money at it," said Lawrence, who knew that dredging could pay better than other occupations on the water, at least when oysters were plentiful. He bought the fifty-five-foot *Thomas Clyde* in November 1991, for $25,000 from a Deal Island family. The boat was in fair shape, so Lawrence Murphy put her to work right away.

On this warm December day in 1991, Lawrence had been at the helm of the big skipjack only three weeks. The wind breezed up and he told his crew to shorten, or reef, the mainsail, a procedure that involves dropping the sail several feet and tying reef points all along the bottom of the sail to literally shorten the triangular sail. One of the crew, Mike Irwin, was out on the davits (the metal assembly from which the push boat hangs when it's not in use) tying the last reef point, when another crewman walked by and knocked against the sheet (the line that regulates the angle of the mainsail to the wind). The sheet was led through a block that travels back and forth across a traveler rod, an iron bar attached to the stern deck, as the boat changes tack and the boom swings from one side of the boat to the other. Knocking the sheet would have been no problem, except that this time the block had jammed on the wrong side of the bar. When the man hit the sheet, the block unjammed and slid several feet across the traveler, allowing the boom to fall out a few more inches. It was just enough that Irwin, stretched out over the water to reach the last reef, lost his balance and fell into the river.

"Wadie," Lawrence shouted over the VHF radio to his cousin on *Rebecca*. "I got a man overboard."

Wade hesitated, trying to decipher the muddle on the radio, then reached for the mike. "What'd ya say, Lawrence?" he asked.

"Man overboard."

Wade hollered at his crew, motioning them to the stern. He knew someone had to reach the man in two, maybe three, minutes, otherwise the heavy oilskins would cling to the man and suck him under. Over the past century, too many dredgers had died this way, pulled to the bottom by their own work clothes. Fear of drowning is why dredgers work in loose boots they can kick off instantly if they go overboard. No one laces up their boots onboard a skipjack.

Later, Wade would realize what an impossible task it was for his crew to save a man in the water so far away. Not only did they have to cover a distance of about a quarter-mile, but they also had to lower the push boat and position it against the stern.

Aaron, a young, spry crewman, leaped into the push boat as the rest of the crew lowered the boat to the water and positioned it in its chock against the skipjack's stern. Someone let loose the main halyard and the mainsail dropped to the boom. The whole procedure took only about a minute, but it was one minute gone.

*Rebecca* was steaming toward the *Thomas Clyde* when the radio brought the news: "He's got the life jacket, thank God." Lawrence's voice was shaking. Someone on the *Thomas Clyde* had thrown Irwin a life jacket and he was clinging to it when *Rebecca* pulled up alongside him. Six pairs of hands reached down to drag him aboard. He came up dripping wet and coughing.

As they got the man aboard, Wade recognized him as a relative he had helped rear ten years earlier. As a youth, Mike had lived with the Murphys on Tilghman Island and worked with Wade, crabbing in the summertime. He was a little guy, no more than 140 pounds soaking wet. He leaned over and coughed for a minute or two, then he straightened. He was shaking with cold under his black oilskins, but he seemed okay. He was lucky. It had been unseasonably warm for December. Working on the water in the winter, many men who fall overboard drown because the icy waters numb them, and they can't even grab a life ring.

He was lucky, too, to be so small. The tattered life jacket lying on *Rebecca*'s deck was waterlogged and ripped almost to shreds. "It wouldn'a' held up anyone heavier than Mike," observed Kenny, who had fallen off *Rebecca* the year before.

The two skipjacks, *Rebecca* and the *Thomas Clyde*, moved gently together. Mike, insisting he was all right, crawled out on *Rebecca*'s push boat, already hoisted to her davits in preparation for sail dredging again, and got back aboard the *Thomas Clyde*. "Give me a hug, boy," Lawrence said, as the two boats separated.

Wade had already turned *Rebecca* onto a broad reach, heading back to his buoys, back to work, when the big husky blond captain embraced his young crewman. A few minutes later, Mike was on the radio. "Wadie, thanks."

"I didn't save you," Wade said. "That life jacket saved you."

The wind freshened and whitecaps blanketed the river as the crew on *Rebecca* went back to work. The gray sky began to sweat. Wade Murphy shouted over the clatter of the winder engines, "Next time we come about, reef the main."

The men jumped to the task, dropping the mainsail several feet, tying off the halyard. They threw the dredges overboard and then lined up along the boom to tie reef points in the sail. The captain reached for the throttle line and the cable spun in; the dredges clattered aboard; the men emptied them and culled through the pile, tossing good oysters off to the side. As *Rebecca* rounded into the wind, making her familiar U-turn, the crew didn't need to be reminded of the main, which had been left sagging so as not to lose precious time holding the boat into the wind to haul up the sail. Now, in the few seconds it took *Rebecca* to tack, three men grabbed the halyard and hauled down with all their weight, heaving and wrestling the huge, luffing sail snug again the masthead before she filled with wind again on a new tack. *Rebecca*'s sails billowed out, powering the fifty-two-foot hull through the increasingly rough chop.

Back at work, no one played or dragged their feet. No one second-guessed the captain. They all knew what could have happened and what has happened all too often on this Bay and its tributaries. For centuries these murky Chesapeake waters had been rich in seafood—crabs, clams, and dozens of species of fish—but none had been more prized than the oyster. Locked tight in a hard shell and quick to die in heat, the oyster forced men to work in the bitter cold, unpredictable winter. Like all valuable things, even those provided by Nature, there is a price to pay: hard work, long hours, bad weather and, on occasion, life, itself.

Today, the price had not been so high.

Captain Lawrence Murphy reacts to the rescue.

The skipjack's big mainsail rides up the solid pine mast on wooden hoops which allow it to be quickly dropped in an approaching squall. The rig is the same one used at the turn of the century when boatbuilders on the Eastern Shore would choose masts from among the straightest, strongest trees in the old growths of heart pine.

# One

# BEFORE THE SKIPJACK

*It's like chasing the rainbow, looking for a pot of gold.*
—Captain Art Daniels about dredging

For the last hour, the watermen in the log canoes had been watching the steady progress of the four vessels as they sailed before a fair wind up Tangier Sound. The watermen talked about the foreign schooners as they dipped their long, wooden shaft tongs into the shallow waters around Smith Island, scraping about until they found what felt like a good clump of oysters. Then, operating the tongs like a pair of pliers, they lifted the oysters out of the water and dumped them onto their boats. It was a back-breaking, tedious job that seldom rewarded two watermen working together with even as much as forty or fifty bushels at the end of a day.

The four big vessels were within a quarter-mile of the watermen when they suddenly altered course, turning on a reach to the steady ten-knot breeze. The schooners were close enough that the watermen could hear the shouts of the crew as they blocked in their sails and lowered a clattering iron device into the water. Several of the men in the log canoes leaned on their tongs and squinted against the sun at the vessels, trying to catch every detail about this unusual contraption that the boats appeared to be pulling on a long line or cable. After a few minutes they saw the men aboard the ships feverishly working on deck, and then the steel device broke the surface of the water. Now the watermen of Smith Island could clearly see the prize that these Yankees were after: oysters filled the bags of the dredge to overflowing. The bags came up so full of shellfish that oysters slipped off the top of the scoop as the men heaved and grunted against the hand winders,

wrestling hundreds of pounds of metal and shellfish aboard ship. The pile of oysters that splattered on deck as two men turned the device upside down was enough to make the wonder in the eyes of the Smith Islanders turn to worry. There must have been hundreds of fat oysters lying on deck. In a few minutes, there were more oysters aboard a single Yankee schooner than they could harvest in an hour with their hand tongs.

The Smith Islanders poled their boats together to talk amongst themselves.

So, this was the "drudge" they had heard so many rumors about around the islands of the lower Chesapeake. The men of Tangier had talked about the Yankees who raped the rich oyster bottoms of the Pocomoke Sound with their drudges. When their boats were laden to the gunwales, they would turn south again toward the mouth of the Chesapeake, carrying thousands of bushels of Chesapeake oysters home to New York and Massachusetts, where they had already depleted the oyster bars with this new invention. And now they had moved north into Maryland, prompted by the actions of the Virginia legislature which had banned dredging in Virginia waters during its last session in 1810.

The Smith Islanders fell silent as they watched the vessels sailing rapidly back and forth across the oyster bar, hauling the dredges loaded with oysters aboard every few minutes. Within an hour, the oyster piles were knee deep on deck. So, the rumors they had heard were accurate; the Yankees certainly appeared to be scraping the oyster bars clean.

Reluctantly, the islanders went back to work, but the tongs that had served them so well a few hours earlier now seemed clumsy and inadequate. Ever since they could remember, the men of the islands had been content to hand tong for oysters, a labor-intensive job they executed from log canoes, boats fifteen to thirty feet long, built with three to five logs that were hewn to the shape of a canoe, and equipped with sails that helped carry them to and from the oyster bars. On the low-lying islands, there was little land to plant, and no other means of making a livelihood in the winter, unless they hunted the thousands of ducks that descended on the marshes during the cold months. Oystering was almost the only means the men had of making a living on these isolated, marshy islands.

Consequently, the appearance in the early nineteenth century of Yankee ships, whose captains were intent on taking thousands of bushels of Chesapeake oysters using a device called a dredge, was a real threat to the Chesapeake watermen, struggling all day with their tongs to harvest a few oysters out of the shallow waters of the lower Eastern Shore.

The Yankees weren't interested in the local oyster market or the livelihoods of the Chesapeake watermen. They had markets for the oysters up north, where their own natural resource had become depleted. In fact, it was the depletion of oysters in New England waters and the continued high demand for the succulent delicacy that encouraged the Yankees to turn their schooners south toward the Chesapeake. To

harvest the oysters quickly and efficiently, the Yankees brought with them the same device that had so effectively wiped clean their own oyster bars.

The dredge was a scooping device, attached to a sailing vessel with rope or cable. It was thrown overboard when the vessel was over an oyster bar, and dragged along the bottom until its bag filled with oysters. Then men working a hand winch, or windlass, cranked in the line until the dredge was hauled aboard the vessel at midship. Two dredges, dragged on either side of the vessel, could scoop up several bushels in one "lick" across the oyster bar. Tongers, by contrast, had to work all day to harvest a few dozen bushels of oysters.

Smith Islanders had good reason to worry. Within a few short decades, the dredge, like no other

*Left,* the *Lady Katie,* a traditional two-sail bateau dredging beside the *Mamie A. Mister, right,* a three-sail bateau.

maritime invention, other than the engine, would alter the course of history for Chesapeake watermen and the shellfish they sought so persistently to harvest. For many who lived in the poverty-stricken marshes off the Eastern Shore, it would bring prosperity; for others, it would wreak pain and death. But for now, the invasion by Yankee dredgers was met with tremendous hostility. In 1810, Virginia, hit first and hardest by the Yankee invasion, prohibited foreigners (which included New Englanders) from dredging in its waters. That only encouraged the Yankee captains to sail farther north up the Chesapeake into Maryland waters, where they took what they wanted for another ten years, carrying tens of thousands of bushels of oysters home to New England. Sometimes the oysters were sold, but many were used to reseed the depleted oyster bars up north.

Maryland finally banned dredging and transporting oysters out of state in 1820, and when the dredge stirred up feuds between Marylanders and Virginians who used it illegally, Maryland legislators banned it again in 1833. Regardless of the law, however, dredgers continued to operate on a limited basis until the Civil War erupted in 1861, disrupting commerce and the fishery industry. When the war ended, it brought a new climate to Maryland. Somerset County had already authorized the use of a smaller dredge-like device, called a scrape, in its waters in 1854. No doubt, the economic success of the scrape in Somerset County won over watermen who joined businessmen in lobbying for legalization of the dredge. They got what they wanted in 1865 when Maryland passed a law permitting the use of the dredge, but only under sail and in waters too deep for tongers to harvest oysters. For the most part, dredgers worked out in the open waters of the Bay and sounds, while tongers continued to operate in shallower waters in rivers and creeks.

That first year, 391 vessels were licensed to dredge in Maryland alone. Ten years later, 691 dredging licenses were issued in Maryland, far outpacing the number of licenses issued for the smaller scrape, for which there were 429 licenses issued.

Dredging quickly became big business. In 1874, Orris A. Brown of the Virginia Oyster Force reported that in Pocomoke and Tangier sounds alone dredging afforded a living to 1,400 men "who received an average of $15 per month, making a monthly income of the labor alone of $21,000, and this, in an oyster season of nine months, amounts to $187,000." Brown estimated the total dollars generated by dredging in the region for both labor and capital at $289,000. "The oyster

Crew throw the dredge overboard, while another skipjack works nearby.

beds are paying about $29.50 per acre per year," he wrote, which was apparently a good income in that era.

Nine years after legalization of the dredge, oystering was fast becoming one of Maryland's biggest—and most violent—industries. Dredgers in big pungies, schooners, and sloops worked the Bay and its tidewaters in 1874. Overharvesting was already creating shortages of oysters in deeper waters set aside for the large dredge boats. While most dredgers were law-abiding people, some were opportunists who would slip into waters set aside by law for hand tonging, and steal oysters, often under cover of darkness or bad weather. Eventually, hand tongers, seeing their livelihood taken from them, fought back with shotguns and called upon the General Assembly to impose peace and order on the Bay. The state created an Oyster Navy in the late 1860s, but it would take more than twenty-five years and a scarcity of oysters to establish an uneasy peace with the dredgers.

Through the 1870s, watermen harvested at least nine million bushels of oysters annually from the Chesapeake and its tributaries. While oysters thrived in the

Chesapeake and its tributaries from the Potomac River north to Swan Point, located across the Bay from Baltimore, the two sounds off the lower Eastern Shore, with 9,700 acres of highly productive oyster bars, quickly became the hub of the oyster industry. Not only were the oysters in abundance in Pocomoke and Tangier sounds, but they were also considered of better quality than oysters in some parts of the Bay, according to early records of the Maryland Oyster Fisheries, which showed substantially better prices paid for oysters from this region.

Even as the dredge brought prosperity, however, there were deep concerns that it would deplete the natural resource here, as it had elsewhere. The dredge had already acquired a well-deserved bad reputation for destroying oyster bars in the English Channel, where it was developed, and later in New England waters.

In his report of the Oyster Fisheries of Maryland in 1874, William E. Timmons, commissioner of Maryland's Fishery Force, hoped to quell fears that the dredge could possibly deplete the Chesapeake's vast supply of oysters: "The Chesapeake Bay and the rivers emptying into it are said to produce more oysters than any other waters in the world of the same area," he wrote. In arguing in favor of dredging, Timmons observed that, along waters where dredging was permitted by law, communities prospered.

"There appears to be a marked difference in the price of real estate in those sections where they have local laws to dredge and scoop their oysters. Land is much higher on Deal's Island, Elliott's Island and Holland's Island, than it is on Poplar Island or Kent Island, where the oystermen confine themselves to tonging, and I think it grows out of the fact that where they scoop and dredge oysters the resources are utilized to the full capacity of the production of the oyster beds, which makes money more plenty in that particular section," Timmons wrote in his report on the oyster industry.

In the climate of abundance that prevailed in the 1870s, Timmons had only one suggestion for conservation of the oyster: "No one should be allowed to carry the old or dead shell ashore from the oyster beds—they should be left for the spawn to catch to," he said. His suggestion was ignored. Timmons even argued that the dredges promoted the growth of bigger, better, more edible oysters because they "thinned" the oyster bars—an opinion that is still held today by those who believe the patent tong, which bangs against the oyster rocks while it harvests the shellfish, has contributed far more to recent oyster population declines than the dredge.

"The only question to be settled is, 'will the oysters be destroyed by this fast way of catching them?' I think the time has not yet arrived to consider that question, nor will it be upon us until many of the beds in the Chesapeake Bay and its tributaries, that have not yet been touched by the dredgers or scoopers, are torn to pieces and made to produce oysters fit for market," Timmons told the Maryland General Assembly.

The time to settle that question, however, came much sooner than Timmons expected. Just a couple of years later, fewer and fewer vessels applied for dredging licenses and in 1879, the oyster industry suffered an economic nose dive. Only 327 dredging licenses were issued in Maryland, fewer even than were issued in 1865 when dredging was legalized.

A study by W. K. Brooks, an associate professor of biology at Johns Hopkins University, confirmed everyone's worst fears—oyster beds in Tangier and Pocomoke sounds, the Bay's most productive areas, were rapidly becoming depleted. Brooks suggested stiff regulations and policing of those regulations, the immediate closing of bars when they appeared overworked, and a new law that would force the return of shells to the bars so oyster young, known as spat, would continue to have hard surfaces to "set" on, thus improving oyster reproduction.

Few watermen paid any heed to Brooks's prediction of hard times ahead. The oyster industry quickly revived from its all-time low. Harvests on the Chesapeake wouldn't peak until 1884 when fifteen million bushels were taken from the Bay. That year also produced a record number of licensed dredge boats in Maryland: 955 vessels. Not surprisingly, two new vessels had evolved exclusively for dredging oysters— the bugeye and the smaller brogan. Both were originally built of logs, like the fifteen- to twenty-five-foot log canoes used by tongers. Eventually bugeyes were made of planks as virgin forests disappeared in the country and large timbers became scarcer.

It would be fifteen years before Brooks's prediction would come true. In 1889, 860 vessels were still dredging Maryland waters, but oyster harvests had declined considerably to 6.5 million bushels annually. The harvest continued to slip until 1891, when fewer than 4.4 million bushels were taken from the Bay and its tributaries.

Without the rich bounties of the past, captains could no longer afford to maintain large elaborate vessels for dredging. Almost overnight, the round-bottomed sloops and bugeyes, which took so much time and skill to create, ceased to be built. When dredgers began to order boats again, they would ask for an entirely different sort of vessel, one that had evolved from the flat- or V-bottomed bateaux that had become popular all along the East Coast in the 1870s and 1880s, and which were so easy to build that almost anyone could construct one in their backyard.

As early as 1883, a few Eastern Shore boatbuilders had begun to experiment with the cheaper V-bottom vessel. J. L. Harrison of Tilghman Island was one of the first boatbuilders to construct a dredge boat with the now familiar V-bottom or deadrise hull. In 1883, he built two vessels—*Lillie* and *Yttria*, both carrying two masts on forty-five-foot deadrise, or bateau, hulls. About 1888, the *Eva* was built in Cambridge by a man named Johnson. The builder used scrap lumber left over from the construction of the schooner *Rover* to build *Eva*, which had many characteristics of what would later be called a bateau, or skipjack. Cambridge dredgers considered *Eva* the first skipjack, according to Howard Chapelle, who spoke with her captain in the 1940s. Chapelle, who became one of the top authorities on boats, took off detailed lines of the dredge boats while living in Dorchester County and wrote the first comprehensive accounts of skipjacks.

*Eva* appears to have been a transitional hull; she originally carried the rig of a three-sail bateau, but her hull had many sloop characteristics, including frames and fore-and-aft planking.

Like so much in boatbuilding, it was an experiment, an attempt to build a cheaper boat that would still sail well enough to dredge oysters under sail. Evidently, the experiment worked. In 1891, the *Ruby G. Ford* was built in Fairmount. Somerset County dredgers remember her as the first bateau, which is what most Eastern Shoremen call the skipjack. By 1896, this new type of vessel was being built in dozens of boatyards and backyards on the Eastern Shore. For the next fifteen years, as steam and gasoline power steadily replaced the sail as a means of propulsion on most bodies of waters around the world, wooden boatbuilding thrived on the Chesapeake and, in particular, on the islands and marshy lowlands of the Eastern Shore where dredging was a major occupation.

The skipjack owed its creation and continued existence to the law of 1865 that forbade dredging by any power other than sail in Maryland. A hundred years later, long after the golden age of the sail had passed, that single law, written as a conservation measure some thirty years before the first skipjacks worked the oyster bars, would eventually help preserve a unique and fascinating way of life and encourage the preservation of one of this country's last remaining commercial sailing vessels: the skipjack.

The dredge, which Yankees brought to the Chesapeake in the early 1800s, has changed little since it was invented.

*Two*

# THE EARLY YEARS

*I remember working near Poplar Island when you could almost reach
out and touch a boat in every direction and we were all working
together with the sail . . . a hundred in a little section.*
      —Captain Art Daniels on the old days of sail dredging

**M**EN LOADING the dredge boats that tied up to Long Dock in Baltimore Harbor couldn't help but notice the unusual new type of boat that sailed in and out of the harbor with barely a breath of wind in her sails. It was short and beamy and could sail when other boats lay dead in the water. Then in the fall of 1901, so many of them descended on the port of Baltimore that the sight of the vessels, with their bright new masts and white canvas sails, prompted one reporter for the Baltimore *Sun* to write that it was as if "there had been a rain of them."

"Their quickness to go about may have earned for them the name of skipjack, which is applied by fishermen on the New England coast to the bonita, a fly[ing] member of the fish family, when bait is out," the reporter wrote.

The truth is, Eastern Shoremen who built the new boats called them bateaux. One Smith Islander never even heard the term "skipjack" until the thirties, which is not surprising since the term was never used on this isolated island in the Chesapeake that was a major home port for dredge boats. On the mainland, however, Eastern Shoremen had a boat they called a skipjack, but it wasn't a big dredge boat. It was a smaller sailboat, twenty-five or thirty feet long, which carried hand scrapes, smaller dredges hauled in by hand that were used for harvesting oysters or crabs. Smith Islanders called these boats hand scrapers or barcats. The old hand scrapers looked like miniature bateaux, which may have been what led to the misuse of the name by Baltimoreans at the turn of the century.

Despite the mistake, the city nickname is the one that eventually stuck—everywhere, that is, except in Somerset County, which produced more bateaux than any other region of the Shore. Today, the boats that sail over the oyster bars in the fall, with their sharply raked masts, long bowsprits, and simple sail design, may be what most people call a skipjack, but call them that in front of an old Crisfield dredger, and you'll likely see a little smirk on his face as he silently labels you as "city folk."

The bateau had features that made men in the oyster industry stop what they were doing and take notice.

"The proportions of the skipjack make it possible for the newcomer to turn within its own length, a fact of great value to the oyster dredging vessel," wrote a *Sun* reporter. He noted that the skipjack had been observed in Baltimore for "perhaps three years." In fact, Eastern Shoremen were building the bateaux in earnest by 1896 when at least twenty of this new style dredge boat set sail. For the next few years, hundreds of skipjacks were launched from boatyards on the Eastern Shore.

However, it's not surprising that the 1901 season caused quite a stir along the Baltimore wharves. More than sixty skipjacks, most of them thirty-eight to forty-five feet long on deck, were built that year. Never again would so many dredge boats be constructed in one year. Undoubtedly quite a few of them found their way from the marshy islands of the lower Eastern Shore to the wharves of Baltimore City.

Every year, a week or two before the November 1 opening of the dredging season, large fleets of dredge boats left the islands of Deal, Smith, Tangier and Tilghman on the Eastern Shore to be outfitted in Baltimore.

In 1896, there were just a handful of bateaux among the fleet of bugeyes, sloops, and schooners, but by 1910, the bateaux dominated the oyster bars.

Today, the skipjack is thought of as one of the prettiest vessels plying the Bay, but set against the magnificent schooners, pungies, and sloops that sailed the Chesapeake in the late 1800s, she was nothing more than a workhorse. The skipjack was specifically developed as a cheap, ugly half-sister of these other working craft.

In 1884 when oyster harvests peaked at fifteen million bushels and Maryland had its largest dredge fleet (955 vessels), a few boatbuilders were just beginning to experiment with the deadrise hull on a dredge boat. The cheaper bateau didn't catch on, however, until hard times hit the oyster industry in the 1890s.

The bateau with its simple flat or V-bottom could be built for about $600, half the cost of a sloop or bugeye which had an expensively framed, round-bottom hull. However, the skipjack, with its boxy hull, was not nearly as seaworthy as its predecessors, and was only expected to last half the life of the better-built dredge boats. But these drawbacks didn't matter to the captains of the 1890s who, after years of plenty, faced a severe shortage of oysters.

Even the rig of the skipjack was designed with economy in mind. Fewer crew members were needed to handle the fewer sails of a skipjack that was rigged more simply than the traditional sloops, which carried a gaff-rigged mainsail and a topsail for light winds. The skipjack had a small, self-tending jib and a huge triangular, or "leg-of-mutton," mainsail on a sharply raked mast. The mainsail rode up and down the mast on wooden hoops, so it could be dropped quickly in an approaching squall. But the main purpose for such a severely raked mast was probably twofold: it helps keep the sail's center of effort in a favorable position for dredging under varying wind conditions and points of sail, while still placing the top of the mast over the middle of the boat so it could be used as a primitive crane for the purpose of unloading bushels of oysters from the hold, or hull, of the dredge boat.

A few two-masted skipjacks, called three-sail bateaux, were built, but most disappeared over the years. The huge mainsail of the two-sail bateau was

The bateau or skipjack, showing the "leg-of-mutton" jib in foreground.

simply a superior rig in the light winds so characteristic of the Chesapeake, allowing the boat to catch more breeze and pull a dredge when three-sail bateaux with their smaller sails could not budge on the oyster bar.

Skipjacks generally were smaller than the bugeyes of the late 1800s, ranging in length on deck from thirty to sixty feet. However, the vast majority of the more than six hundred skipjacks built for dredging oysters were between thirty-eight and forty-eight feet on deck. A dozen or so measured between fifty-five and sixty feet, with lengths over seventy feet when bowsprits and stern counters were included. However, most of these bigger skipjacks were built around 1915 or later when boatbuilders discovered that the bigger hulls could still carry the two-sail rig, which dredgers

preferred, without the mainsail becoming too big and awkward for a relatively small crew to handle.

Through trial and error, boatbuilders at the turn of the century developed a simple formula for constructing a skipjack, and it was passed on by word of mouth: the beam or greatest width is equal to one-third the length of the boat on deck; the mast is the length of the boat on deck plus the boat's beam; the boom is the length of the boat on deck; the bowsprit equals the beam; and the width of the transom is equal to three-fourths the beam. The length of the centerboard equals one-third the length on deck, and the mast is raked about 75 degrees to the load waterline so that the top of the mast is directly over the point of the boat with the greatest beam. This is where the hatch is generally

located so that a halyard attached to the masthead could be used to lift bushels of oysters or other cargo out of the hold.

Of course, dredgers and boatbuilders made adjustments, particularly to the shape of the hull, which helps determine how well a boat sails. Over a period of time, each skipjack would develop a reputation: she might be an excellent or poor dredge boat, a heavy weather boat or a fair weather boat. Some skipjacks were criticized as being too "full" forward in their hull construction or too flat on the bottom for seaworthiness.

Determining how to build a boat had always been a matter of selection and compromise. Dredgers had to consider such factors as what type of water and

A volunteer works on the hull of the *Nathan of Dorchester,* a skipjack under construction by the city of Cambridge in 1992-93. The *Nathan* was expected to dredge during the season and carry passengers for tours in the summer. Like early boat-builders, this volunteer used a hatchet to stave, or shape, the planks that will form the curve of the bow.

weather they would primarily work in: would they work in protected areas, like the Choptank River, which has nearby ports to slip into when bad weather hit, or would they work out in the Bay where rougher seas would demand a bigger, more seaworthy boat? Would they be working in shoal or deep waters? They considered the availability of crew: some skipjacks, particularly those used in the southern Eastern Shore where crews were scarce, were rigged with two masts in

order to reduce the size of the sails so that fewer men were required to raise the smaller sails.

Dredgers also had to consider existing laws governing the oyster industry. For many decades, big boats over ten tons were excluded from working in the Choptank River and other protected bodies of water. If a dredger wanted to work in the river, he had to build a smaller boat, or he artificially reduced the boat's tonnage by placing false bulkheads inside the skipjack or creating more cabin space, as opposed to cargo space. Of course, it also helped to pay off the inspector who measured the vessel. Not surprisingly, many big skipjacks, which could easily carry twenty or thirty tons, were officially registered as seven- or eight-ton vessels, allowing them to work in the Choptank and Tangier Sound.

For the most part, the days of pirating oysters were over by the time the bateau arrived on the Chesapeake scene, but evidently a few bateaux were built for the purpose of pirating oysters, according to Howard Chapelle, who describes one such pirate skipjack in his book, *The National Watercraft Collection*.

Because of the different characteristics of the waters they worked, skipjacks reflected regional influences. Many skipjacks from the lower Bay islands of Deal, Smith, and Holland were virtually flat-bottomed because of the extremely shoal waters around the islands and in Tangier and Pocomoke sounds, records Howard Chapelle. The skipjacks with the most extreme regional influences, however, were built in Pocomoke City and became known as the "Pocomoke round-bottoms." These skipjacks were framed, had round-chine hulls, and were planked fore and aft, similar to *Eva*, the first Dorchester County skipjack.

Often, dredgers would pick a skipjack they liked and have their new dredge boat patterned after it. While some skipjacks were considered sister boats—built from the same plan—few, if any, Eastern Shore boatbuilders worked from blueprints. Some builders made models or half-models from which they worked, but skipjacks were such simple hull designs that even models were generally unnecessary.

Jim Richardson, who was considered the last of the master boatbuilders on the Chesapeake, talked about how to build a skipjack in interviews with Robert C. Keith, who edited *The Jim Richardson Boat Book*. "On a skipjack, after you set up your keelson and your stem and your transom, the very next thing you do is bend on the side planking, just bend it in the air without frames, only a couple of braces in the middle. At that point the shape of the boat is determined. You do it by eye. From then on you just follow standard procedures—nail on the bottom planking, turn her over, do the decking and so forth."

The skipjack may not have been as big or as seaworthy as its forerunners, but when it started to be built in earnest in 1896, it had some definite advantages over the dredge boats of the time. Its flat or V-bottom hull and broad beam meant its draft was only two to four feet, so it could dredge in shallower water. This was a real plus since many oyster bars in deeper waters had become depleted by the 1890s. With the introduction of the shallow-draft skipjack, oyster bars in shoal waters were now reachable with dredges.

By 1900, almost every community dependent on the water for its livelihood on the mid- to lower Shore, no matter how small or remote, had at least one boatbuilder. Many of the skipjacks built between 1896 and 1915—the boom years for skipjack construction—were built on islands: Deal Island, Taylors Island, Hooper Island, Tilghman Island, and Crab Island.

Volunteering their time on the *Nathan of Dorchester*, workers nail on the bottom herringbone planking typically used on skipjacks. The *Nathan* was modeled after the *Oregon*, an early Dorchester skipjack.

Some of the islands where boatbuilding thrived, such as Watts, Smith, and Holland islands, were so remote that the only way to reach them was by boat. This was no deterrent for watermen, however, who handled all their business, and much of their pleasure, by boat in the early 1900s. In fact, many mainland villages were so isolated by surrounding marshes, they were also easier to reach by water.

While some skipjacks were built in the western shore towns of Virginia, including Urbanna, Reedville, and Deep Creek, the vast majority were built in the communities of the mid- to lower Eastern Shore. Not surprisingly, Somerset County, the center of oyster dredging at the turn of the century, produced more skipjacks than any other county.

Some of the earliest, most prolific builders of bateaux included John Branford of Inverness, a tiny settlement on the southern side of the Manokin River. Many of the early boats were built on and around St. Peters Creek and the village of Oriole at the source of the creek, which may explain why the Baltimore *Sun* reporter, in his 1901 article, noted St. Peters as the origin of the skipjack, or bateau.

Out on the isolated islands off Crisfield, before the turn of the century, James H. Price produced boats like the *Carrie Price* on Holland Island, which was deserted twenty years later when erosion and encroaching salt waters forced its more than one hundred inhabitants to flee. Frank Tull and Lawson Tyler were from Smith Island, though Tull was known to do much of his big boatbuilding in Crisfield.

Builders kept few records; consequently, many of their names have been lost over the decades. However, many boats were named by the builder for members of his family, a practice that has helped not only to preserve the name of some of these early builders who otherwise would have been lost in obscurity, but also to identify who built which boats. Jimmy Daugherty at Crisfield, for example, built the *Fannie L. Daugherty* and named it after his daughter. The *Minnie V* was built at Wenona on Deal Island in 1906 by John Vetra, who named the boat for his wife, Minnie, with V, of course, standing for Vetra.

Usually boats were named for mothers or daughters, rather than wives, since builders knew that marriages could grow sour over the years. Some boats were named after the buyer, as was the case with the *Robert L. Webster,* considered the biggest skipjack ever built. However, every captain who knew the *Robert L.* insists that the *Florence Louise,* built nine years later by

Frank Tull of Tylerton, Smith Island, could hold more oysters. Tull built the *Florence Louise* at Crisfield, making her wider and deeper than the *Robert L. Webster.*

Talbot and Dorchester counties also had builders. Oliver Duke was building in Royal Oak as early as 1896 when many of his dredge boats showed the influence of buyeyes and sloops. Duke told John G. Earle, a marine engineer who dedicated many of his retirement years to researching maritime history and collecting data on the boats that worked the Bay, that all of his skipjacks had an inboard rudder and a transom with camber, creating an elliptic stern. According to Earle's early notes on Duke, the *Emily,* built in 1896, also had a figurehead, which was unheard of on a skipjack.

Other early Talbot builders included John T. Landon of Wittman, near Tilghman Island, John Harrison of Tilghman Island, and George A. Cummings of Fairbank on Tilghman.

Not surprisingly, most of the skipjack fleet was centered in areas where dredge boats were permitted by law to work. Consequently, Smith Island became a major dredging center, with as many as fifty dredge boats in the early 1900s. Deal Island harbored the largest fleet. Most older dredgers remember at least a hundred in the 1920s or 1930s. Even places like Mount Vernon, on the Wicomico River north of Deal Island, had a fleet of skipjacks. Crisfield, while a major processor of oysters in the early 1900s, was not known for its oyster fleet, though undoubtedly there were dredge boats that harbored at Crisfield. Dredgers primarily sailed into Crisfield to sell their oysters to one of the hundred shucking houses that operated along the town wharf, including small, family-run operations.

North of Deal, Cambridge developed as the major port for dredge boats on the Choptank River. Dredge boat captains hailed from many of the small villages in the marshy wetlands of southern Dorchester County, including Wingate and Bishops Head, but many of these southern Dorchester captains worked out of Cambridge or Tilghman Island during the season, turning these ports into little cities.

Many Eastern Shoremen remember when you could walk across Cambridge Creek on the decks of the dredge boats that tied up there on a weekend. In the first half of the twentieth century, Cambridge was a major canning town, home of Phillips Packing Company, once a leading cannery in the United States. Of course Phillips also canned oysters. During the week the dredge boats would leave Cambridge and sail downriver to work the oyster bars, returning home Friday or Saturday.

Often the dredging fleet would anchor off Tilghman Island, which was also an important dredge port. Many islanders still remember when Blackwalnut Cove, at the southern tip of Tilghman, looked like a city at night because of all the lights glowing from the dredge boats anchored in the harbor. Dredge boats could sell their oysters at the packinghouses on Avalon Island, south of Knapps Narrows, just off Tilghman, and many of them would tie up along these packinghouses. The little island was connected to Tilghman by a long dock or thoroughfare.

In the early part of the twentieth century, few dredgers came home at night to sleep in their own beds. Most of them, even dredgers who lived in Cambridge, stayed on their boats for a week at a time. Somerset County dredgers, whose oyster rocks in Tangier Sound were exhausted or diseased through most of the early twentieth century, often were forced to head north up the Chesapeake to find oysters. Consequently, the Somerset dredgers usually spent two months away from home before returning in their boats for Christmas.

Tilghman Island dredgers were probably the luckiest in regard to working out of their homes. There were many rich oyster bars around Tilghman, both in the Choptank and out in the Chesapeake, so most Tilghman Islanders had only to slip out of port a short distance in order to reach good dredging grounds.

Dredge boats would generally stock up on food and equipment weekly, but usually two weeks before the season opened the dredge fleet would sail to places like Baltimore or Solomons to outfit their boats for the season.

Charles "Chuck" Hughes of Vane Bros., a ship chandler that was founded in 1897 and is still in business in Baltimore, remembers the days when dredge fleets sailed into Baltimore Harbor for outfitting. During the season, the skipjacks would leave every Monday morning from Pier 4, Pratt Street, known as Long Dock, and head out into the Bay to dredge. They wouldn't return until Friday. At the ship chandlery, "Everybody worked seven days a week," recalls Hughes. On Friday, the ship chandler would have the orders ready for the boats and would spend the weekend loading the dredge boats with another week's supply of food.

A week's grub bill for a typical dredge boat would include a thirty-pound slab of dried salt-bellied pork,

and four to six dozen eggs, salted because of the lack of refrigeration, and usually stored in a barrel. They bought forty pounds of salted codfish, which they ate for breakfast as codcakes. The dredge boats also took on sugar and four or five pounds of cookies, called caddies. The caddies were a vanilla cookie with lemon wedged between, known as "a poor man's Oreo cookie," according to Hughes.

The dredgers ate beans, one of the cheapest, but healthiest, of foods, for lunch and dinner, and would order hundred-pound sacks of black-eyed peas, large lima beans, and other varieties. A good dredge boat cook knew how to vary the color of the beans from one dinner to another to give the impression of variety in the meals. "Bean soup was made for every meal except breakfast," Hughes said. The salted pork was used in the beans to give some flavor.

The chandler kept a fifty-gallon barrel of King Po-t-rik blackstrap molasses, from which they would pour out a gallon into a jug furnished by the dredger. The molasses, of course, was used on codfish cakes, like people use it on pancakes today, but it was also believed by the sailors to have a medicinal effect on them. In the cold of winter, the job of pouring molasses seemed to take the longest. "I remember as a kid, it was such a long, drawn-out affair," said Hughes, who used to help.

Many boats were equipped with the Elisha Webb Webbperfection stove which used coal or chunk wood for cooking. Each vessel had a coal caddy to store coal.

The dredgers never paid the chandler until the spring. Often the chandler worked on shares, which made the dredgers indebted to buying their goods from a particular merchant. "As long as you owned a share and no other chandler did, you were guaranteed the business," recalled Hughes.

Ship chandlers also sold boat and personal equipment, such as lines, sails, deadeyes, blocks, hip boots, potbellied stoves, bushels of coal, gimballed lights for the bulkheads or cabins, even mattresses.

Among the personal effects sold to dredgers were sou'westers or oilskins and the oil to keep them flexible. "They would get stiff in the winter," remembers Hughes. "In those days, they had to be fed a special oil that would keep the suits supple." The oil was a waterproofing sealer that the ship chandler sold by the gallon. These early oilskins were actually made of fiber-coated cotton, a smooth material which, if it did not get oiled regularly, became brittle and stiff, Hughes said.

The chandler might also have kept a list of available men who would hire out on the dredge boats, but Hughes remembers that shanghaiing drunks into service was not uncommon in the early 1900s. Drunks who frequented the bars along Pratt Street would "sign on" while inebriated, not realizing what they had done until they woke up out at sea.

By the 1930s, some dredge boats had mechanical bilge pumps, though many dredgers say they used hand pumps as the main equipment for ridding a boat of water as late as the late 1940s.

In the years since dredging was legalized in 1865, the oyster had become one of Maryland's greatest resources and the state's second biggest industry, behind farming. No one wanted to see this natural resource destroyed; consequently, for forty years, state legislators passed more and more laws and restrictions on dredging, which quickly became Maryland's most regulated industry. These included rigorous cull laws restricting the size of the oysters that could be taken; requirements that culled shells be returned to the beds; requirements that oysters should be culled on the natural bar as they were harvested, and that all empty shells and all oysters below the legal size should be replaced on the natural bar; a limitation on the times within which oysters might be taken, including the prohibition of night work; a limitation on the use of the scoop or dredge to certain open areas; the prohibition of the use of steam or power for the operation of scoops or dredges; the creation of an important and expensive "Oyster Navy," and the prohibition of firearms of a sufficient size to resist the navy; and the creation of an elaborate system of licensing and numbering of dredging vessels.

Sometimes the regulation had immediate results. In 1892, Joseph B. Seth, commander of the Maryland State Fishery Force, credited the culling law of 1889 with reversing the downward spiral in the oyster industry, which had plummeted from 6,559,733 bushels harvested in 1889 to 4,382,980 in 1891.

"For a number of years, the supply of oysters in this state has been annually decreasing, and this great industry which is second only to our farming interest, in value and in number of people employed, has become so crippled and impaired as to give cause for fear of its entire destruction." Seth said the culling law, which returned shell and small oysters to the bars, "not only stopped the heretofore steady decrease, but has added at least 30 percent to last season's catch."

No matter how many laws were created, state officials seemed unable to completely reverse the loss of natural oyster bars in the Bay. Three surveys conducted between 1880 and 1907 documented the drastic decline in Pocomoke Sound. In 1880, a state survey showed 7,360 acres of natural oyster beds. In 1891, another survey showed the acreage had shrunk to 5,120. By the 1906 survey, natural oyster bottom in Pocomoke Sound covered only 1,408 acres. That represented a loss of 112 acres per year between 1880 and 1890, and 232 acres per year since 1891, the *Crisfield Times* noted in 1907.

In the autumn of 1906, 320 of the 566 dredging licenses in Maryland were issued to Somerset County residents. Dorchester County, with the next highest number of licensees, had only 83 dredge boats, one-fourth the fleet of Somerset County.

As lean times pressed on the watermen, the simple life of following the water was no longer simple. A dredger needed to make a minimum annual income of $1,836. This was at a time when the average wage was about $5 a week. Even though Somerset County oysters were commanding high prices, about $1.25 per bushel compared with $.60 elsewhere, lack of the shellfish was taking its toll on the oyster bars, as well as on the men who worked them.

In its first report in 1907, the Maryland Shell Fish Commission observed, "Dredgers practically exhaust the ground available for dredging by the time the dredging season is one-third over, and those who continue to dredge longer than this go over grounds already covered, one or more times. This accounts for the fact that dredging grounds are everywhere more depleted than tonging ground."

With only about 90,000 acres of oyster bottom in Maryland reserved for dredging, the commission calculated that 140 acres had to support each of the 638 dredgers licensed in 1907. But dredge boats equipped with two five-foot-wide dredges could cover a swath ten feet wide by ten miles long every day, the commission observed. The average ten-ton dredge boat covered an average of eight acres a day, or 464 acres a season, when you considered time lost for bad weather and breakdowns in equipment.

While most Somerset County men pursued the independent life of the dredger, few of them prospered enough to own their own dredge boats outright. As one state official in the early part of the century observed, "The actual working oysterman, as a rule, is a man of limited business experience and very limited

At the southern end of Deal Island, once the home port for more than a hundred dredge boats, the village of Wenona hasn't changed much since the heyday of dredging, except that now only a handful of dredge boats harbor there.

financial resources. Occasionally, he is able to own and equip a dredge boat, but more frequently he is assisted in this by someone connected with the packing industry, who thus acquires at least a partial control over the disposition of the catch."

Besides the packinghouses, dredgers also found themselves controlled by the ship chandlers who often had shares in a boat's catch; some ship chandleries owned whole fleets of dredge boats.

Former Deal Islander Tom Webster, who owned N. W. Webster and Bro., a ship chandlery with offices in Solomons and on Boston Street in Baltimore, gained legendary status among Deal Island dredgers as the man who owned a hundred dredge boats. Old-timers who worked for Webster and his brothers often tell the story about how every time he acquired his one hundred and first dredge boat, one would sink, reducing his vast fleet once again to a hundred.

Although it's impossible to determine whether Webster ever owned that many boats, records documenting ownership of the working vessels in the United States do confirm that the ship chandlery did own some dredge boats, and dredgers who worked for Webster don't doubt the claim that he owned a hundred.

Webster was one of the first to try out the new invention, the dredge winder, built by the Page Engineering Co. of Baltimore and first marketed in 1906. In September 1907, Webster left the wharf at Canton in Baltimore on his schooner, the *Kate Vickery*, accompanied by Captain George M. Frances of Chance, bound for the oyster rock near the mouth of the Chester River. According to the *Crisfield Times*, he intended to test this new mechanical winder under practical working conditions.

The mechanical winder was heralded as a labor-saving invention. Dredge boats would no longer have to carry large crews to work the hand winders, laden with a hundred pounds of shellfish. But while the mechanical winder would revolutionize the dredging industry, it also took its toll in terms of human suffering. Occasionally dredgers were mangled by the huge flywheels that spun on for long seconds after the winder engine was turned off. Eventually, dredgers learned to encase the engines so that this didn't happen, but many men lost arms in the machinery as they tried to work around the winder.

Webster, who died in 1924, was not the only man who amassed a huge dredging fleet. There were many entrepreneurs who gambled in dredge boats, hoping to cash in on the rich, but now dwindling, oyster crop under Somerset County waters.

If watermen felt manipulated by packers and ship chandlers, there was another element in the oyster business that the dredgers viewed as an outright threat to their livelihoods. These entrepreneurs had a different idea of how to cash in on Somerset's dwindling underwater wealth—through oyster culture, a method

A half-moon rises over Tilghman Island as the *Virginia W, left,* and the *Hilda M. Willing, right,* return home with their catch after a long day of dredging.

of farming and managing the underwater beds so that they continued to be productive.

As early as 1860, watermen discovered they could remove oysters from the natural bar to a new location without injuring the oyster. "It therefore became the habit of many oystermen, instead of selling the oysters taken by them early in the season or in open weather when the ease of securing them had a tendency to glut the market with a corresponding reduction of price, to deposit oysters taken at this time in sheltered waters, at depths easily workable and with sufficient tidal flow to provide an adequate supply of food," a state official observed. "Later in the season, when the best of the year's crop had been gathered from the natural bars . . . increasing the price, . . . these bedded oysters were taken up and placed on the market. . . . Packing houses also did this, buying large quantities when prices were low, and bedding oysters until prices increased."

While oyster culture had merit as a conservation measure, watermen felt it threatened to rein in their independent lifestyle and reduce them to common laborers, forced to work for fixed wages. Oyster culture had been practiced on a very restricted basis in Maryland for almost fifty years when it suddenly became a real threat to watermen with the passage of the Haman Oyster Culture Law in 1906. The law was named for B. Howard Haman, the attorney who proposed it as a means of replenishing the depleted oyster bars in Maryland waters and generating revenue for the state. The intention of the law was to "encourage an industry in oyster culture upon the barren bottoms beneath the tidewaters and to prevent the leasing of natural oysters bars."

While anyone could apply to the state for an oyster lease for a five-acre lot to cultivate their own oysters, watermen feared that a strong oyster culture law would allow owners of packinghouses to maintain their own supply of oysters, thus forcing the independent watermen to work for the packers or go out of business. In 1907, as the local elections coincided with the start of a new oyster season, the oyster culture law had become the second most important political issue in Somerset County, after Prohibition, which was sweeping the country. Democratic candidates, in defending their party's decision to support the law, tried to convince watermen that oyster culture would ultimately help them maintain their way of life by increasing the supply of oysters in the tidewaters and

allowing them a chance to lease bottom and cultivate their own acreage.

Hosea C. Webster, with N. W. Webster & Bro. ship chandlery in Baltimore, in a letter to the editor of the *Crisfield Times* in November 1907, declared that "discontent over oyster culture is dying." He was wrong. The watermen had vigorously opposed the law, and the bill that passed the legislature was a compromised, watered-down version of the original. The restrictions on the planter, written into the bill by the lobbying efforts of the watermen, made planting so unattractive that the number of acres of bottom leased in Maryland for oyster culture actually dropped substantially in the years after the Haman bill became law. Some 2,116 acres of bottom were leased in Maryland in 1906, compared with only 174 acres in 1911.

Watermen had won the battle against the movement toward farming the oyster bottom of the Bay for now, but the issue would prove a thorn in their side that simply would not go away.

A crewman culls oysters aboard the *Rebecca T. Ruark*.

A crewman aboard the *Rebecca T. Ruark*, captained by Wade Murphy, Jr., relaxes near a pile of oysters while the fleet is becalmed on the Choptank River near Howell Point.

# Three

# THE TERRIBLE TEENS

*People ask me, "Don't you think dredging is glamorous?" I've been dredging forty-six years, and I ain't seen nothing glamorous about it yet. All I can see is it's hard work and you can make money at times. I'm still waiting to see the glamour part.*

—Captain Pete Sweitzer on dredging

IT WAS lucky for young Dan Dize that he got off his father's bugeye when it returned home to Smith Island in 1916. At age nine, Dan Dize often accompanied his father, Captain Theodore Wesley Dize, and his older brother as they hauled lumber or bought oysters in the Potomac River. But young Dan had to go to school, so the captain left him in port, then sailed all night in order to be ready to buy oysters in the Potomac River the next morning.

The trip left the captain so exhausted that he never heard the crewman get the pistol he kept near his bunk and pull the trigger—eight times. Each time the broken .38, which Captain Dize had held together with a piece of rubber band, failed to fire, leaving the imprint of the firing pin in the cap. Then the crewman got a hatchet, and using the blunt end, struck the captain thirteen times in the head and beat his twelve-year-old son eight times, before robbing them of $630 and leaving the two for dead. Both father and son recovered from the attack, but Captain Theodore Dize, who was obviously weakened by the assault, would die two years later of tuberculosis, one of the scourges of living in the poor conditions common to the Eastern Shore.

The assault on Captain Dize and his son is clear evidence that the Chesapeake Bay that awaited the men and young boys, like Dan Dize, who went out to work the oyster bars around 1915 was still a dangerous, uncomfortable, often violent world. While the oyster wars that plagued the Chesapeake in the latter half of the nineteenth century were virtually over by 1915, there were plenty of other dangers to be faced, including exposure to severe weather.

A court case heard in Baltimore in February 1917 revealed just how bad life could be for a man who signed onto a dredge boat. On January 27, 1917, William McPhearson appeared in the U. S. District Court of Baltimore to tell how he lost nine fingers and nine toes to frostbite following his winter aboard the bugeye *Ariel*, owned by Captain Noah Holland of Fairmount in Somerset County.

McPhearson, about fifty years old, signed for service on the *Ariel* at $15 a month from December 31, 1915, until the middle of March 1916. He came to Crisfield by steamer to board the bugeye, but he had no decent clothes to work out in the weather. McPhearson said he told the captain, both in Baltimore and again in Crisfield, that he needed oilskins, boots, and clothes, but Captain Holland wouldn't provide him with the proper garments for the weather conditions he would face, the *Crisfield Times* reported.

The bugeye sailed to the Potomac River to dredge, where those aboard encountered very cold weather. When McPhearson asked Captain Holland for boots and gloves, the captain gave him a pair of cotton gloves, for which he was charged ten cents. A week later it began to snow and McPhearson asked again for a pair of boots. The captain told him he had a pair, but he would not let McPhearson have them. On January 7, 1916, McPhearson said he was forced to work although he was sick. Three days later his fingers were frostbitten, but the captain forced him to work, threatening to kill him if he didn't cull oysters and work the winders.

The cruel treatment continued until January 17 when the captain's son reported that McPhearson was unable to work. From then until January 22, when the bugeye arrived at Fairmount, on the Manokin River in Somerset County, McPhearson remained in the forecastle of the boat. He was kept aboard for two days after arriving at Fairmount. Then he went to Norfolk, where all his fingers except his left thumb, and nine toes were amputated in a hospital, where he was confined for four weeks.

McPhearson said the bugeye was dredging within two miles of Colonial Beach in Virginia and the captain could have easily sailed him into port where he could have received medical attention.

Judge Rose, who heard the case, said the captain impressed him as "being a man who did not care one bit" for the welfare of his crew. He ordered the captain to pay McPhearson $1,500—about the minimum seasonal earnings of a dredge boat at that time.

It was not uncommon for captains, like Holland, to sign on men from Baltimore to work the middle deck of their dredge boat when they couldn't find enough crew around home. Shipping offices in Baltimore would provide men for a dollar a head, but most of these men, who worked for fifteen or twenty dollars a month, represented the lowest life off Baltimore streets. Dredgers had little respect for these city drunks and hoboes.

Captain Ellis "Bill" Berridge, a former Tilghman Island dredger, remembers that his father didn't get his crew through the shipping offices, but rather through the chief of police in Baltimore. "The chief of police in Baltimore, he knew Dad's crew. They were migrant workers. They picked potatoes and tomatoes. When it got time for drudgin', he'd call Dad up and he'd get his crew up and he'd put 'em in jail. They were what you call hoboes, drunks. Dad would pay their fine and get them out," said Captain Berridge. "Put into a situation, if they wanted to get out of jail, they'd work their fine off."

Berridge, who turned ninety in 1993, was thirteen when he started dredging on his father's bugeye, *QuiVie*. The *QuiVie* was a big, sixty-five-foot-long dredge boat, yet even as late as 1917, when Berridge joined the crew, she had no push boat or mechanical winders. Young Berridge worked the hand winders and the sixteen-foot oars on the *QuiVie* alongside the other men. The bugeye had two oars forward and two aft. "I remember working *QuiVie* on Stone Rock [off Tilgh-

man Island]. We'd row her out in the morning, wait for a breeze, and have to row her back," said Berridge.

But in 1917, there were few oysters to be found anywhere in the Bay or her tidewaters. Tilghman Islanders usually worked around their home waters, but that year many of the dredgers, including Captain Berridge, went north to find oysters, then came home early, unsuccessful.

While some captains treated the men they hired off the Baltimore docks not much better than animals, the captains did take care of their fellow islanders. After his father's death, Dan Dize, at age twelve, had no trouble finding work on the middle deck of a Smith Island dredge boat.

By 1920, Smith Islanders spent most of the season dredging in the Potomac River. More than fifty years of exploitation by the dredge had virtually swept clean the oyster bars in Tangier and Pocomoke sounds. Before the start of the season on November first, Dan Dize would leave home and not return until Christmas.

"It was always cold. I never took my clothes off aboard a dredge boat," recounted Captain Dize, who turned eighty-six in 1993. Several of the skipjacks he worked aboard had cabins that leaked badly. "I had to sleep with my oilskins overtop me to keep me dry," he said. And when he left his bunk in the early morning hours, he would spread a pair of oilskins on top of his bunk to keep his bedding dry. Dize and the rest of the crew would wash up from a big barrel of fresh water that was kept aboard the boat, but often in the frigid cold, the wash buckets would be frozen and Dize would have to crack through the ice to wash.

Abroad, the outbreak of the Great War in August 1914 had interfered with trade. The war, combined with Virginia's efforts to perfect an aquaculture program, forced down the price of Maryland oysters. Somerset County dredgers, who had received as much as $1.25 per bushel for oysters in 1907, saw the price of oysters decline over the next two decades until they were lucky to get a quarter a bushel.

But for crew, like Dize, the most pressing issue was being able to find work in the bitter cold, ice-laden teens, and when they were able to work, to keep warm through some of the coldest winters on record.

In February 1917, four Deal Islanders were forced to abandon their bugeye in Breton Bay, off the Potomac River and walk across the ice to Washington, D.C., in a raging snowstorm. The men, Real J. Webster, J. W. Shores, Frank Horner, and Benjamin Webster, had been dredging in the Potomac when their

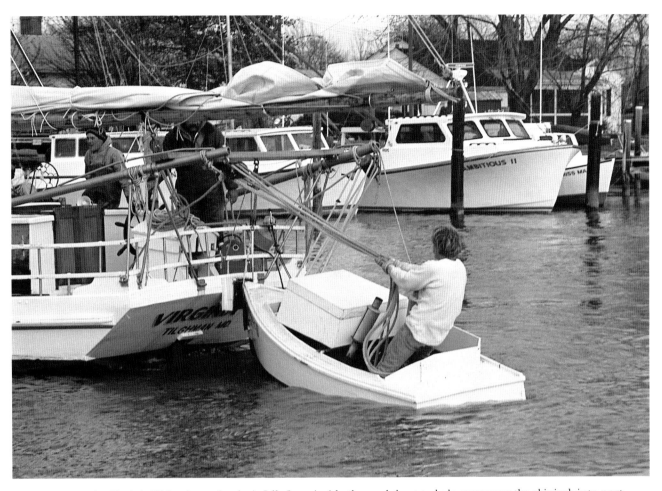

A crewman on the *Virginia W* hauls on the davit falls from inside the push boat to help maneuver the skipjack into port.

vessel became entrapped in an ice floe. The bugeye remained caught in the ice for nine days as temperatures plummeted around the Bay.

The *Crisfield Times* reported that the Deal Island men stayed with the boat until their fuel and food ran out, then the crew finally decided to try to reach the shore over the heavy layer of ice. On Monday morning they started to walk to the nearest shore and continued until Tuesday, when they reached Washington, D.C. From there, they went on to Baltimore to find the relatives of one of the dredgers, but in the process of looking for the relatives, they managed to get themselves arrested. Evidently, the four men looked suspiciously out of place, wandering about from house to house wearing their heavy oilskins and rubber boots. Residents began to worry and called the police, who arrested the dredgers and brought them before a Baltimore magistrate. The judge, however, was sympathetic to their plight and released the men, who had spent the night in jail.

The storm that began Sunday, February 5, left many vessels in distress, including four dredge boats caught in Tangier Sound opposite Cedar Straits. A schooner, two bugeyes, and a bateau were wedged in the ice a short distance from the sound channel, which was open, the *Crisfield Times* reported. Meanwhile, the schooner *Clara J. Howeth* was dismasted while making for Kedges Straits in the storm. The cutter *Apache* had to assist many vessels trapped in the ice around Crisfield.

During the height of the storm on Monday morning, February 6, the steamer *Eastern Shore*, belonging to the B.C. & A. Line, was blown off her course while entering Crisfield harbor and went ashore on a point near the inner light, about half a mile from her dock, according to the *Crisfield Times*. The heavy freeze of the following few hours imprisoned the steamer until the flood tide of Wednesday afternoon. Passengers left the vessel Monday afternoon and walked to the shore on the ice.

The storm raged for three days, and was followed by a severe cold spell that caused a hard freeze. Crisfield harbor and portions of Tangier and Pocomoke sounds were frozen over. Ice blocked many sections of the Bay. Nobody went dredging.

As bad as it seemed at the time, the winter of 1917 was nothing compared with the cold and ice that would envelop the Chesapeake for more than seven weeks in the Big Freeze of 1918.

In the final days of 1917, temperatures began to plummet below zero. January 1, 1918, was "the coldest New Year's Day ever before known," according to the *Star-Democrat* in Easton. Temperatures as low as 10 degrees below zero were recorded in Talbot County. By January 5, 1918, the Chesapeake Bay and its tributaries were impassable. Since boats were still the primary means of carrying supplies, including fuel and coal, to the Eastern Shore, the freeze caused hardship on the Shore as supplies ran low.

"Besides the privation among the poor and those unable to secure fuel, there is imminent shortage of foodstuffs due to the paralysis of activity on the Bay, the accepted source of supply," the *Star-Democrat* reported on Saturday, January 5. "The Chesapeake and all its Talbot tributaries are frozen over; if not altogether impassable, it is fraught with great menace, and the floes in the river, even could they be reached, are too formidable for any craft that might make the venture. Steamboat schedules are practically out of the question. In the meanwhile, the temperature continued around zero, to the accompaniment of driving, bitter winds."

By its third week, the frozen Bay was taking its toll on the people of the Eastern Shore. Dredgers, hard up to make a living, ventured out on the ice with sleighs and automobiles at Oxford and Tilghman Island to try an unusual method of dredging. Many years later in a 1954 Baltimore *Sun* article, Ivy B. McNamara recalled how he and other dredgers ventured out with a sleigh on ice that was fourteen inches thick on the Choptank River, pulling their dredging equipment with the sleigh. The men chopped several holes through the ice, then pulled the dredges by hand across the beds. Tongers also cut holes in the ice and tonged over the beds. The ice was so strong that trucks drove out to the watermen to take their catch.

At Oxford, the dredgers were afraid to venture out of the Tred Avon River to their dredging grounds in the Choptank River, so they stopped on the tongers'

At age seventy-seven, Dave Barkley, here culling oysters aboard the *Wilma Lee,* was the oldest dredger working the Chesapeake in 1991.

rock at Bachelor Point and dropped their dredges through holes in the ice.

The hardship was so great on the watermen that even the Conservation Committee, which maintained law and order on the tidewaters, refused to convict the dredgers as long as the tongers did not object. However, some of the tongers did object and went to the police captain to have the dredgers arrested. Neither the police nor the Conservation Committee wanted to make the arrests, so the tongers decided to make the arrests themselves. They sent one man out to get the names of the offending dredgers, but after the names had been obtained not a single tonger would swear out a writ.

Unlike most cold spells, this one started early and wouldn't let up. On Saturday, January 19, Talbot County residents were awakened about 2:30 A.M. by a terrific wind- and rainstorm. "The wind at times assumed the velocity of a cyclone," reported the *Star-Democrat.* "At Tilghman's Island the storm was unusually severe. Most of the piling under the long wharf of the Baltimore, Chesapeake and Atlantic Railway . . . was carried away, as well as the foundation under the oyster house of Faulkner & Covington. The deadrise [another term for skipjack] *Lillie,* [owned by] Capt. Benjamin T. Harrison, lying alongside the oyster house, was smashed to pieces. The deadrise *Water Lilly* [Capt. John Lowery], lying at the steamboat wharf, was likewise destroyed. The deadrise *Coronet* had a hole punched in her side and was otherwise damaged. The big schooner *Henry I. Phillips* [Captain Frank Page] had her rudder carried away and also lost her mainmast, bowsprit, and longhead. The police sloop *Eliza Hayward,* also in the harbor, was slightly damaged . . . The heavy ice was broken up by the wind in many places and piled high on the shores. One iceberg near the wharf at Tilghman is estimated to be at least 25 feet high and 100 yards in length."

The strong southeast winds broke up the ice in the Choptank River and piled it up on Benoni Point. Monday after the storm, the great mass of ice began to push over the Benoni Lighthouse. The keepers of the light realized they were in danger when coals began to fall from the stove. Tuesday evening, after receiving permission from the government, the keepers abandoned the house and started to walk ashore. They had to climb from cake to cake until they came near the shore, where the ice was very smooth. Wednesday, the lightkeepers made numerous trips back to the lighthouse to remove the furniture and fixtures from the lighthouse, which was leaning so far over that observers believed it would fall at any moment. Photographs taken during the worst of the freeze showed that the ice floes reached thirty feet high, banked around Benoni Point Light, and the fields of ice stretched unbroken for miles, interspersed with peaks as much as twenty feet high on the Choptank River near Oxford.

Watermen not only had to deal with the cold and the ice, but a war, as well. The United States, which had entered the Great War a few months earlier in the fall of 1917, was not only recruiting all the young watermen into service, but was also asking those left behind to conserve energy.

Beginning January 19, 1918, the State Fuel Commission ordered the Eastern Shore communities to close down all factories, stores, schools, and similar buildings for five days for the purpose of saving fuel. Businesses and public buildings were to remain closed every Monday thereafter.

Meanwhile, the weather continued to batter the Shore. On January 21, Talbot County and the Eastern Shore suffered its heaviest snowfall in eight years. The storm hit the Shore early Tuesday morning and lasted until well into the afternoon, leaving six inches or more of snow on the ground. "It badly crippled traffic on the roads, and, in fact, threw a monkey wrench into the cogs of the machinery perfected by the local fuel administration to save fuel," the *Star-Democrat*

reported. "The storm started about 1 A.M., and with a little more wind, would have assumed blizzard-like proportions."

The cold continued and by January 26 the *Star-Democrat* was lamenting the "deplorable condition of about 40 colored dredgers at Claiborne. They have been out of work over four weeks and were without food or fuel and were suffering greatly from lack of both. The matter was taken up by Gen. Seth and relief was immediately planned."

As if the Eastern Shore communities had not had enough of the winter of 1918, two more blizzards ravaged the tidewater towns during the last week in January, dropping another ten inches over the Shore. The snow fell on Monday, January 28, and Wednesday, January 30. While the snow did little damage other than to hamper the flow of traffic on land, it caused considerable new problems out in the Bay, reversing efforts to open channels through the ice fields.

Meanwhile, on the islands of Somerset County, food was beginning to run out in some households on Smith Island. Finally, three young men rigged a skiff with a sail, put on their ice skates and crossed to Crisfield to get food. About eight hundred Smith Islanders were isolated for seven weeks before the U.S. battleship *Ohio* entered the Bay and cut a ship channel.

In its February 2 issue, the *Star-Democrat* called on state lawmakers to extend the oyster season in order to help watermen recover economically from the Big Freeze of 1918: "The loss in the oyster business due to the freeze, which has existed practically all winter, has run into very big figures, and will create a hardship that will require a long time to recover from. To offset this distress, the people of Tilghman, and . . . St. Michaels, Claiborne, and other points, feel that no better work could be done by the General Assembly than to extend the oyster season to June 1, in order to cover the time lost by the present freeze. The dredging season closes Mar. 15. As already two months have been lost by the freeze, and under the best conditions it will be at least some weeks more before the boats can resume operations, an extension of the oyster season to May 1 would but cover the period lost by the freeze.

"There are numerous reasons why the present oyster season should be extended. In the present food crisis, the country needs as much foodstuff as it is possible to produce, and the shortage occurring in the supply of oysters, occasioned by the extreme weather, will deprive the markets of that much food. The welfare of the boatmen, the oyster packers, and shuckers too, should be considered, because they have been deprived of more than a month of business in the very middle of the season.

"Oysters are reported to be very plentiful in the Choptank and the bay, yet the freshets which come down with the spring thaw will kill thousands of bushels if left on the bottoms. An extension of the season will save these oysters for food and give those engaged in the industry an opportunity to make up for the lean season caused by the freeze," the *Star-Democrat* concluded.

January had come in like a lion and gone out like a lion, dumping 13.6 inches of snow over the Shore, much more than the 8-inch norm. By February 16, the Oxford/Bellevue ferry was running again across the Tred Avon River, but a week later, Benoni Point Lighthouse, at the mouth of the Tred Avon River, finally collapsed.

A new day dawns on the Chesapeake Bay as crew aboard the *Wilma Lee* prepare to throw the dredge overboard.

*Four*

# THE DEPRESSING THIRTIES

*We've had our ups and downs in oystering. You have your good years and your bad years, but I always made a living. It's a livelihood; you're your own boss, and that's the main thing.*
*—Captain Stan Daniels, known as the singing captain because he often sings at the wheel and sometimes over the marine radio*

T HE BOY awoke to the feel of stinging cold on his skin. Sleepy-eyed, he reached up and wiped away the layer of snow that had sifted through the cracks of the closed hatchway during the night and covered his face. Many decades later, he would suffer frostbite and skin cancer from constant exposure to the raw elements, but for now, young Jesse Thomas didn't mind the snow, nor the cold, nor the leaky cabin of the *Mary Sue*. For a twelve-year-old boy, life aboard a skipjack was exciting. The boat carried him far away from the dull, dreary life of the classroom, far from his island home of Deal, into a big world of endless ports and new adventures.

"I woke up with snow in my eyes many a time," said Captain Jesse Thomas of Princess Anne, who turned seventy-eight in 1993. "You couldn't stop the cabins from leaking. I guess they were getting in bad shape. I don't know a time when I didn't have leaks in mine."

Like most adolescent boys on Deal Island in the early part of the twentieth century, Jesse Thomas quit school to work full-time on the water to help feed the family. Yet even at twelve, he was no rookie to life on a working sailboat. Ever since he had been old enough to climb aboard at age three, he had been exploring the great world of the Chesapeake Bay from the deck of a dredge boat, particularly in the summertime when his father, Ira, freighted watermelons and other Eastern Shore products to ports around the Bay on the sixty-foot skipjack, the *Robert L. Webster*.

"The whole family would come along on trips freighting," he said. In Washington, D.C., "we used to get off the boat and walk up to the Washington Monument." There the kids would skip the elevator and take the stairs to the top of the monument, where they had a clear view of the capital city below. There were eleven Thomas children, so there was always a crowd of little Thomases accompanying their parents on the freighting trips.

By the time young Jesse joined the crew of the *Mary Sue* in the autumn of 1927, he already knew a lot about handling the sails and, typical of a waterman, he was too proud to let another man beat him working, as he culled oysters with the older men.

By the 1920s, many of the big dredge boats on the Bay had engines to ease the workload on the crew, but the *Mary Sue* was a smaller vessel, only forty-two feet on deck, and had neither a winder engine nor a push boat equipped with an engine during Thomas's first years aboard her. The dredges, loaded with oysters, were cranked in with hand winders, a grueling chore that left even grown men exhausted.

Calms were also hard on the crew, since they had no engine to push them in and out of port. The men would position a set of oars fore and aft and row the big boat back into port. "You couldn't row them against the tide," said Captain Thomas who, nevertheless, often had to row against a running tide. "We worked ourselves to death."

Two years later, Jesse Thomas was working the middle deck for his uncle aboard the *America*, a little skipjack that only carried about two hundred bushels. They loaded her to her gunwales and headed back into port that Saturday only to find that their hard day's work was all but worthless. President Roosevelt had closed the banks. The day before, oysters had sold for twenty-five cents a bushel in the shell. After the banks were closed, oysters sold for seventeen cents, shucked and shipped to Baltimore. When the captain got his check two weeks later, it was for only thirty-five dollars for a whole boatload of oysters.

In the small ports and on the islands around the Eastern Shore, where there was already so little money and so far to make it stretch, the collapse of the nation's banking system and the onset of the Great Depression proved an economic blow that would shake these communities, dependent on the water for their livelihoods, for at least the next decade. Oysters, after all, were a luxury that people now found they could do without.

Captain Clyde Evans, a Smith Islander who was twenty when the Great Depression began, remembers times when dredgers couldn't sell their oysters. "I've seen it when a packer wouldn't take 'em if you gave them to 'im," Evans said. "I've seen them catch 'em, bring 'em over here [to Crisfield], and couldn't sell 'em. Take 'em home, shovel 'em out, carry 'em out to the bar, and lay 'em out on the bar, and take 'em up fifteen to twenty bushels at a time and bring 'em over here" when there finally was a market. "Sometimes we would put out 100, 150 bushels at a time" on the shoals around Smith Island, Evans said. The watermen on Smith Island never worried about their oysters being stolen. On Smith Island, everyone knew each other and respected each other's work. When the packers did buy, "Shuckers only got twenty cents a gallon for shucking 'em," Evans recalled.

Evans believed Smith Islanders fared better through the depression than folks on the mainland partly because the islanders had always been self-sufficient. Most of them raised their own chickens, ducks, and sometimes small livestock. They also kept gardens. And, of course, they could turn to the water for their food supply, so no one went hungry.

Evans can remember working six days, from sunup to sundown, for five dollars. But while money was tight, things were also fairly cheap. On Smith Island, you could live on five dollars a week. Evans can remember when his mother sent him to the store with a wheelbarrow and a dollar. When he returned home, he'd have the wheelbarrow full of stuff and have some change.

As the Great Depression dragged on through the thirties, more and more dredge boats were left on the mud flats. Dredgers just "wouldn't rig 'em up," Evans said. Without a market, it wasn't worth the cost of working and maintaining the vessels. "A lot of them went to the North Carolina oyster bars, where they also dredged for oysters under sail," according to Evans.

On Tilghman Island, Captain Ellis Berridge remembers when his father quit dredging. "He laid the boat up, it got so bad," Berridge relates. The depression also forced the younger Berridge out of dredging for a while. When oysters and the market improved in the sixties, Berridge would come back to captain the *Anna May Rich* and the *Martha Lewis,* but for the time being, he looked for other work.

Captain Stanley Larrimore, who was born during the depression, remembers his father, Glendy, also quit dredging: "The *Fannie Harrington* [a bugeye], he put her up and let her die. They pound netted, caught fish. . . . They laid them up those coves, sails and everything," said Larrimore, who remembers that many of the Cambridge boats were abandoned on Tilghman Island during the thirties. "Five or six died in Blackwalnut Cove, and some in the upper part of the island."

Watermen, like Jesse Thomas, who had grown up with pride, working hard and trying to outdo the next man on the skipjack, learned to survive, sometimes by doing anything, and sometimes by doing just nothing.

Shortly after he was married in 1934, Thomas and his wife found work in an orchard, picking peach kernels off the ground where they had fallen from the trees. They worked six days a week for eleven dollars. "You worked all the time for something," said Thomas.

Crabbing, a dredger's summertime employment, was just as bad as the oyster industry. When the price of crabs fell to only two cents apiece, Thomas, who ran a crab shedding business in the summer, made so little money, it was hardly worth his time to work. "I used to sit in the front yard. My wife thought I was lazy."

In the shipping offices of Baltimore, where captains, pressed to find a crew, had often settled for drunks, hoboes, and jailbirds, they now found a new class of poor standing in line with the destitute: doctors, lawyers, and other men who once had no reason to use their muscle and brawn were signing up to work on the dredge boats. Many were paid less than twenty dollars a month. They worked in the cold months of winter with holes in their shoes, without oilskins to keep the spray off, and with hardly enough clothes to keep them warm.

Even Nature worked against the dredgers in the thirties. When there was a market in the late thirties, there were few oysters on the bars, which served to lengthen the depression for watermen. Larrimore can remember going out with his father, Captain Glendy Larrimore, in the *Laura J. Barkley*: "I don't remember a whole lot of oysters in them days. There would be just a little pile. They weren't catchin' that many."

Worse, the thirties that awaited the impoverished watermen would prove catastrophic in more ways than just economic. Three natural disasters befell the watermen of the Eastern Shore during this decade. The first arrived in the late summer of 1933 and in the memories of the men and women who lived through it, it was known simply as "the August Storm."

On Wednesday, August 23, 1933, the Chesapeake region suffered under a "downpour of rain of almost cloudburst proportions," according to the *Crisfield Times*. The heavy rains of the hurricane had begun pelting the Eastern Shore three days earlier, on Sunday afternoon, August 20. Rain fell all day Monday, but Tuesday dawned clear, leaving many people with the misleading belief that they had missed the full force of the storm. Late Tuesday afternoon, however, dark, heavy clouds appeared on the northeast horizon and by dusk "a heavy wind was blowing, accompanied by a fine mist of rain," the *Crisfield Times* related. The wind increased steadily all Tuesday night and by midnight it was blowing a gale, the rain coming down in sheets.

Wednesday, at the height of the storm, practically the entire city of Crisfield, as well as the surrounding inhabited islands in the Chesapeake, were inundated with high tides. The tide, which was not due to be high until late Wednesday afternoon, started up at an alarming rate early in the morning and continued until late in the afternoon. Many businesses in downtown Crisfield were forced to close before noon as the tide crept up until there was two to four feet of water in many parts of town.

Sixty-mile-per-hour winds blew out windows and doors, while the unusually high tide destroyed merchandise and goods in the town. Along Crisfield's waterfront, docks were torn down and washed away; scores of oyster and crab houses were badly damaged by the wind and tide. Workboats were lost, many of them drifting out to sea, while others were swamped and sank where they lay at anchor. Many a captain who raised his boat in the aftermath of the storm found it to be a total loss.

On Smith Island, crab houses were swept away, homes damaged, and boats lost. Many of the residents had their household belongings—everything they owned—swept away, leaving them practically destitute.

Tangier Island, flooded by the tide, fared the worst. Crops were ruined, crab houses wrecked, and boats lost. According to the *Crisfield Times*, "The storm has left people on the island in a pitiable state and one from which it will take them some time to recover."

In Salisbury, dozens of men worked desperately through the storm digging a ditch to divert the Wicomico River and save the business section of the Eastern Shore's largest city from flooding. The storm had weakened dams on the Wicomico and officials feared they might go out.

On Hooper Islands, a string of three low-lying islands in the vast southern marshes of Dorchester County, one businessman looked out his window and found the entire upper island submerged, except for a few ridges. As far as he could see there was no land visible, nothing but water. The residents of Hooper Islands waded through water, sometimes chest-deep, to set livestock loose. One man died on Hooper Islands during the storm, and hundreds were in jeopardy as the water rose at the rate of eighteen inches an hour. Some reported it rose a foot in fifteen minutes.

One boat carrying fifty to sixty people sank off the islands in twenty-five feet of water. The passengers saved themselves by "walking ashore on the boards and timbers that were floating around them, jumping from one piece to another," the Cambridge *Daily Banner* reported.

"At the A. E. Phillips crab house about 30 people were loose on a platform and jumped from that to the floating roof and then, as the roof was swept by a point of land, they jumped to the land thereby saving their lives.

"Boats were resting in the yards, on the road, many of them having floated right over the tops of fences, four or more feet high," the *Daily Banner* reported on August 26. "A 500-bushel capacity boat had floated right into the yard of the electric plant, and was left undamaged." A 4,000-bushel cargo ship from the Nanticoke River broke loose from its anchorage on the Honga River and was carried so far across the marshy island that it ended up closer to the Chesapeake Bay side of Hooper Islands than to the river.

Deal Island, the most populous island of the Chesapeake, and home port for most of the Chesapeake's skipjack fleet, found itself suddenly isolated and reduced to rubble in the aftermath of the hurricane. The high tides and winds had swept away the wooden bridge to the mainland, forcing its fifteen hundred residents to rely on boats to ferry people, mail, and goods across the Upper Thorofare. The seafood industry was wrecked, since every oyster and crab house on the island was either swept away or so badly damaged that salvage was doubtful in the days and weeks that followed. The hurricane also claimed the half-mile-long steamboat wharf built through the shoals to the channel in Tangier Sound, and swept away the big hotel.

Captain Norman Benton was nine and living with his grandmother when the storm hit. Behind his grandmother's house was a big field, but the high tides of the hurricane inundated the fields of Deal Island. "It was just a river," behind her home, he remembers. The tide "come up to the house to about fifty feet. I thought it was fun," said Benton, but it was hardship for his grandmother, who was out of a job, along with hundreds of other Deal Islanders. "She worked at a crab picking house and wharf extending out into the sound near Wenona. It took it all."

At the time, there were about twenty-five dredge boats at Wenona, on the south end of the island, and about seventy-five at Chance, most at anchor in the Thorofare or out in the Manokin River. In the aftermath of the storm, "boats were all up in the land, skipjacks and other boats scattered everywhere. A lot of boats were destroyed," Benton remembers.

Captain Stanley Larrimore was only three when the storm hit, but he remembers the tide rising until it was only two houses down the street from his parents' home at Bar Neck on Tilghman Island. "They brought their rowboats up to the house" two doors away, he said. When the waters receded, his father, Captain Glendy Larrimore, walked up Bar Neck Road and found his skipjack, the *Laura J. Barkley,* lying in the field, surrounded by cows, but unharmed.

In the months following the August storm, one thing was certain: thousands of watermen along the Eastern Shore faced economic hardship unless drastic measures were taken to improve their lot. Watermen looked across the Bay for help, not just to the Maryland legislature, but to the river that had once proven to be the richest oyster grounds outside Tangier and Pocomoke sounds.

In 1931, Maryland had closed the Potomac River to dredging after biologists produced evidence that the dredgers had not only depleted the bars, but were

destroying them with their incessant dredging. The ban was supposed to last two years while the oysters repropagated. The two years were over in 1933, and, in the wake of the August storm and the devastation it left behind, Somerset County dredgers and local politicians pushed for the reopening of the river.

On September 17, Robert H. Jones, chairman of the Democratic state central committee for Somerset County, wrote a passionate plea to Governor Ritchie for help in reopening the river: "This plight of our citizens who resort to the taking of oysters for a

Crew prepare to hoist the
jib at sunrise.

livelihood is desperate in the extreme, and it is the consensus that the opening of the Potomac river to dredging is the only means through and by which the oystermen can be self-sustaining and a sufficient supply of oysters made available for the packers to operate and give employment to labor. Oysters are not on the bars of Tangier Sound and the Chesapeake Bay in sufficient quantities to make the taking profitable."

Jones's plea to the governor was quickly countered by Senator J. Allan Coad of St. Mary's County, who stated his strong opinion in a letter to the editor

of the *Crisfield Times,* which appeared in the October 27, 1933, issue: "... of all the various means and methods employed now or in the past in Maryland waters for the taking of oysters, none has been so terribly destructive and detrimental as the use of heavy dredges made possible since the advent of the power winder.

"As proof of this one has only to recall that oyster areas that for a half a century had successfully withstood the annual operations of literally thousands of dredge boats during the days when only hand power was employed, within a mere decade and a half after the universal use of power winders, became so depleted that it no longer was possible to operate a dredge boat at a profit, and as a consequence, Maryland's dredging fleet, that had numbered thousands in years gone by, gradually decreased until in the year 1932-33, less than one hundred dredging licenses were issued.

"The Potomac was closed to dredging in 1931 upon evidence produced by the U.S. Bureau of Fisheries, and the Conservation Department of Maryland. It was shown that continual use of heavy dredges in the Potomac River had not alone depleted the oyster producing areas therein, but in many instances had destroyed the natural rocks to such an extent that their rehabilitation was well nigh impossible. . . . No definite length of time of closing was fixed in the act," though most dredgers remember that the river was supposed to be reopened in two years.

On Saturday evening, November 18, 1933, some two hundred dredgers from around Somerset County crowded a meeting room on Deal Island to testify in support of opening the Potomac River. They talked of suffering immeasurable financial loss.

The watermen had hoped the state legislators would meet in a special session to reopen the river, but as the season dragged on, it became obvious that nothing would be done. A bill to open the Potomac to hand scrapers (small motorboats with small dredges, or scrapes, that were hauled aboard by hand) was defeated on Monday, December 11, 1933.

The permanent closure of the Potomac River—as it turned out to be—would create tremendous hardship for Somerset County dredgers whose own bars in Tangier and Pocomoke sounds were so depleted or diseased that they only occasionally yielded a decent harvest during much of the twentieth century. Deal and Smith Islanders had relied on the Potomac River for half or two-thirds of their oyster harvests until the closure. Now they would have to spend all their time working farther north out in the Chesapeake Bay. They were not permitted in the Choptank River, which was restricted to Dorchester and Talbot County dredgers only.

"Oystering in the Potomac would be the same as finding a gold mine in Alaska," said Art Daniels, captain of the *City of Crisfield,* who can remember his father dredging in the Potomac. "If we could work in the Potomac River, there'd be so many oysters, the market would be the problem," he said.

Ironically, the Potomac would continue to be dredged. From the 1940s through the early 1970s, any

man who was daring enough to sneak out at night in a powerboat equipped with a small hand scrape could make a living as an oyster pirate on the Potomac. For a while in the forties, Virginia police appeared to promote the illegal activity by looking the other way as Smith Islanders power-dredged on the Potomac.

"The police would allow us to work until eleven o'clock," when they would come out and do their duty, chasing the offenders off the bars, said a Smith Islander. By then, the islanders had caught enough to make a living. The arrangement worked well for Virginia, which got the islanders' business, but it hurt the Smith Island dredgers who chose to work legally in their skipjacks. The dredgers could no longer find crew; every young man who could afford a powerboat was out on the Potomac. For many Smith Island dredgers, it was the last straw. In the three Smith Island communities, which had once had more dredge boats in Somerset County than any other place besides Deal Island, the dredge boats began to disappear. One by one, they were sold away from the island or left to rot. One dredger, Captain Dan Dize, chose to move with his two skipjacks to Tilghman Island, where crew could still be found and where there were still oysters to be harvested. By the 1960s, only a handful of dredge boats were left on Smith Island. The last, the *Ruby G. Ford,* was sold to a Tilghman Islander in 1971.

It seemed as if every three years during the depressing thirties, Nature collaborated with the pitiful economic scene to wreak death and disaster on the watermen. After the August storm of '33, which damaged boats and floated them far ashore, came the big freeze of '36 when a rescue party set out to save the islanders, who were believed to be starving. The rescue ended in the death of one of the rescuers.

The depression and the natural disasters that accompanied the thirties did more to destroy the dredge fleet than any other period in its history. The number of dredge boats working in Dorchester County waters alone dropped from 131 in 1930 to only 7 in 1934, the year after the August storm. Dorchester County would never recover. This county which at one time in its history boasted a fleet of 250 dredge boats, would never again have more than 34—in 1955.

The worst decade in the hundred-year history of the skipjack closed with the deaths of nine dredgers, victims of an unseen, unheard gale that broke through a fog, upsetting three dredge boats in the queen of gentle waters, the Choptank River.

# Five

# DEATH IN THE FOG

*When you work on the water, making a living, you'll get caught in bad storms. Common sense, a lot of times, will take you out of them, and respect of the water and the good Lord.*
—Captain Stan Daniels

ALL MORNING, heavy fog had enveloped the small fleet of dredge boats working the oyster bar off Chlora Point near Castle Haven in the Choptank River. As of February 3, 1939, the crews aboard seven dredge boats, most from Wingate and other towns in the marshy wetlands of lower Dorchester County, had had little luck making a living off the river bottom. "The oysters had died off," remembers Wilson Todd, who was sailing with his father, Captain Purnell Todd aboard the *Ethel Lewis.*

The wind had been so light out of the northeast that the boats could barely drag one dredge across the oyster bars under sail before the weight of the shell-laden dredge slowed them almost to a halt. "There was just enough wind to drag and stop and wind [the dredges in] and go ahead a little bit, and drag again," remembers George Wheatley, of Bishops Head, who was an eighteen-year-old working the middle deck aboard the *Annie Lee.*

It was bad enough that oysters had been scarce all season, but recently, while the fleet worked near the mouth of the river, ice had forced the fleet to stay in harbor for several days. Finally, the weather had warmed enough to loosen the ice in the Choptank and allow the fleet to work again. And now, no wind.

Off and on throughout the day, the skies would darken, threatening rain, only to lighten again. Around noon, the fog lifted a little, but visibility was still poor.

Wheatley didn't think anything of the fluky weather, but Wilson Todd, who was thirty-five years old and had seen plenty of bad weather, didn't like the looks of the sky. He went aft to talk to his father about the weather. "I said, 'We might as well get away from here and get home. We ain't doin' nothin'. Looks to me like we're gonna have a thunder squall.'" His father agreed, so they left the fleet around noon, and headed home for Cambridge.

Later, aboard the *Joy Parks,* Captain Orville Parks also saw something that made him very uneasy. "The glass [barometer] was down, way down, as low as I had ever seen it and jumping around, which is a bad sign," he later told a reporter for the *Daily Times* in Salisbury. "We better get out of here," he yelled over to Captain Lloyd Kerwin, aboard the *Reliance.*

The two boats, which left about two o'clock, were soon joined by the rest of the fleet heading up-river to Cambridge, where they usually tied up for the weekend. As they turned homeward, many of the skipjacks still had canvas up, but several captains had dropped their sails and had their yawl boats pushing.

*Annie Lee*'s push boat needed fuel, however, so Wheatley jumped inside the little yawl, which was still strapped to the davits at the stern of the skipjack, and filled her gas tank. In the time it took him to fill the tank, the sun disappeared behind thick clouds and the day darkened. Wheatley tossed the empty container on deck, then glanced behind. What he saw was like nothing he's seen before or since. "It looked like smoke on the water," remembered Wheatley, and it was less than a hundred yards away. "It come just like a bank. Rolled right into us."

At the moment he saw it, there were no white-caps on the water to warn the dredgers of the approaching high winds. A photograph taken at the time by an observer on land seemed to confirm that what Wheatley saw, churning the waters into the appearance of smoke, was a mini-tornado, known as a waterspout when it develops on water because of the way it pulls the water upward into a spout.

*Annie Lee*'s captain, Theodore Woodland, shouted to his crew to drop the sails, but it was already too late. When the squall hit, packing seventy- to eighty-knot winds out of the northwest, *Annie Lee* immediately began to yaw off course, spinning into the wind. Had she been able to complete her turn into the wind, she probably would have stayed afloat, but the wind was too sudden, too heavy; with the skipjack carrying so much canvas, the waterspout flattened her against the churning seas.

"She lost her buoyancy and went right on down; I mean, she went right on down flat," said Wheatley, who jumped out of the yawl boat. Somehow, the four crewmen and captain were able to stay afloat as the skipjack sunk beneath them.

*Annie Lee* had been dragging a small skiff behind when the storm hit. Captain Woodland grabbed hold of it and the men climbed aboard her. Somebody grabbed *Annie Lee*'s anchor rode as it floated by.

Within minutes of the storm hitting, the seas became rough. By hanging onto the anchor line, which was still tied to the sunken skipjack, the men were able to steady the wildly rolling skiff. Then, suddenly, they lost hold of the anchor rode. The skiff, thrown sideways on the big waves, rolled right over. The five men were thrown out.

It was only a few seconds, but Wheatley vividly remembers the twenty-two-foot drop to the bottom of the river. Like the other men, he was still wearing the rubber hip boots he had been working in on the *Annie Lee*. Now the heavy boots, which had protected him against the rain and the dirty job of culling oysters, acted like an anchor, drawing him straight to the bottom of the river.

"When I hit the bottom, I shot myself right out of my boots," he said. When he surfaced again, the skiff was only ten feet away, now upside down in the water. He swam to it and grabbed the skeg, a small board protruding from the flat-bottomed skiff.

Miraculously, all the other men surfaced, too, and swam over to the skiff. By now, there were well-developed whitecaps. Forty-knot winds were "blowin'

the top right off the seas" and rolling big seas over the little skiff, which was the men's only hope of survival. Wheatley remembers how several of the men—frightened, tired, and freezing in the icy water—pulled at the tiny skiff, trying to drag themselves atop it.

"You're scared. Everybody's scared. If you're not scared, you're crazy," Wheatley said of the twenty minutes he spent in the water. "You know how a drowning person would be. The mistake they made is they tried to pull themselves up. Every time they did, the skiff would roll right over, just like a log." As the boat rolled, it would knock some of the men away from her. Wheatley, who somehow managed to stay calm enough to think, simply let go of the skeg and grabbed it again when the boat stopped rolling.

Captain Woodland, who was thirty-five, disappeared first. "The last I saw him, it looked like his hair was underwater about two feet, going down," said Wheatley, who tried to save him. "I always did think the captain was hurt in some way. He was an excellent swimmer." Wheatley surmised that barrels, or other debris on the deck of the *Annie Lee*, might have hit the captain when the skipjack heeled in the wind.

Next to disappear was Emerson Wingate, who was washed away from the skiff and never resurfaced. Another crewman managed to crawl up on the skiff, but was washed overboard by a wave, never to resurface.

Within ten minutes, all four men who had been with Wheatley were gone. For the next ten minutes, Wheatley gripped the little skiff, scanning the horizon for his fellow crewmen and for rescuers. The fog had broken into streamers, some high, some low, which allowed Wheatley, from his vantage point in the water, to see bits and pieces of dredge boats around him. "I could see the *J. T. Leonard* way off. She had her topsails blowed all to pieces, like a sock in the breeze," said Wheatley of the sloop which, unlike the simply rigged skipjacks, carried one sail far aloft. "I could see Captain Lloyd in the *Reliance*," but Lloyd couldn't see Wheatley. The wind was still blowing too hard for anyone to look into the wind, Wheatley soon realized.

Wheatley spotted the *Agnes*, a one-masted bugeye, capsized south of the *Annie Lee*. He didn't know it then, but everyone aboard the *Agnes*, which had sunk in deep water, had perished, including Captain William Bradford who, at age seventy-three, was considered the dean of the dredge boat captains.

Then he looked north and saw the bugeye *Nora Lawson* capsized off Howell Point. Captain Bevel North aboard the *Nora Lawson* had managed to lash down his sails and anchor in shoal water off Howell Point, but the wind was so terrific, it had capsized the boat under bare poles. The dredge boat was in shallow water and went aground. Enough of the vessel remained above water that North and his crew were able to cling to the side of the boat until they were rescued by Captain William Parks in a motorboat.

A dredger who survived the gale would later tell the *Daily Banner* that all three capsized boats were in a line, supporting the theory that they were hit by a twister.

"Then I looked back the way the wind was blowin'," Wheatley said. "I seen the top of a mast, that's all I could see. Then the bowsprit jumped through the fog on me."

It was Captain William "Bill" Hubbard in the *Geneva May*. Two men were standing at her bow; two at her middle deck. Hubbard had just come by the boom of the sunken *Annie Lee* and was looking for survivors. When he spotted Wheatley hanging onto the skiff, he threw him a line. It was an anchor line, called a hawser, and it was almost as thick as a man's wrist.

"She [*Geneva May*] was runnin' down with the wind. She was flyin'," said Wheatley. "I didn't have nothin' to hold onto but plain line. If I hadn't held it, I would have drowned, too." As the skipjack hauled him away from the skiff, Wheatley stuffed the thick line between his teeth. "I locked it in my jaws, so it wouldn't slide," and he gripped the line tight with his two hands on either side of his mouth. The crew winched in the line on the rollers at mid-deck—normally used to roll in the dredges—and hauled him aboard.

As he lay on the deck of the *Geneva May*, Wheatley remembers hearing the captain say, "My gosh, I don't know who it is. One of Theodore's crew." Someone said, "Don't let his face hit them oysters." Then he passed out. Later, he learned that his skin had turned so dark in the freezing water, that they thought he was a black man. He didn't gain consciousness until they reached Cambridge, an hour later.

Back in Cambridge, the Todds had just about reached Long Wharf at the entrance to Cambridge Creek, and were only about a hundred yards from the dock, when the squall hit. "It blowed the hardest I've ever seen it blow," said Wilson Todd, who did not realize the plight of the other dredge boats in the fleet.

The first word of the tragedy was brought to Cambridge by Captain Hubbard, who carried Wheatley ashore, and summoned medical help. Wheatley was treated aboard the boat, then taken to his brother's home to recuperate from exposure.

The state police boat, the *Tangier*, under the command of Captain D. Clinton Kinnamon, went down the river in a vain search for survivors.

"I never expected to step foot here again," Sangston Todd, a crewman, told a reporter for the *Daily Banner*. "All of us are lucky to be back." Crewman Ivy McNamara told the newspaper reporter that the wind was so strong, "I didn't think a single boat would come back." Captain Lloyd Kirwan, a son-in-law of Captain Bradford, called it the worst storm he had ever seen on the Bay. Many of the boats that made it back came into port with their sails ripped and their rigging damaged.

Captain Bradford of Crapo near Deal Island was finishing his sixtieth year on a dredge boat, working the bugeye *Agnes* for its owner, William L. Jones. He had planned to retire after this trip. Before leaving port the week before, he told the oyster inspector, Captain Hallie A. Creighton, that he thought this trip would be his last. Tragically, it was.

Others who died on the *Agnes* were four black crewmen: Aaron Ennalls, Rodney Jones, Robert Elliott, and Sam Brown. Killed on the *Annie Lee* were Captain Theodore Woodland and Emerson Wingate, both of Bishops Head; Herbert Robinson and James Scruggs. In all, nine dredgers lost their lives that day.

For the next several days, patrol boats of the Maryland Conservation Commission, which policed the waters, and volunteers, including practically all the captains who had survived the storm, returned to the site of the tragedy to drag for bodies and to help recover the vessels. Saturday, they were only able to recover two bodies, but Sunday, using special grappling hooks made by a local blacksmith the day before, the recovery team dragged the river bottom and found six more bodies. The body of one crewman was found caught in the rigging of the *Agnes*.

In retrospect, Wheatley said it never dawned on him that he might die, even as he watched the others disappear. Against great odds, he had been the sole survivor in a tragedy that can easily be billed as the worst disaster in skipjack history.

"I guess, what saved me is I was always fightin'. I was one of these people who thought nothin' could happen to me. You have to keep movin'. If you stop fightin', lots of times, you be dead. That's the way I look at life. Life's a fight from the time you start, till you die."

Two months later, Wheatley joined another dredge boat crew, planting seed oysters for the state.

The *Lady Katie*, with Captain Stanley Larrimore at the helm.

*Six*

# FEUDING OVER THE OYSTER BARS

*I dredged with a man who run over another boat. He said, "You better hold on this time because I'm gonna run into him." And we pulled our mast out.*

—Captain Norman Benton about
fighting over the oyster bars

STANLEY LARRIMORE was working the middle deck of his father's skipjack when Captain Glendy Larrimore suddenly hollered for the crew to drop the sails. The *E. C. Collier* was on a collision course with Larrimore's vessel, the *Laura J. Barkley*. Young Larrimore and another man were trying to take in the sail when the vessels collided. Seconds later, the mast came crashing down around the young men, breaking into three pieces. "All that stuff fell down on us on deck," remembers Larrimore, who escaped without injury. The other crewman was skinned pretty badly.

It was clear to the men aboard the *Laura J. Barkley* that this had been no accident. "He just run right down on us," said Larrimore.

The captain in the *E. C. Collier* had been working the oyster bar at Todds Point on the Choptank since daybreak. When the *Laura J. Barkley* approached, he pulled the worst of the dirty tricks dredgers used against each other as they battled, sometimes using their own boats as weapons, for the right to work a piece of bottom.

The crew of the *Laura J. Barkley* had just thrown their dredges overboard and were adjusting the lines when the *E. C. Collier* bore down on them, Larrimore remembered.

If a captain knew what he was doing, he could dismast another vessel without causing any damage to his own boat. To do this, a captain had only to "come by and cut you close" or slack his boom out until the big wooden spar hung way beyond the deck of his own vessel, far enough to become entangled in the rigging of the other vessel as they passed each other over the oyster bar, Larrimore said. "They'd go by you and hook their boom into your jibstay or jumping stay (a steel cable hooked to the top of the mast and rigged down to the bow of the boat to steady the mast), and that would pull your mast down over your bow."

This incident happened on the first day of the season in the late forties, forcing Captain Glendy Larrimore to return to port for repairs.

No one really knows why the captain of the *E. C. Collier* dismasted the *Laura J. Barkley*, but it was surely over oysters.

Greed sometimes provoked these attacks. If a captain hit a particularly good lick of oysters, he might not want to share them with other dredgers because the more he shared, of course, the less he would have for himself. But the oysters belong to no man, and every dredger has the right to work the public oyster bars of Maryland.

"Nobody owns nothin' out there. That's the way I look at it," said Larrimore. "If I put a buoy out, I can't claim that place; it's just a marker. Some of them put buoys out and they feel that's theirs and you shouldn't be around, but it doesn't work that way. Not with me."

Of all the laws written around the oyster, not one deals with the rights of a dredger working his buoys. Over the years, however, dredgers have developed their own unwritten code of ethics.

"If I came to someone's buoy, most of the time I could work it with him if I got behind them or I let them work it the way they want to . . . let them go about

The *Lady Katie* passes through the drawbridge that spans Knapps Narrows.

when you wanted to," Larrimore explained. In other words, a captain who moved in behind another shouldn't bully the first man off the oysters, or interfere with his pattern of dredging. You were supposed to respect a man's right to work oysters he had staked out with buoys.

Ethics over the oyster bars, however, often didn't last long. A captain might make a quicker lick, come about before the first boat, and move in ahead of the other dredger. Since bigger dredge boats were generally faster and carried more sail, they could easily push around the smaller boats, even force a captain off his own buoys.

Captain Dan Dize remembers a story his father, Captain Theodore Dize, told of how he took revenge on a schooner captain who was pushing him off his oysters. Dize was dredging in a pungy, a gaff-rigged

vessel often used for dredging in the 1800s and early 1900s, when a schooner joined him on the oyster bar. The schooner was bigger and had far more canvas than the pungy. Each time he came about, the schooner captain would go to windward of the pungy, taking the wind from the pungy and leaving the pungy dead in the water. After a while, Captain Dize could no longer pull a dredge. Finally, he aimed his bowsprit for the schooner's midsection and rammed it. Dismasting and ramming were two methods used by captains of smaller boats to stop the bigger dredge boats from pushing them around.

Sometimes friendships were ruined on the oyster bars. Captain Stanley Larrimore remembers the time one old captain was catching oysters and nobody could figure out where he was working.

"John Larrimore, my cousin, and this captain were friends. He told John, 'The first time you get a chance, slip down here and I'll put you on them.'"

His cousin got in on the cache of oysters for a day or two, then one morning Stanley Larrimore followed him out, hoping to find the rich oyster bar. The old captain and John Larrimore, however, would not go on the bar.

"I fooled around all day. At eleven o'clock, lunchtime, I never had one bushel on my boat. I went out in the Bay, way out from them," Stanley Larrimore recounted. With him gone, the other two captains went on the bar. "I caught a marker on them, jibed, and put my yawl boat down, and went right for them. When I got there, they had oysters piled above their sideboards. They tried to pull their buoys up, but it was too late."

The first captain blamed John for letting Stanley find the oysters, charging that John had been too slow getting up his buoys and moving off the oysters. "They fought the rest of the evening. They ran over each other," ramming each other's boats, Larrimore said. Before the end of the day, Stanley Larrimore had as much as either of them. The other two were so busy fighting, they didn't do much more dredging.

As oysters became scarce in the early twentieth century, it was not surprising that skipjack captains often turned to dirty tactics—tactics that could easily have damaged their own vessel, as well as that of the offending captain—to keep other dredgers off their oysters. It was not always easy finding oysters. Even with fewer than a hundred boats dredging in the 1940s and 1950s, dredgers still quickly depleted their oyster bars. Some dredgers, however, continued to do well throughout the season, by working the edges of oyster bars—finding the slim ridge of oysters left behind when the bar was originally dredged, or by finding new beds of oysters where no one had ever worked before.

Before the days of video depth-sounders, dredgers used sounding poles to locate new oyster beds. To make a sounding pole, they'd "cut two straight little saplings about maybe an inch and a half in diameter and splice them together," Larrimore said. This produced a pole almost as long as the boat, about thirty-five feet. "Then you went to the windward side and you sounded end-over-end. You dropped the pole in the water on an angle and as the boat was going, when you got the pole on the bottom, it was pretty well straight up and down and you'd make your sound. When that end picks up, then you overhand it. If you're going

along on real muddy bottom, then come up on something hard, a lot of times that would be oysters. Once you located that bar, it was always in your mind. You took landmarks, north and south and east and west. That's how you go back. Or you put a little vanilla bottle to mark it." Dredgers would anchor the tiny bottle on a line no longer than the depth of the water, so that it was hard to see.

One of Larrimore's crew was sounding for oysters in the Choptank in the late seventies when he hit a mess of oysters that no one else knew about. "I was looking for these oysters," remembered Larrimore. "I had worked there with my father." When his first mate hit the oysters, "you could hear those boys hollering for a mile," Larrimore said. But then trouble arrived.

"We hadn't made two licks, and here comes this boat. "I told the fellas, 'I ain't gonna let that man go on these oysters. We'll go off of them.' Then I picked

Captain Stanley Larrimore remembers his father, Glendy Larrimore, having his boat dismasted in a disagreement with another dredger on the Choptank River.

up my spyglass and looked and it was my nephew. Darryl had had a lot of bad luck that year." Larrimore asked his men if they wanted to let Darryl Larrimore work with them, and they agreed, since they were friends with his crew.

"I caught my limit and was in about eleven A.M. Darryl, it took him longer. He ain't come in till evening." When he finally got into port, Darryl had oysters all the way across deck on the *Claud Somers*. It was only 150 bushels on deck, but since the skipjack was so small, "it looked like she had a million bushels," Larrimore said.

"The next morning, here they come," recalled Larrimore, referring to the rest of the fleet. By then, all the captains had heard how many oysters the Larrimores had docked. "Well, I wouldn't go on them," said Larrimore, who dredged a mile and a half away from where he had hit the oysters.

At one point, dredger Robbie Wilson hit a few oysters. "Dern, Robbie, you found it," Larrimore assured him, trying hard to mislead the others. "I had them off of 'em till two o'clock that afternoon."

Then a hand tonger, who had passed Larrimore the day before, went by again and realized what was going on. The tonger called his cousin, dredger Bart Murphy, on the CB. "You fellas ain't lookin' in the right place," he said, then he proceeded to tell his cousin where the Larrimores had been working the day before.

"We caught a good many oysters off of that spot," recounted Larrimore with a grin. "They still kid me about that sometimes."

Like many of the Tilghman boys, Larrimore dropped out of school at seventeen to join his father on a skipjack in 1947. "I can remember when the school bus went out around the corner. I wished I had gotten back on it, but I was too stubborn to do it. [Dredging] was hard work and it was cold."

Glendy Larrimore tried to discourage his son from dredging by making him do all the hard work. The *Laura J. Barkley* was anchored off Tilghman, and they would run two anchors out from her bow to keep her from fouling. Somebody had to row the second anchor out, and usually Glendy sent his son.

Crewmen wrestle a dredge laden with oysters aboard the *Howard*.

"He'd say to me when it got real cold, 'Don't you wish you were on that school bus?' and I'd say, 'No,' all the time I was thinking, yeah, on the back seat, somewhere."

"You'd think he'd cut a little slack on his son, but he was really trying to get me to go back to school," Larrimore realized.

When Larrimore grew up, Blackwalnut Point, at the southern tip of Tilghman Island, was a community with its own harbor, as well as stores to stock the homes and boats. Larrimore remembers four or five skipjacks anchored in the shallow cove when he started dredging. "There would be times when they were on the bottom," said Larrimore of the harbor that is now barely deep enough to accommodate the deadrise workboats.

"From the shore we'd have to go out in a skiff. We always towed a little skiff," he said. Often when they were out dredging away from home, they used the skiff to go ashore, to get wood for the cabin stove and water. "We'd come ashore and get half a cord of wood in the skiff, and then we'd throw it up in the bow. Half the time, it'd be so wet, we couldn't get it to burn," Larrimore remembered.

However, the skipjacks didn't always have to come ashore for provisions or to let off their oysters. Big buyboats would go out to the dredge boats and purchase the oysters from them. "A lot of time, he [the captain of the buyboat] would bring our water and our wood to us. We had big fifty-five- or thirty-five-gallon barrels." The crew used the halyards, lines rigged to the top of the mast and usually used to haul up the sails, to take the big barrels of water off the buyboat and put them on the skipjack's deck.

When the crew returned to port, they would put two anchors out and row ashore. Anchoring is "easier on the boat," believes Larrimore, who now ties his *Lady Katie* to a dock, like all the other captains. "She turns around with the wind, and the sun hits her every different way."

Buyboats began disappearing in the fifties as oyster packinghouses relied more on trucks that could follow the boats to different ports to buy the oysters. "That was the end of a lot of things," according to Larrimore.

Back in 1947, the push boats had small engines that didn't have transmissions. "We hooked them up direct, no reverse. Just went forward. They had automobile engines, Model As, and Pontiacs."

"The first boat I worked on had a Hettinger one-cylinder motor [used for winding in the dredges].

They had a piston, must have been eight or ten inches. They were temperamental, they run good, but half the time they wouldn't pull." Today, with big automobile motors in their push boats and better winder engines, captains can haul in their dredges and come about on a new tack fairly quickly. "With them Hettinger winders, unless they worked real good you couldn't do that. When you kept the boat off, she gathered headway and that made more of a strain on the winders. You'd have to let her shake in the wind until she got her dredges aboard. You'd always take your leeward dredge aboard first, and then the windward. Now, you can bring them both aboard at the same time."

When the old winders failed, the crew had to pull the dredges, loaded with a hundred pounds of shellfish, aboard by hand. "I've even towed them into shoal water so they wouldn't have to pull them in from thirty foot of water," Larrimore said. "When you get into shallow water, you can throw an anchor in the back of the bag and dump it out."

Sail dredging—which is all dredgers did before the law was changed to allow two days of power dredging in 1966—took skill. "The bar might be one way, and the wind may only let you work it crossways. It's a challenge," Larrimore said.

The ideal speed for dredging is three knots, which is why dredgers start reefing in their sails even in moderate winds of ten to twelve knots. If they sail too fast over the oyster bar, the dredges start floating off the bottom. "After you put your third or fourth reef in and take your jib in, that's about the last thing you can do, as far as slowin' her down. From there on, it's not too good. At thirty miles per hour [wind speed], you're floatin' your dredges. Can't get them on the bottom right. You can let her come up [into the wind] and let them get down on the bottom, but once she keeps off [the wind], she'll pick' em right up and pull them off the bottom," Larrimore said.

During 1948-49, oysters were scarce. "The very first day of the season, we caught maybe fifteen-eighteen bushels," around Tilghman. "We didn't find much so we decided to go up the upper part of the Bay looking for oysters. We couldn't find much, so we decided to come home."

The skipjacks usually carried a cook who served up hot meals, whether the crew lived aboard the boat or came into port each night. The cook would often have breakfast cooking on the stove before the vessel left port in the early morning hours. Dinner or lunch was often served around eleven A.M. The meals were cheap, but hearty. "Them days, it was mostly beans, corned beef hash, hot bread, codfish cakes, cabbage, and potatoes," Larrimore recalled.

Larrimore would have continued dredging with his father, but in 1951 he received a draft notice. Rather than be drafted into the marines, "who were really catching it then" in Korea, Larrimore enlisted for four years in the navy, and ended up staying for six years. When he returned to Tilghman Island, he bought the *Reliance* from his uncle, Reds McQuay, and went back to dredging.

The *Reliance* had been badly damaged by Hurricane Hazel in 1954. During the flood tide, she had broken loose and floated up over the main road through Tilghman Island. By the time the men of the island got her off dry land and back into the water, she had a cracked keel and was leaking badly. Larrimore purchased the boat for $2,500, the going price for skipjacks.

"The next year, we put her on the railway and started to work on her and we couldn't find a stopping place," said Larrimore. "She was rotten and they busted her keel, right where her centerboard is. I bolted her back together. I finally stopped in October. I had spent $3,500 on her. The following year, we finished her up."

Larrimore totally rebuilt the *Reliance*—only to have her sunk by a rodent. He was heading back into port one day, after catching his limit of 150 bushels, when the boat started to feel funny. "I told the crew, 'Look in there and see if this boat's got any water in her. She don't feel right.' They were playing cards, so they just said, 'She's all right.'"

The *Reliance* was just about off Sherwood, coming between Poplar Island and the mainland, about ten minutes out of Tilghman, when Larrimore realized she was filling up with water. "I thought we could make it to Tilghman, but just before we got down to Tilghman, she got even with the water. I just sailed her up until she hit bottom. Jackie Thompson came down and took the oysters off her," and Larrimore limped her home.

He put her on the railway, got a flashlight, and took a look inside. And there, through the capping (a two-inch piece of wood on the centerboard well), he saw the hole. "That's where the rat eat that hole."

Rats were a nuisance when the skipjacks tied up to a port. "Lot of times, they're looking for a place to get, and they'll get up in your motor." This one, however, had hidden in the centerboard well. "When he

got in there he was closed in. He gnawed a hole right through it."

Larrimore, who was born in 1930, has seen oysters become scarce in the Bay, then recover at least three times in his lifetime.

In 1956, the *Reliance* could bring in $300 to $600 a week, but the captain's share was only about $33 a week. The boat got one-third of the haul, averaging between $100 and $200 a week in November 1956. The captain and crew split the remaining two-thirds of the

Two dredge boats race home with their catch after a day's work harvesting oysters from the Chesapeake.

money from the catch, after taking out costs for food and fuel. "I've heard my father say, if he had sold $300 by Christmas, he was doing good," said Larrimore.

"We went on through the sixties pretty good, up to 1963-64, then the oysters died off again. It was better in 1974-75," remembers Larrimore, who was often back in port by ten o'clock in the morning. Ten years later, they would be scarce again.

"It's been cycles. It's never been really something that was great," Larrimore said of dredging. "It's an interesting life; you're working outside. You're not going to a factory, eight to four. But it's got a lot of disadvantages when you get older: there's no retirement fund.

"Unless you were smart enough to invest in something . . . houses that you could rent, or something. There just wasn't enough to save. We've had good years, but we've had a lot of bad years, too. When you wind up, it's a livin'. That's barely what you get out of it."

Crew venture out onto the long bowsprit of the *Kathryn* to reef the jib as the wind breezes up.

# Seven

# HURRICANE HAZEL

*I caught 619 bushel in an hour and thirty-five minutes in the* Mamie Mister. *That was around 1960 on Flat Rock. We got three dollars and some a bushel then.*
—Captain Jesse Thomas recalling his best lick
in fifty years of dredging

FOR THE captains harbored at Kent Narrows, it was a simple decision: believe the weather reports and get in a day's work, or play it safe and stay in the harbor.

Hurricane Hazel was working her way north, packing winds of over a hundred miles per hour, but she wasn't due to hit Chesapeake Bay until late that night.

When dawn broke on October 15, 1954, the wind was fresh, between twenty and twenty-five knots, but not too rough for skipjacks working under the power of their yawl boats. So that morning, several of the big dredge boats joined the scows, workboats, and buyboats assembled off Parson Island in Eastern Bay, near Kent Narrows, to plant seed oysters for the state of Maryland.

Captain Norman Benton, who was crewing for Captain Jesse Thomas, remembers that the men aboard the *Esther W* were not concerned about the hurricane as they left to move seed. "Weather didn't call for it to come. We thought it would hit that night and we'd be back by that time."

Likewise, the men aboard the smaller boats had little concern for the approaching storm. They would put off their seed oysters to big scows and buyboats, which would carry the load across the Chesapeake Bay. The small boats would be back in port before midafternoon. But the scows and the bigger skipjacks, which carried up to a thousand bushels of oysters, would cross the Chesapeake to the South River, where the state had decided to plant the seed oysters, or spat, as young oysters are called. Over the designated bars, crews would shovel the spat overboard.

That morning as the hurricane worked its way north, Captain Ira Thomas in the *Mamie A. Mister* and his son, Captain Jesse Thomas in the *Esther W* worked over Parson Island Bar, dredging the seed-laden shells off the bar and dumping them on deck. Most of the year, the big wooden boats were pretty vessels to look at, but during the seed oyster season, the boats were outfitted with ugly plywood boxes on their decks. The boxes were needed to hold the oysters that would be piled up on deck almost as high as a man is tall. They were also required by the state, which measured these boxes to determine how many bushels of seed oysters the boat could carry. The state paid the captains according to how many bushels they planted.

The state of Maryland had been planting seed oysters since the 1940s in an effort to improve the diminishing harvests on the Bay. By removing seed oysters from bars that reproduced well and hauling them to places in the Bay where the oyster population had become exhausted, the state hoped to bolster the oyster crop.

It wasn't long before the skipjacks were loaded and ready to cross the Bay. The wind was freshening as they left the bar. Besides the *Esther W* and the *Mamie Mister,* a third skipjack, the *Thomas Ruth,* also made the trip over.

"We were trying to make it over and get back," said Benton. "It started gettin' bad when we left in the morning. The wind was increasing all the time." Benton may not have been concerned when they left that morning to start work, but now, as they crossed the open Bay, "I worried all the time," he said. "When we got across the Bay, it was blowin' fifty miles an hour. By the time we got to the creek, it was ninety or a hundred."

At age thirty-eight, Jesse Thomas had seen a lot of bad weather, but never had he been aboard a dredge boat in an approaching hurricane. Winds as high as fifty knots didn't worry him, but he knew a skipjack, even under bare poles, had been known to capsize in winds over eighty miles per hour.

While crossing the Bay, the skipjacks passed scows struggling into a head wind back to the Eastern Shore after planting their seed oysters. By the time they made the mouth of the South River, the winds were howling fifty knots. "We were supposed to plant them in the South River, but it got bad so we dumped 'em as we went along," said his crewman, Norman Benton.

Jesse Thomas pushed on up the river as far as he could take the *Esther W,* knowing the farther inland he could get, the better protection he might find from the raging winds of the hurricane. Just below the South

River Bridge, the crew spotted a yacht anchored inside a creek and Thomas steered the *Esther W* inside the creek. They dropped four anchors, but it wasn't enough to hold the big workboat, which was considered one of the four or five biggest skipjacks ever built.

"I drug back into land," Thomas said. "She was hittin' bottom hard. I thought she was gonna knock the rudder off."

Thomas tried to turn the boat around in order to head back across the river where he had spotted a good harbor sheltered by high banks.

"I was trying to get her around any how, but she was rounding," he said. Thomas struggled with the wheel, desperately trying to turn the big boat into the wind so he could make his turn. The thing he feared most was jibing the boom in high winds. If the hurricane-force winds managed to turn the *Esther W* the wrong way, the big boom, powered by the ninety-mile-per-hour winds, might swing violently across the stern

While waiting for the dredge to fill, crew aboard the *Lady Katie* take a few minutes to rest from the grueling job of shoveling seed oysters into huge piles on deck.

The crew of the *Rebecca T. Ruark* wrestle with the jib.

of the boat, probably tearing out the mast, damaging the vessel, and maybe hurting someone.

Finally, the bow of the *Esther W* struck a tree. The tide was so high, the boat was actually floating over what had been dry land just a few hours earlier. The impact pushed the skipjack on around into the wind, so that Thomas could safely turn and sail her across the river. "I got back in that harbor and got into a place that was as good as if I were in a cave," he said.

Meanwhile, his father in the *Mamie Mister* rode out the hurricane in the river, at the mouth of the creek. Neither the *Mamie Mister* nor the *Ruth A. Thomas* broke anchor that night.

The wind howled throughout the night. In Annapolis, the winds were clocked at 108 miles per hour; in Washington, 105 miles per hour. At the height of the storm, the winds swung around from the southwest.

The next morning, it took an hour for Captain Thomas and his crew to unload the tree limbs and debris that were scattered across the deck of the *Esther W.* Despite the high winds and tide, there was no damage on board and everyone was safe. Likewise, the other two skipjacks had weathered the storm without damage. After clearing away the debris, Thomas helped his father get underway.

When they finally got back to the Kent Narrows, they found that the boats tied up there had fared worse than the three that made the run across the Bay. Captain Eldon Willing, Sr., had been prudent and kept the *Robert L. Webster* tied to the dock, but the tide rose so high that the *Robert L.* ran up over the dock, destroying the dock and damaging the skipjack.

The Thomases had taken the risk and won. Not only did they get in a day's work and a day's pay, but their boats were unscathed—amazing considering the

Aboard the *Rebecca T. Ruark*, seed oysters pile up on deck as high as a man is tall.

damage Hazel left in her wake. Every port on the Chesapeake was in shambles. Just weeks before the start of the new oyster season, boats were smashed, docks were destroyed, and many vessels were washed hundreds of yards ashore into fields and marshes by the extremely high tide.

On Tilghman Island, Captain Reds McQuay found his skipjack, the *Reliance,* lying in the middle of the main road on the island. She was intact, but her keel cracked as they hauled her back into the water where she belonged. At Deal Island, where some forty skipjacks and numerous workboats were harbored, the hurricane left hardly anything untouched.

Earlier in the day, as the tide began to rise, Gordon Gladden, his older brother and a friend, went down to tend to their father's skipjacks. Elbert Gladden, Sr., had four skipjacks tied up in a little creek near Chance. Normally, there was just enough water to float the shoal-draft vessels, but in the face of the oncoming hurricane, the tide had already risen five feet above normal. It was over the heads of the teenage boys as

they tried to secure more lines to the boats. When Elbert Gladden came down to the docks and saw what they were doing, he told them to stop. Instead of tying more lines, he directed the boys to release all the lines so the skipjacks would be carried by the tide. Tying down the boats, he feared, could cause them to be ripped apart by the tide and winds. The next morning, the Gladdens found their boats all intact, but washed about a hundred yards into the nearby fields.

"We had to get house movers from Fruitland to move the boats. We got skids and rollers and thirty men," Gordon Gladden recalled. It was an undertaking that took days, but Elbert Gladden managed to turn the fiasco into a party. The year before had been a bad one for the strawberry crop and Gladden, who kept an acre in strawberries, had refused to sell for a market that was paying only two dollars per crate. Instead, he had turned all his strawberries into strawberry wine. After two days of moving the big boats, Gladden broke open a few jugs and passed around the home brew.

With her sails lashed down, a dredge boat makes for port before an approaching storm.

# Eight

# TWISTER OFF THE CLIFFS

*If they don't see any fear in your eyes, then everything goes along all right. But, boy, if the captain get afraid, then everything goes haywire and you lose your boat.*
—Captain Art Daniels about bad weather and the crew

CAPTAIN ROBBIE WILSON and other dredgers can remember when the looming banks of Calvert Cliffs served as a protective wall against the weather, offering them refuge and an opportunity to work the oyster bars above Solomons Island, even in a gale. The wind could blow seventy knots out of the west, or northwest, and the men could dredge with a three-reef mainsail some two hundred feet below the top of Calvert Cliffs. But for at least one dredger, Calvert Cliffs was nothing less than "a mean, dangerous place."

"I didn't like to work under them," said Captain Clyde Evans. "It's high there, and the wind would come down and turn round and round." He has good reason to label the cliffs dangerous. While every dredger has experienced high winds, rough seas, hail, sleet, snow, and ice, few had witnessed what he saw come off the cliffs one day in the late sixties while dredging with other Smith Islanders.

It was a perfect dredging day as the five skipjacks from Smith Island worked together under the cliffs near Drum Point Light at the mouth of the Patuxent River about noon. "It was windy, but it weren't no gale," said Evans who estimated the wind was ten to fifteen knots.

"I was lookin' ashore and seen it comin'. One of them twisters come off the top of the cliff. I hollered to drop the jib and the mainsail all at the same time," said Evans who believed the little twister was on a course for his boat, the *Lorraine Rose.* "It hit the water several hundred feet from us. You could see it comin'

right across the water, twisting. When it went by me, I could have throwed a shell and hit it," it was that close.

But while his skipjack and three other vessels were spared, the twister hit the *Eldora.* Captain Edgar Bradshaw evidently never saw it coming; he still had the sails up on the *Eldora* when it hit her. "It flipped her right over, just the same as you'd pick up a cup and throwed it. She went right over," said Evans, who was working beside the *Eldora.* "She went over like a top."

Captain Bradshaw had three of his four sons aboard as crew, as well as another man. All of them were tossed into the water as the *Eldora* capsized in ninety feet of water. It happened so fast, however, that air was evidently caught inside the cabin, for the skipjack did not sink. In the aftermath of the twister, she was listing on her side at a forty-five-degree angle, with one side still breaking the surface. The men—none of whom could swim—were clinging to this side of the boat when Evans and Captain Daniel Harrison in the *Ruby G. Ford* went over to pick them up. The rescue was fairly easy since the water was calm. Evans picked up the captain and two of his sons; the rest climbed aboard the *Ruby G. Ford.*

With the crew safe, the Smith Island men turned to the task of saving the *Eldora.* If they didn't act fast, she would sink and with the bottom some ninety feet below, she might not be able to be salvaged.

While most watermen help each other, the comradeship of the Smith Islanders was particularly well known. Generations of living on a group of isolated islands off the Eastern Shore in the Chesapeake Bay had taught Smith Islanders that working together often meant survival.

"I quit many times an hour before I would have quit to help pull somebody," so they could get their boat or engine repaired, said Evans. He knew that his help could mean the difference between the other man working or losing a whole day.

So the Smith Islanders talked and came up with a novel way of rescuing the boat. Rather than dragging it to shore and risking tearing it up, they decided to try putting a line under the skipjack and winching her up.

"One of us got to her stern and one to her bow on either side of her," said Evans. Evans unhooked a dredge and passed the cable to Harrison who went to the other side of the *Eldora*, letting the line pass under the hull of the vessel. Then he attached the end of the cable to his winders and both captains started blocking her up, winding the cable in. She rose so easily out of

the water, Evans surmised that her hull must still have been full of air, which would also have helped to keep her buoyant.

"Soon as the hatch came up, we throwed the pumps on her and she come right up," he said. An hour or so after the capsize, the *Eldora* was floating on the surface again.

"It never hurt nothin', other than his sails got wet," he said. Inside the cabin, the stove and other items were tossed about, but nothing was damaged. Bradshaw went back into port to clean up his boat and check it out. The others went back to dredging.

The sudden and violent capsize apparently upset Bradshaw and his crew. The next day, he sailed home to Rhodes Point on Smith Island. "I don't think he ever worked her again," said Evans who lived at Ewell, a few miles from Rhodes Point. "I think he laid her up and the next fall he sold her."

Seawater runs from the dredge bag as a crewman, working the winder engine, dips the dredge in and out of the river to rinse mud out of this lick of oysters.

Two skipjacks are mirrored in the river as a "slick ca'm," as dredgers call this weather, envelops the fleet on the Choptank River.

# Nine

# DAYS OF POWER

*Dredging is not as hard as it used to be. You used to have to stay aboard an old boat, anchor off, and never go ashore. Now you can go home in your bed every night. You can get your rest.*
—Captain Stan Daniels

A S FAR as the eye could see, the river was as still as glass around the skipjacks that lay on their dredges over the oyster bars. Bad enough that it was "slick ca'm" for a day, but it had been like this for three weeks.

Every day for three long weeks the Tilghman Island captains had pushed out to the oyster bars before dawn in hopes of catching a breeze. And for three long weeks, they had sat, becalmed over the oysters that they were permitted to harvest only under sail. Without wind, there was no work for the men on the dredge boats. So, to while away the hours, Captain Pete Sweitzer would move his skipjack, the *Hilda M. Willing*, alongside the *Joy Parks* and play poker with Captain Dan Murphy.

Sweitzer had been caught out in bad storms and in eighty-mile-per-hour winds, but none of the worst weather nature had drummed up during his long years as a skipjack captain matched the misery of three long weeks without wind—and without work.

"It was the worst time I've ever seen on the water," said Sweitzer, who bought the *Hilda M. Willing* in 1946, shortly after he returned home from naval duty during World War II. Sweitzer's parents were farmers, but there was little land to farm on Tilghman Island, so when Pete Sweitzer returned home after the war, he went to work on a dredge boat, then bought his own skipjack.

During that three-week period in the late fifties, "We couldn't catch a damn bushel. We couldn't move for three weeks," said Sweitzer. Experiencing such a long stretch of windless days during the first two months of the season was particularly devastating because dredgers knew they would lose still more time to ice and bad weather once winter settled in.

"Two-thirds of the money you make oystering, you make before Christmas. If you don't make any money by January first in the oyster business, you might as well forget that year," Sweitzer states. "November and December are really the only two months we got. After December, the weather takes charge," he said, referring to the ice that locks most Chesapeake harbors for several weeks each winter. "We have eight weeks to make a season's work with a dredge boat. If we lose two-three weeks to this moderate weather, you'll never get it back, not this season."

A long period of calm weather in November and December meant the captains couldn't pay their bills. Crews were also likely to jump ship and find another job.

For almost a hundred years the dredge boats had worked under the 1865 law forbidding dredging under power. A few years later, spurred by the memory of that long calm, Pete Sweitzer went to a state legislator in an attempt to have the old law changed, at least for two days a week. Fortunately, Tilghman Islander Randolph Harrison, who was also a former dredger, was chairman of the Chesapeake Bay and tributaries house committee in the state legislature which oversaw all legislation dealing with the Bay in the sixties.

"How about lettin' us have push boats? Just let us try it two days a week for two years," Sweitzer suggested. Harrison arranged to hold a public meeting on the suggestion. Dredgers on Deal Island liked the idea, but

Sweitzer's neighbors on Tilghman Island were staunchly against it. "Some of them were fightin' mad," Sweitzer said. "One of them threatened to fight with me because it was my idea."

The reason for the resistance is that dredgers understood the efficiency of their own equipment. Those who stood up against power dredging feared it would be too efficient and wipe the oyster rocks clean.

"They jumped on me tooth and nails. 'That was going to kill the oyster business; we'll wipe out everything,' the opponents said.

"Either that, or we're doomed," countered Sweitzer, who believed "everybody was gonna have to get out" if something wasn't done to give dredgers a more dependable income. "We were at the total mercy of the weather."

While the Tilghman captains may not have liked the idea of power dredging, the Somerset County dredgers saw it as their chance for survival.

At the turn of the century, Smith Island, out in the Chesapeake, had been one of the biggest home ports for dredge boats. Before the Great Depression there were about forty or fifty dredge boats on the

The jib of the *Helen Virginia, background,* may well be the first red sail hoisted on a Chesapeake Bay dredge boat. Dredgers have started buying sails made in China to save on the high cost of sails sewn locally, but the color, which caused quite a stir, was accidental. The *Kathryn, foreground,* wears the traditional white.

A dredger waits out a calm on a sail day, knowing he can power dredge Mondays and Tuesdays. Prior to the 1966 season, when dredging regulations were changed to permit some power dredging days, extended periods of calm weather often encouraged crew (who earn a share of the harvest) to jump ship and find other employment.

island. But oysters were scarce in Tangier Sound, and Smith Islanders, along with other Somerset County dredgers, were finding it hard to make a living at their longtime occupation. Many Smith Islanders had gotten out of legal dredging by the sixties, lured by the prospect of making bigger bucks dredging illegally with a powerboat in the Potomac, a practice that stretched from the 1940s through the 1970s, or by patent tonging, a form of oystering using a powerboat equipped with hydraulic tongs.

Smith Island dredger Captain Clyde Evans said he considered quitting, too. "Power dredging was the only thing that saved it," Evans said of dredging in Somerset.

So, despite local opposition on Tilghman Island, the hundred-year-old sail dredging law was modified in 1966 to allow the skipjacks to dredge under power on Mondays. A few years later, Tuesdays were added. The men continued to dredge only under sail the rest of the week, but now, no matter how calm the weather got, captains could be relatively certain that they could work and make a living on Mondays and Tuesdays.

"What it does is, it guarantees you're going to make some money that week," said Sweitzer. "The same captains that cussed me for thinking of the idea were the very first ones to get out there and do it, and within a year, they were all for it."

Sweitzer believes the law may not have been changed if it weren't for the help of Delegate Randolph Harrison who once owned a skipjack. "He knew all about dredging boats. His father had dredging boats. He thought this may help. . . . That's the only damn thing that saved dredging. Without that, these dredge boats would have been gone twenty years ago."

A second change in Maryland law that encouraged the continuation of dredging happened in the early seventies when the Tangier Sound Watermen's Association, led by Smith Islanders, took Mary-

The *Wilma Lee,* with Captain Robbie Wilson at the wheel, becalmed on the Choptank River.

land to court over its law requiring every waterman to stay within his county lines when working, and won. Up until 1971, when the *Bruce* decision overturned this law, only the Chesapeake Bay was open to everyone and, in some cases, the counties had extended their lines out into the Bay, forcing watermen from other areas to stay off their shores.

The *Bruce* decision particularly benefited Somerset County dredgers who had watched their oysters in Tangier Sound and surrounding waters die off at least three times during their lifetimes. In fact, most of the Somerset County dredgers spent their careers working away from home out in the Bay because there were seldom enough oysters to dredge in their home waters. While oysters had also died occasionally in the Choptank, the mortality in the river appeared to be not nearly as great, nor as frequent, as it was in Tangier Sound. When the association won its court case against Maryland, Somerset County dredgers were finally able to join Dorchester and Talbot County dredgers in the rich Choptank River.

If the two changes in the century-old law gave skipjack captains a certain amount of financial security, it also ushered in a new era of daring. For the first time, captains had a good reason to push out of port on Mondays and Tuesdays, no matter how bad the weather, for they seldom caught as many oysters nor made as much money sail dredging as they did dredging under power. With so much money to be made on a power day, occasionally some captains became bolder, choosing to power dredge in the face of approaching storms or under heavy gales when, if it had been a sail day, they would have stayed in port. Meanwhile, electronic equipment, increasingly used onboard the skipjacks in the sixties and seventies, helped bolster this false sense of security created with the loosening of the power dredge law, and encouraged men with little experience sailing or dredging to buy a skipjack and go dredging.

"Years ago, the reason why captains were so apprehensive about wind is because they didn't have radios, and didn't have sounders and didn't have all this electronic equipment and the captain had to go by the seat of the pants," said Sweitzer. "It was up to him and he decided when to go out and when to stay in. Now it's too damn easy. You listen to the radio and he [the weatherman] will tell you where the wind is, and a guy in Annapolis says there's thirty- to forty-knot winds and you know you'll get it soon. I've been out in a thick fog when the damn wind would come fifty miles per hour right out of the fog and you didn't have any warning. A captain had to be on his toes those days.

"They don't have any fear of nature, but years ago, the fear of nature was instilled in the captains when they were young. For one thing, they didn't have the powerful push boats they have now. When it blowed forty-fifty knots, you couldn't push head to wind. You slacked the damn sail down and went with the wind; you scudded. Nowadays, everybody says, 'I got power. I don't have to worry about no damn wind, I can push head wind.' I been out there when it's blowing seventy-eighty miles per hour. You can't push through that.

"Now they have all this electronic equipment and they think it will save them. They go out in times when they're taking a hell of a chance going out. They go right out in the face of it—forty-fifty miles per hour winds, thinking, 'I got a radio. That'll save me. I can hear the guy talking.' They take a lot of chances with these skipjacks, more than the older captains."

A crewman stretches out to nap on the bowsprit of the *Virginia W* while the skipjack is becalmed on the Choptank River.

Long periods of calm weather encouraged dredgers to break the law and power dredge, particularly before the advent of the airplane as a policing tool in 1949-50.

# Ten

# ON THE WRONG SIDE OF THE LAW

*If they don't like you, they'll come aboard and make your oysters small. He can take my oysters which are three inches, and with that little thing he's got, he can make them two and three-quarter, and in fact, they do it. They chip on them [the oyster] and knock the edge off. If they choose to, you've broke the law. The bad part about it, it's not a little misdemeanor, it's a criminal charge.*
—Captain Art Daniels about the law: the Maryland Department of Natural Resources Police

A T SUNRISE, the three skipjacks left Tilghman Island, splintering a fifteen-foot-wide swath through the half-inch-thick ice as they headed for France Bar off the mouth of Broad Creek in the Choptank River. For most of the skipjacks, the ice wasn't too thick to push, particularly since they were sheathed in metal at the waterline. But one of the boats was the *Sigsbee,* whose bottom had sagged so badly over her seventy years that she was virtually concave and couldn't push ice well. Consequently, the *Sigsbee* occasionally got herself wedged in a thickening wall of ice before her bow.

In the seventies, oysters were fairly plentiful, particularly on tonging ground, which was seldom over-harvested like the dredging bottom. On that day, with the ice to help hide their activity, the captains planned to get their limits early. They were headed out for an illegal oyster run.

Most of the skipjack captains were Christians who believed in following the laws of God, but the "line" was an arbitrary, man-made regulation. Some of the dredgers, like Captain Wade Murphy, Jr., could remember their fathers talking about how the dredging lines were moved in on the dredgers back in the thirties. "We figured that, by right, it was ours to work," Murphy argued. "It's illegal because the people [DNR] say it's illegal."

In the Choptank, the line between tonging bottom and dredging bottom ran down the middle of an oyster bar. Even though the skipjack captains were few in number, their dredges, dragging along the bottom

for hundreds of feet at a time were sometimes able to wipe the bottom clean of oysters. Meanwhile tongers, who used old-fashioned, hand-held, scissorslike tongs, fifteen to thirty feet long, to pluck a few oysters at a time from the bottom, left many oysters behind on their side of the bar. While there were still plenty of oysters to be had on dredging bottom, it was far easier for the skipjack captains to fill their dredges and get their limit quickly and easily by dredging illegally on the tongers' side of the line.

Since the line ran right across an oyster bar, few dredgers could resist the temptation to cross the line from time to time and reap an easy harvest at the tongers' expense. Usually, they only had to go about ten feet across the line to hit plenty of oysters.

And there was no better time to dredge illegally than when the weather was poor. A light snow or fog shielded their illegal activities from the marine police, who scouted the river with binoculars from a speed boat or from shore. Likewise, the police planes couldn't fly in bad weather to snap photos to be used in court against the dredgers.

The *Sigsbee* had not yet reached the line when she ground to a halt. The ice before her bow had become too thick, and she could no longer push through it. Captain Wade Murphy sent three men to the bow to try to free the boat. Leaning over the rail and using shovels, they pushed at the ice, trying to crack and shove the ice floes away from the bow. Meanwhile, crewman Gordon Simmons got in the yawl boat and opened the throttle to try to force the boat through the ice.

Suddenly, the bow line securing the yawl boat to the stern of the skipjack snapped. Fueled by the big automobile engine and unable to push the skipjack ahead, the yawl broke loose from the chock that held her wedged against the starboard side of the skipjack. Instantly, she shot off to starboard, her bow flying in the air as she reached the limit of her davit falls, the lines used to haul the little boat out of the water when she wasn't being used. Simmons, who had been standing in the yawl boat, working the controls, flipped in the air, doing a complete somersault, and landed feet first in the water behind the yawl boat. He just managed to grab the stern of the little skiff whose engine was still wide open, its propeller spinning, pushing the

bow high into the air. It was all he could do to keep hold of the boat. The spinning propeller was churning the water, pushing Simmons away from the boat.

Simmons was in a precarious position: if he let go, he would surely drown. With the skipjack hung in the ice and the yawl boat out of control, nobody would be able to reach him. At the same time, Captain Murphy knew if someone slowed the engine, the boat would fall and drag the young man underwater where the spinning propellers would chop him up.

Murphy jumped in the push boat and reached for the controls, knowing he had to do it right. "I had to slow her down and take her out of gear at the same time," he said. As the boat fell back into the water,

In the early years, dredgers often power dredged under cover of darkness; but here, Captain Wade Murphy, Jr., guides the *Rebecca T. Ruark* back into port as the sun sets and a full moon rises over Tilghman Island.

Simmons felt the turning propeller slap against his leg. The cold water had numbed him so "he didn't know if it had cut his leg off," Murphy said. When they dragged him aboard, not only was his leg still intact, but he didn't have a scratch on him.

Simmons, chilled to the bone, went down in the cabin to warm up. Each of the men took off a piece of clothing and gave it to him so he would have dry clothes to wear. Meanwhile, another skipjack captain had come over to help cut a swath around the *Sigsbee*, setting her free of the ice.

A few minutes earlier, the day had looked like a disaster. Now things were brightening. Murphy could see that Simmons was cold, but unharmed. And his

skipjack was free. "We'll work awhile, then take you in," he told Simmons as he turned on a course for the wrong side of France Bar.

In a few hours, the crew of the *Sigsbee* had gotten their limit and Simmons, who escaped a brush with death with only a bad cold to show for it, got the next day off, a rare treat on Murphy's dredge boat.

Working illegally was so widespread that, as one retired captain put it, "If you say you haven't done it, you're lying." The most common way they broke the law was to dredge under power. One former captain explained his real secret to successful dredging was "to put that yawl boat down every time you could."

Today police use planes, speedboats, high-powered binoculars, and cameras to catch and document violators, but back in the first half of the century, it was fairly easy to get away with dredging under power and working illegal bottom. Dredgers simply hauled their dredges onboard when they saw a police boat in the distance. Since they weren't breaking the law unless both the yawl boat and the dredge were overboard, they were usually safe.

Even when they did get caught, dredgers often got off easy because everyone knew each other, so the magistrate who handled the fine for the offenders would more than likely be a relative or neighbor.

Captain Wilson Todd of Cambridge remembers the time when a marine policeman told Captain Orville Parks he could dredge at night. Todd heard about the illegal oyster run and decided to join Parks that evening, even though he had not been issued an invitation. When Parks saw Todd and his crew assembled aboard the *Sallie Bramble* he asked him what he was doing. "I'm going to stay here just as long as you do," Todd told Parks. "The way I figured it, if he could pay his fine, I could pay mine."

Parks finally headed on out to the oyster bar, followed by Todd in the *Sallie Bramble*, a one-masted bugeye. "We were dredging with the yawl boat and throwing them in the hole. I had a load, about three hundred bushels," said Todd, who was never even fined for the offense.

Ice was bad to work in, but if it had one redeeming point, it was that it helped the dredgers hide their illicit trips across the line—at least, that's what two dredgers thought when they crossed over to tonging bottom one day in the seventies.

For Captain Stanley Larrimore and Captain Wade Murphy, the fact that the plastic line buoys, called spar buoys, were caught beneath the surface of the ice—

even though they were both working close enough to clearly see the buoys—was as good as any excuse for dredging over the line on tongers' bottom.

Eventually, a DNR airplane flew overhead, but neither captain was concerned. They figured the buoys could not be seen, so the pilot would not know they were over the line. When they were summoned to court over the infraction, "We made like we didn't know where we were at," remembers Larrimore. Then the DNR police produced evidence the dredgers had never seen before: photographs in which the buoys were clearly visible through the ice, and the dredgers were clearly on the wrong side.

Greed wasn't the only factor pushing the dredgers to power dredge illegally. Long windless days were tough on crew members who put in a day's work and got nothing to show for it when they couldn't dredge. Some calms lasted for days. The dredgers also lost days when it blew so hard that the skipjacks couldn't work. On top of the wind factor, it was also common for dredgers—like most watermen—to lose several weeks of work during the winter due to icy conditions. Unlike the other watermen who were not restricted to sail power, however, dredgers couldn't work calm days. Consequently, the dredgers found themselves constantly caught between the laws of man and the forces of Nature. With four to six crew aboard, who needed money to pay bills, it was sometimes difficult to resist the temptation to dredge illegally.

The winter of 1977 was a particularly cold, hard winter for the watermen. The dredging fleet was locked in the harbor for six weeks as the ice thickened to over a foot deep. Many of the dredge crews were running out of money when Captain Bart Murphy, who dredged the *Ruby G. Ford,* decided to try something his father had done back in the Big Freeze of 1934: dredge with a car.

"I knew how to do it," said Bart Murphy, who had heard his father talk about how he used an automobile to pull a dredge under the ice. "We had

Dredgers admit they often succumb to the temptation to power dredge on tonging bottom, which is illegal. Here, a skipjack working within the law pushes out to a seed oyster sanctuary while a patent tong boat works nearby.

Becalmed, a skipjack uses its push boat to move over an oyster bar, a maneuver which would be illegal if the dredges were overboard on a sail day.

a hole in the ice and a two-hundred-foot rope. We cut a hole, shoved it under the ice with a thirty-foot pole. Then we cut another hole where the pole ended." They pulled the pole and line through, then shoved the line with the pole under the ice again, and dug a hole where the pole ended, again. They did this another six or eight times until the two-hundred-foot line was stretched out under the ice. Then, they attached an old hand scrape, a small dredge once used on small hand scraping boats to drag for crabs or oysters, and started pulling the scrape along the bottom with an old Simca.

Murphy and his crew power dredged with a car over tonging bottom off Poplar Island for eleven days before the temperatures rose to thirty-two degrees, and the ice started cracking. They finally quit when several tongers, who were doing the same illegal activity, lost their automobiles and barely escaped with their lives.

In times of hardship, the marine police seemed to look the other way when dredgers broke the law, but most of the time the police were trying to outsmart the dredgers, which wasn't easy. Before the advent of the police airplane in the late forties, it had been difficult for police to catch dredgers operating illegally. It was particularly hard to prove they were power dredging.

"He's got to see your dredges coming aboard," said Larrimore. "What would happen is, we'd see the [police] boat coming, and we'd pull our yawl boat up and there was nothing he could do." It was so easy to power dredge, in fact, that "it was very seldom we had a ca'm day," Larrimore said with a smile.

The advent of the airplanes around 1949-50, however, changed the battleground maneuvers and gave police an edge in the silent war of wits. "We all knew it was coming. We knew they had an airplane," said Larrimore, who was dredging with his father, Glendy Larrimore, at the time. "We'd go through drills to see how fast we could get our yawl boat up. We had lines tied on the switches [to start the engine] so nobody had to get in the yawl boat."

The airplane pilot "was a handful for us. He would come out of the sun" so the dredgers couldn't see him as well. "We knew where he would be coming from, but we didn't know when." Mason Shehan piloted one of the early police planes, a seaplane which he would land right on the water beside the offending dredger. With the airplane in the sky, "we got caught more often than before," Larrimore admitted.

But even with the airplane, dredgers sometimes got away. "One time the marine police pilot was flying to Annapolis and we were working on Sharps Island Narrows. It was foggy," but the fog was low over the water. The pilot "could see these masts going by. He flew down over us, but he couldn't see what boats it was. All he could see was the top of the masts," said Larrimore. "He turned in the wrong boats. They weren't even there." So the dredgers got off, again.

While dredgers usually know where they are, they do occasionally end up on the wrong side of the line quite by accident. "In the Choptank, they paint them [the line buoys] white. If you're up the river looking back this way, in the whitecaps of a nor'wester, they're hard to see," Stanley Larrimore said.

Captain Jack Parkinson was dredging off Castle Haven in the Choptank River one time when he found so many oysters that in just two days, "the crew made $1,000 and the boat made $4,000. I didn't know where I was at, not then. I worked there two whole days." By the second day, Parkinson realized he was over the line, but other dredgers had joined him. Eventually, the police boat came over and ticketed everybody except Parkinson who, at that moment, happened to be on the right side of the line.

For dredgers, the sight of an airplane in the sky or a motorboat on the water is enough to signal them to alter their illegal activities. But a few decades of dredging has taught Stanley Larrimore not only to look for the boats, but for the birds, as well.

The Tred Avon Light, near the mouth of the Tred Avon River, marks one end of the dredging line in the Choptank River. Dredgers occasionally cross the line by a few feet and scoop some oysters off tonging bottom, and that's what Larrimore intended to do one morning. "What happens is, you've drug down here and you've scraped all this, and the hand tongers may not even have worked the other side of the line. Over the line only ten feet or so, there's a lot of oysters," Larrimore said.

It looks like another "slick ca'm" day at sunrise.

"Their job is to catch you, of course, and your job is [that] they not catch you. They get pressure put on them. Hand tongers say, 'Look, dredgers are working over the line,'" which forces the DNR to act, Larrimore said. "You can go in there today and work all you want, but the day after, you better look out."

Dredgers who skirt the law on the oyster bars complain bitterly when DNR police seem to target them at the dock, trying hard to nab them for undersized oysters. (If more than five percent of a bushel is found to be under the three-inch size limit, a dredger is in violation of the law.)

"The department don't realize, them oysters, . . . we haul them up in those dredges, they're dumped out on that deck, then they're thrown back in those piles, then they usually shovel them up in the piles, then you take the shovel and put them in a tub and a lot of times you dump them in the conveyer and then they dump them in the truck. For [a bushel of] oyster[s] to go eight percent [of undersized oysters] after being handled that many times . . . the fellow who culled them oysters was trying. A person who works on the water or who's been around, they usually understand. After you handle it six times and an oyster go eight percent, it's ridiculous to charge a person for something like that."

One year, Larrimore was issued three tickets. The penalty for three tickets is loss of your license for a period of time. Larrimore, however, managed to convince the judge that he hand tonged before the start of the dredging season, which was not uncommon among dredgers. Since the tonging season begins earlier than the dredging season, the judge agreed to take his license for the hand tonging season when he didn't have men dependent on him for their living. "I think I led them astray," said Larrimore with a twinkle in his eyes. "I wasn't going to hand tong, anyway."

Captain Walt Benton of Mount Vernon wasn't as fortunate when he was slapped with three violations in one year while dredging the *Somerset* on Tangier Sound. When Benton appeared in court for his trial, the judge compared him to a drug dealer—right in front of the jury. He lost his license for two weeks, was forced to be under supervised probation for two years, and was fined $500.

It happened at a time when Benton believes tidewater police were harassing the Somerset County dredgers. Benton said the police would pull dirty tricks to try and find them guilty of keeping undersized oysters. They would come aboard their boats and step all over the oyster piles, breaking the oyster shells.

There were already a number of skipjacks working over the line when Larrimore got to the Tred Avon Light. "When I got to the light, there weren't no sea gulls sitting out there. I told the boys, 'I ain't goin' out there,'" said Larrimore, who sensed a trap. After more than three decades of dredging, he had seen just about every trap the police could possibly concoct to nab offending dredgers. Sure enough, about ten o'clock a police boat sped out to the light to pick up the officers who had been left in the structure before dawn that morning. "I thought them birds would have been there if they hadn't been in the light," Larrimore said.

Crew cull through oysters after unloading the dredge on deck.

Dredgers are usually careful not to step on their oysters because if you break the bills, or ends, a legal oyster quickly becomes an illegal, undersized oyster.

"My brother had eight police went aboard his boat. He only had ten or twelve bushel, all in one pile. They walked all over them, breaking them up," Benton said.

A marine policeman usually culls through a bushel to find out if the dredger is in violation of the law. If the bushel produces more than five percent undersized oysters, the dredger can be found in violation of the law.

Benton said he caught one police officer trying to put all the small or empty shells in one spot on his boat, so that when they took a sample, it would have more undersized oysters than the law allowed. Another time, an officer shoveling his own bushel sample was obviously looking for undersized oysters between shovelfuls. "He'd shovel, look at every shovel, see a few boxes [oysters which have died and left only the box shell], and shovel them in," said Benton, who stopped him. "I told him, 'You can have the third tub, the fourth tub, any tub you want, but you're not going to pick your shovels. . . . The day they got me, we were working an area with a lot of spat [young oysters which attach to the shell of a mature oyster]," Benton said. "They were cutting the spat off and calling it part of the five percent."

Most captains treat the marine laws like traffic violations—minor infractions handled with the payment of a fine. But the court takes a different view. The violations are considered criminal acts. If a captain racks up three violations in one season, he must go to court and be tried like a criminal. He not only risks having his license revoked, but may also be sentenced to jail. Even captains who try to abide by the law will often get tickets for having undersized oysters aboard when their crews fail to cull them properly. Not surprisingly, some dredge boat captains have criminal records as long as that of a thief.

"Most of the time we don't appear [in court] because the fine would be $50. I could make more than that dredging," Larrimore said. But on one occasion it was well worth the dredgers' time to go to court. Several of them, including Larrimore, had been arrested for dredging over the line. "We got a lawyer and come to find out, the line was down on us at one end." When the lighthouse at the mouth of the Tred Avon River was replaced, the new structure was located some fifteen hundred feet inside the dredging line. DNR police evidently assumed the new structure marked the dredging line.

The ice floes were running with the tide one day when twelve skipjack captains ventured out into the river, heading for France Bar. Oyster packer Buck Garvin, who owned several skipjacks and also flew an airplane, decided to go up and see how the skipjacks were doing. Captain Wade Murphy, who had kept the *Sigsbee* in port that day, went with him. "Eleven boats were working illegally over the line," Murphy said. "One was working legally." The legal dredger was Captain Art Daniels, who is also a Methodist minister from Deal Island.

Most of the illegal dredgers had caught more than their limit of 150 bushels. Some had up to 175 bushels on deck. Dredging legally, Captain Art Daniels had caught only 12 bushels, Murphy observed. When Murphy saw Captain Daniels in a blacksmith shop later that evening, he asked him why he dredged legally when the catch was so low, while other dredgers, including his own son, Captain Stan Daniels, were doing so well on illegal bottom. "My religion says that you live by the laws of the land. Stan's belief is different from mine," Daniels told him.

Murphy had always had a great respect for the older captain and his ability to dredge, but "I respected Art more after that for living up to what he thought was right," Murphy said.

Captain Art Daniels has watched for fifty years as the laws imposed on watermen to help equitably divide the harvest have ultimately done more to divide the communities and the men who depend on the water for their living. "The way it is now, we've got the patent tonger and the hand tonger; we've got the diver and we've got the dredge boat. Every one of them, the law separates them. What we're doing is dividing people," said Daniels. "I think the whole oyster business ought to go to power dredging: do away with sails; put a dredge on everybody, then we'd all be together. Wouldn't it be better to sacrifice to bring people together? The skipjack would be gone, but the thing is, your people would be drawn together."

A crewman throws the dredge overboard as the first light of dawn brightens the sky.

Ruth Daniels tends the helm for her husband, Captain Stan Daniels. A regular member of the *Howard's* crew for ten years, Ruth started dredging in 1983 when her husband had trouble finding crew. Ruth, who gave up professional sewing to dredge, is the only woman to last more than a year or two working aboard a skipjack. She also crabs in the summertime. In recent years, her son, as well as Daniels' son, have joined the crew, which makes dredging aboard the *Howard* truly a family affair.

*Eleven*

# WEDGED IN THE ICE

*It helps draw your family closer. At one time we had four generations on the water.*

—Captain Stan Daniels, who still dredges
with his wife and their sons

IT WAS eight o'clock, already late by a waterman's timetable, when Captain Stan Daniels guided his skipjack, the *Howard,* out of the safe haven of Love Point on Kent Island, down a narrow channel cut through the ice, and out into the Chesapeake.

Before him, the Bay appeared to be "a solid piece of ice," remembers Daniels. Frozen over a foot thick by a week of subfreezing temperatures, the upper Bay was now almost impassable. As he rounded Love Point, Daniels could see the air pockets between ice chunks and the long swath of fairly open water, a quarter-mile wide, which Captain Zack Taylor had promised would lead them safely down through the heavy ice floes to open water below the Bay Bridge. For the moment, tide and wind were in their favor, helping to push the ice out of the channel toward the western shore. But the favorable tide wouldn't last long.

Daniels understood the danger involved in passing a wooden boat through ice. Even with sheaths of metal nailed along her waterline for protection, ice could smash through a boat or cave in her sides. Driven by the tide and wind, the ice chunks could climb over her decks and sink her in a minute, or ride silently under her keel and capsize her.

The Bay was riddled with ice floes, but the real worry to the dredgers were the tons and tons of ice chunks, stacked like blocks against the western shore, which would surely come down on them when the tide changed. Despite the potential danger, Daniels was confident they could make it. He and six other captains in the fleet had only five miles to cover between

Love Point and the Bay Bridge, which acted like a dam, holding back the sea of ice. Below the bridge, the waters were fairly open, with only occasional ice floes to dodge.

As often happens, it was the prospect of making big money that encouraged the dredgers to dice with their lives by pushing out into a Bay strewn with dangerous ice floes. The following day, the state was due to open new oyster bottom at Old Rock off Chesapeake Beach, south of the Bay Bridge. New bottom, which had been seeded by the state, but not worked for years, was always lucrative. Dredgers could be certain they would catch their 150-bushel limit, particularly in the first few days or weeks. If the fleet trapped in the upper Bay could cross these five treacherous miles to the bridge today, they could be in on the fortunes to be made at Old Rock tomorrow.

The severe cold snap had begun with a four-inch snowfall on Wednesday, January 7, 1970. Newspaper accounts called it "the coldest weather experienced in many a year." The *Crisfield Times* reported on Friday, January 16, that boat traffic had been halted between Smith and Tangier islands and Crisfield following four days of subfreezing temperatures that left Tangier Sound coated in ice. The mercury had dropped to a low of ten degrees, which was registered at the Somers Cove weather station.

The freeze-up isolated both islands, and oyster boats all around the Eastern Shore were forced to remain tied up. Ice was reported to be five to six inches thick in Crisfield harbor and on the Little Annemessex

Captain Stan Daniels at the helm of the *Howard*, which was badly damaged by the ice floes of 1970.

River. On Friday, January 9, and Saturday, January 10, there had been no boat traffic at all between the islands and Crisfield. Then on Sunday, a state buoy tender out of Annapolis came down the Bay to Smith Island and made its way into Crisfield harbor. On Monday the same boat made the run from Smith Island to Crisfield, instead of the regular island boat.

For the preceding week, as temperatures plummeted, the skipjack captains, most of them from Somerset County, who had their boats harbored at Love Point, had managed to keep working, despite the thickening ice, by following a private tugboat out into the Chesapeake. The tug, owned by C. J. Langenfelder, a shell company on Kent Island, cut them a path out into the Bay off Love Point. Here, they found patches of open water, some four hundred to five hundred feet long, large enough that they could pull a dredge and harvest a few bushels to make a living.

Captain Norman Benton, working his first season at the helm of the *Fannie L. Daugherty*, was dredging in one of the pockets of clear water. It was bitter cold, but the morning broke clear and as pretty

as any Benton had seen. As the remaining fleet joined them, Benton hauled up his dredges and headed down the Bay, picking his way through the ice floes.

"We thought we could make it before the tide changed," said Daniels. "When the tide changes in the Bay, it'll push the ice up north or push it down south. Well, it'd already pushed it up north."

Daniels had awoken at four that morning at his home on Deal Island, and decided not to move his boat that day, given the bad weather reports across the Bay region. But at six A.M., he got a call from Deal Island dredger Captain Zack Taylor, who was at Love Point. Taylor said the channel was free and now was their chance to move south below the Bay Bridge. He urged Daniels to come with them, and Daniels agreed.

"I called Daddy," said Daniels; his father owned the *City of Crisfield*. "I wish I'd stayed in bed," he recalled later. As it turned out, it would be the worst decision he had ever made while working the Bay.

The skipjacks strung out in a line, heading toward the Bay Bridge. The captains picked their way from air pocket to air pocket, pushing ice when they couldn't go around it. Besides the *Howard* and the *Fannie L. Daugherty,* there were also the *City of Crisfield, H.M. Krentz, Laura Evans, Bernice J, Annie Lee,* and *Geneva May.* The only other boats in the area were about five workboats that were rockfishing above the Bay Bridge between the ice floes.

The skipjacks did not get far before the tide changed and their problems began.

Art Daniels, captain of the *City of Crisfield,* remembers that, about eleven A.M., the wind breezed up and shifted to the northwest. Then the ice began to move in on the boats. The ice moved "so silently, it was eerie," Art Daniels said. At one point, the *City of Crisfield* raised out of the water, on top of the ice. "It sounded like somebody was out hitting the boat with a hammer. We were all praying." The ice packing up around the *City of Crisfield* "was like a man standing alongside your boat; something out of nowhere, peeping up at you."

Captain Benton was just five hundred yards north of the bridge when the *Fannie L. Daugherty* became wedged in the ice. Now, he not only had the strengthening wind to deal with, but the tide had also turned. "I was scared we weren't going to make it, it looked that bad," said Benton, who had his oldest son, twenty-year-old Clifton, aboard, as well as four other men.

Benton, who was one of the farthest along in the channel, had more problems to worry about than just the ice below him, for looming in his path was the Bay Bridge. Benton feared that the ice, driven by twenty-knot winds and an ebbing tide, would drag the vessel southeast into the steel framework of the bridge. The sixty-foot mast of the *Fannie L. Daugherty* couldn't get under the structure. "If it didn't cut the mast out, it would upset us," Benton said. The *Fannie L. Daugherty* drifted about a hundred yards in the direction of the bridge.

The *Howard* was in the middle of the Bay when "the ice come down on top of us," Stan Daniels said. "We tried to get out of it. We tried dodging and everything. Finally, the ice overcomed us. It surrounded us and jammed us so we couldn't move. We couldn't go nowhere. Some of those icebergs were eight-fifteen feet high. My ya'boat, I had her down and when that ice come underneath there it pushed her up to the davits. All I had to do was tighten the ropes."

The ice piled up as high as the bendguard on the side of the *Howard,* just inches from the deck of the skipjack. "We were worried about ice piling up," said Daniels. "Ice will do three things: it's either going through you, underneath you, or overtop of you."

Not only were all of the skipjacks closed in by ice, but the five workboats were also caught, setting the scene for what would become one of the longest and most dramatic rescues by the Coast Guard on the Chesapeake in recent history.

Most of the men aboard the dredge boats were family or friends from Deal Island or nearby communities in Somerset County. In fact, three generations of the Daniels family were stuck in the ice.

Captain Art Daniels, *left,* was trapped in the ice. He is shown here with Mike Taylor, a crewman for the *Howard.*

Stan's father, Art, was captain of the *City of Crisfield*, while his grandfather, Clifton Webster, was at the helm of the *H. M. Krentz*. The boats were all within a half-mile of each other, close enough that they could see each other's plight. Stan had every intention of climbing off his boat and walking over to one of the others if his vessel started to sink. In the meantime, there was little for him to do but wait for aid.

Stan Daniels and his crew were down in the cabin, drinking coffee and playing cards, when they heard a crunching noise. "I asked the cook: 'What's that noise?'" Daniels went down in the hole to take a look. "I heard all this crackin' down in the hole. I didn't know what it was doin'. Well, she was bustin' my sides, the ice was," he said. Down inside the hull, Daniels could see that the weight of the ice, piling up and pushing against the sides of the boat, was cracking the *Howard*'s chine boards.

"We gotta do somethin'," Daniels shouted to his crew, and they began a desperate attempt to save the *Howard* by forcing ice underneath the wooden vessel. "We got shovels and broke ice alongside and pushed it underneath her," Daniels said. "It was comin' in layers. We'd tilt the ice on its side and it started going underneath her. Finally, it raised her right up. The only thing saved me, there was a big sheet of ice there and we went on top of it. It set us right on top of a big chunk of ice, three to six foot thick."

Still, they weren't out of danger. Water was pouring in through a crack in the side of the boat. "I thought we were going to sink right there. I already had my iceberg picked out. I was ready to go. We took a mattress and shoved it inside her to stop water from coming in," he said. It worked.

Meanwhile, two Coast Guard cutters, which had been alerted about the problems north of the bridge, arrived to tow the skipjacks out of danger. However, they both got hung up in the ice as well. Finally, the Coast Guard sent its biggest vessel, a two-hundred-foot buoy tender, stationed in Baltimore.

As they waited for the buoy tender, Captain Norman Benton and his crew were also struggling to keep the ice off the deck of the *Fannie L. Daugherty*. "It was trying to climb on the middle of the boat, where the rollers are," and where the deck is only about two feet above the water, Benton said. Benton had no radio to communicate with the other captains, but he could see them all and they were all in trouble. Near him, the *H. M. Krentz* was listing badly after being lifted up on top of the ice.

The tide was forcing the huge ice floes against the Eastern Shore, where it was climbing fifteen to twenty feet high against the shore, in blocks ten to eighteen inches thick.

If their worst fears came true, Benton and his crew planned to abandon the boat and jump from one cake of ice to another until they reached shore, some three thousand yards away. It was a daring plan that could easily have ended in disaster if one of them had fallen in a hole between ice floes.

The *City of Crisfield* was the third skipjack to hook onto the huge buoy tender, but even after his boat was towed south of the Bay Bridge and set free, Art Daniels found that ice was still an issue. There were many ice floes to dodge south of the bridge. One of the chunks struck and broke the blade on the propeller of his push boat and he could no longer push the *City of Crisfield*. The *Bernice J*, with Captain Mervin Christy at the helm, was nearby and towed him to Annapolis.

At first, the buoy tender hauled one vessel at a time, but the process was too slow. Daylight would soon be gone, so the ship captain decided to pull two boats at a time.

The "last go-round with the ice was right before dark," Benton said. The ice floes, piling up against the *Fannie L. Daugherty*, reached the top of the rollers, which are used to help haul in the dredges. The men had to keep pushing the ice off the deck with shovels.

"When it got dark, we all started worrying," Stan Daniels said. About seven P.M., ten hours after the ordeal started, the buoy tender finally reached the *Howard*. As it turned out, the tow into harbor was as dangerous as sitting in the ice. "When the Coast Guard buoy tender started towing us, ice was hitting the sides of her, knocking her ten foot each way. You could feel her tremble. I thought a hole was comin' in her anytime. I thought it was going to pull her all to pieces."

Twice, Daniels called over the radio to the buoy tender's captain, asking him to slow down, but to no avail. "I was going to cut the rope on her. She started taking on water then. She was half full when I got in Annapolis. I like to sunk in the harbor," he said.

It was eleven P.M. when the *Howard* reached Annapolis. Daniels pumped her out and found a motel for the night. The next morning, he took the *Howard* on to Chesapeake Beach where she sunk on the bottom. "She's been leaking ever since," Daniels said.

The next morning, all the skipjacks went down the Bay to Old Rock, near Solomons. "We made our

150-bushel limit in two-three hours," said Benton, whose boat was relatively unscathed.

But the episode with the ice did not end so well for the *Howard*. For several weeks, Stan Daniels tried to work, keeping a pump running to empty the water in the skipjack's bilge, but he couldn't keep her afloat. Finally, he sailed her to a marina on the West River and "put her in a casket box. That's what I done. I covered her with metal."

Before this ordeal, "My boat was in brand-new shape. You could sleep in the bottom of her," relates Daniels, who purchased the *Howard* soon after the 1909 vessel had been rebuilt. "When I got her, she was in fine shape. Not a piece of rotten wood in her."

The ice did more damage than Daniels realized. While he repaired the cracked sides, he was unaware of how badly the keelson—the main beam which runs lengthwise along the bottom—had been damaged. For the next twenty years, Daniels would have more and more problems with the *Howard* leaking and sinking.

"If you're working, you'll go out in bad times, but I've learned, if there's ice, to stay in the harbor," he says.

Crew raise the sails aboard the *Howard*.

Captain Jack Parkinson, of the *Helen Virginia,* helped rescue the crew of the *F. C. Lewis* in February 1976, when the skipjack was capsized by sudden gale-force winds.

*Twelve*

# RESCUE IN THE FOG

*Being captain is a lot easier than culling oysters.*
—Captain Jack Parkinson on why
he bought a dredge boat

ALL MORNING the marine radio had been broadcasting the threat of gale winds, up to forty knots, due to hit the Chesapeake Bay. Sometimes the weather forecast was wrong, but this day, even the appearance of the sky agreed with the forecasters.

"It was real stormy," remembers Captain Norman Benton of daybreak on December 6, 1976, the day he thought he'd lost his oldest son. "I begged Clifton not to go down. I tried to get him to stay in," said Benton, who refused to take his own skipjack, the *Fannie L. Daugherty*, out into the unsettled weather. Like most of the older captains, Benton had weathered enough squalls, even a hurricane, that he knew when to stay in port.

But Captain Clifton Benton wouldn't listen to his old man and at sunrise, he steered his skipjack, the *Susan May*, out into the upper Chesapeake with three other skipjacks: the *Kathryn* with Captain Johnny Parkinson; the *Helen Virginia* with Captain Jack Parkinson; and the *F. C. Lewis, Jr.* with Captain Stanford White. The weather looked bad enough that seven other skipjacks in the fleet stayed in port at Love Point on Kent Island. Normally, the younger Benton would not have so stubbornly ignored his father, but today was Tuesday, a power day, and he hoped to cash in on a pile of oysters his father had hit just the day before.

Oysters were abundant enough in the seventies that captains often caught their limit. Recently, however, harvests in the upper Bay had fallen to between 70 and 90 bushels, well below the 150-bushel-per-day limit imposed by the state, which the dredgers had been catching regularly the season before. But the preceding day, while the rest of the fleet worked along

the western shore, Captain Norman Benton had struck out on his own, searching for oysters along the Eastern Shore of the Chesapeake. Just north of the Bay Bridge, he got lucky and hit a good lick. He quickly caught his limit and was back in port by 12:30 that afternoon. When the rest of the fleet straggled in later that day with far fewer oysters, they soon found out about Benton's luck. "They wouldn't have been out there if I hadn't hit the oysters," Benton believes. "They went to look for what I caught."

The *F. C. Lewis* and the *Helen Virginia* reached the oyster rock first and dropped their dredges over. As they started to work, there was no wind, at all, remembers Captain Jack Parkinson in the *Helen Virginia*. Then Parkinson saw half the Bay Bridge disappear in a dark fog. It was an odd sight. Even Captain Norman Benton noticed it from the safety of Kent Island. "It got so dark, you couldn't see the other half of the Bay Bridge," Benton said.

Still, the captains didn't understand what was coming silently toward them. "All we saw was a fog bank comin' from the south. Didn't know it was no wind at all," Parkinson said. The cloud bank enveloped the *F. C. Lewis* so that Parkinson, who was north of the other skipjack, could only see the top of her mast.

Then, without warning, the mast disappeared. The *F. C. Lewis*, bare poles, had capsized with six crew aboard.

"I just saw the mast gone," said Parkinson, who knew immediately that the fog bank was carrying a powerful force of wind, far more than the weather reports had predicted. "I just saw them turn over . . .

no sails or nothin'. That's an awful funny feeling, to be working and see a boat turn over," he said.

One of Parkinson's crew was in the yawl boat. "I told my boy to open her [throttle] wide open and get out of her and get on deck," said Parkinson. Even in the seventies, skipjacks had no controls on deck to adjust the speed of the push boat; someone had to climb into the yawl boat to start the engine and open or close the throttle.

Parkinson turned his boat to run with the wind, but the dry squall hit him before he got her completely turned around. "When it hit me, she went on down . . . she went down to the winder box," which sits in the middle of the deck, said Parkinson of his skipjack. "Half of her was in the water. I thought she was gonna turn over because she set there and trembled." With the help of the push boat running full throttle, the *Helen Virginia* righted herself and went running with the wind.

Meanwhile, the crew aboard the *Kathryn*, which had not yet reached the oyster bar, tied themselves to the mast to keep from being swept off the deck. The squall also hit the *Susan May* while she was still heading south toward the oyster rock. "He come near gettin' lost," Norman Benton said of his son, Clifton. The *Susan May*, like the other two, nearly capsized. Barrels of gasoline which Captain Clifton Benton carried on deck for his engine were swept overboard.

Norman Benton was inside a big metal building at C. J. Langenfelder's when the wind hit. "It sounded like somebody was bombarding the building," said Benton who thought the winds might even blow the big structure away. Benton immediately thought of his son and the other dredgers. "I wasn't no Christian, but I was praying for them. I thought they were gone. I thought they were lost . . . all of 'em," he said.

The winds, which lasted only ten minutes, were clocked at 115 miles per hour at the Bay Bridge. When the wind subsided, Benton jumped in his truck and raced down Love Point Road until he could see the Chesapeake Bay. "I could see my boy's boat," said Benton, who saw that the *Susan May* was all right. "Then I got the news of the *F. C. Lewis* blown over."

Not surprisingly, all six men aboard the *F. C. Lewis* were family. Captain Stanford White had his son, Stanford "Sonny" White; his grandson, Jeff White; his son-in-law, Stevie Webster; and his nephew, Earl White, all crewing for him.

When the skipjack capsized, all of them had managed to stay with the boat, except the captain, who was in the water. Sonny, who had managed to stay dry up until this point, swam a few feet out to his father and pulled him back to the boat.

"I looked back and they were all hangin' on the side of the boat," said Parkinson, who turned around and went back with the *Helen Virginia* to rescue the men. "The first time I went by, I threw them life preservers. They grabbed them. The next time, I guess the seas were six foot high. They were hangin' on the bottom of the boat."

The seas had gotten so rough that Parkinson knew he only had one chance to save the men. "I'm only goin' to make but one pass. This is it," he told his crew. "When I come by there, I guess the luck of the Lord, or skill, or whatever it was. . . . I went down her side, stopped her, and everybody crawled aboard my boat at one time. Nobody got drowned."

A half hour after the storm, Norman Benton went out in the *Fannie L. Daugherty* and harvested fifty bushels of oysters. Meanwhile, C. J. Langenfelder's sent a vessel over and raised the *F. C. Lewis* before dark.

Skipjacks sail near Sandy Point Light in the Chesapeake Bay.

*Thirteen*

# THE SINKING OF THE *CLAUD W. SOMERS*

*You love these old boats like an old dog. You fall in love with them
and you hate to see them die. They 'come part of you . . . that's what
it is, like your wife and family. Every captain loves his boat, but a
skipjack's a little special. It's unique. There's not many left.*
—Captain Stan Daniels about skipjacks

**B**UDDY JONES was motoring out of the Honga River when he spotted the dredge boat, the *Claud W. Somers,* drifting in Hooper Strait off Sharkfin Shoal Light. Immediately he knew something was wrong. "We seen them driftin'. No yawl boat down, no sails. Just driftin'," said Jones who suspected Captain Thompson Wallace was having problems. Since Jones's radio didn't work, he steered his workboat, the *Dana Matt,* over to the *Claud W. Somers* to see if he could help.

Like many Deal Islanders, Wallace, fifty-five, had an association with dredge boats that spanned thirty-five years. His father and brothers had worked on the middle deck of skipjacks, and when Wallace was in his early twenties, he also starting working aboard the dredge boats. His love for the sail and his skill behind the helm was obvious to Elbert Gladden, who owned a small fleet of skipjacks. Wallace started substituting as a captain on Gladden's boats, and eventually Gladden offered Wallace the helm of the *Ida May.* For fourteen years, Wallace captained Gladden's skipjack, before buying his own skipjack in 1976.

By the seventies, Captain Thompson Wallace was one of only two black dredge boat captains left on the Chesapeake. The other, Captain Mervin Christy, owned the *Bernice J,* which also worked out of Deal. Earlier in the century, it was not uncommon to find a black at the helm of a skipjack, but the numbers of black captains had dwindled, along with the number of dredge boats still working the oyster rocks. Back in 1916, there were 13 black captains among the 178 men who applied for dredging licenses in Somerset County.

Sixty years later, blacks still made up a large portion of the crew which worked the middle decks of skipjacks, but few went on to captain and buy their own dredge boats, like Wallace and Christy.

Like most old skipjacks, the *Claud W. Somers* needed some work when Wallace bought her, but he was handy around boats and was able to keep her in good condition. When he left that morning, everything was in working order, said his wife, Esther Wallace. Whatever problems he now had with the engine in the yawl boat had developed while out on the water.

"If you got an extra battery, we can get in," Jones remembers Wallace saying when he pulled up alongside the skipjack. Jones always carried a spare battery, so he lent it to Wallace, then he drifted beside the skipjack while they tried to start the engine in the push boat. After a few minutes, it became evident that the problem was more serious than a dead battery.

Jones offered to tow him in, but neither man had any heavy tow line on board. Finally Jones found some half-inch-thick line, and they rigged it as a tow line and started toward Deal Island. "We didn't go nowhere before she broke," Jones said of the line. Wallace then rigged up a line but the two vessels didn't get more than a mile before the tow line broke again. "If we'd'a had a good line, we'd'a got him in," Jones said.

The wind had been a moderate ten or twelve knots when Jones came over to help. But a storm was approaching out of the east. It finally hit when they were still four miles out of Deal Island, Jones said. As they struggled on for two more miles, the wind strengthened until it was almost impossible to make any headway.

"Any time you take a boat, hooked to another boat, and you got three hundred horses in her and you can't even budge her, it's bad," said Jones. "That's when everything started breakin' loose. I had so much gas on her trying to pull. . . . Whatever they hooked to us, it would snap it. It pulled the stern deck loose on my boat. Pulled the snubbing bit right out of my boat," Jones said.

About a mile and a half outside Deal Island, the full force of the storm struck. "When the wind hit us, I don't believe Hazel was blowin' no harder," said Jones, who later heard reports that it had topped seventy-five miles per hour. "The seas were higher than that building: twelve-twenty feet and I was only in a thirty-eight-foot boat."

Jones knew that towing into such a powerful wind was taking a toll on his own equipment. "My transmission was not all that great; I had trouble keeping oil in her," he said. "It was cold and everybody was scared to death. . . . I know I was. I asked them to come aboard me, that way I knew I could get them in. They were all standing by the mast. None of them would come aboard. I guess they figured that their big boat had more of a chance than I did. But we had the power to get in with. He was trying to save his boat," Jones believes.

Wallace's crew was largely family. On board were his brother, George, sixty-four; a nephew, Carter Wallace, thirty-three; Thomas James, who was a cousin of his wife, Esther; and another crewman, Levine Johnson, who was not related. One of Wallace's sons, Gerald, twenty-three, a navy serviceman on leave, was also aboard. "He happened to be home that day and he was used to following his father," said Esther Wallace of her son. "Nobody was expecting him to go," Mrs. Wallace said, but Gerald enjoyed spending time with his father on the water, so he decided that morning to go dredging with him. "Ever since he was a little boy, he loved to follow his father," Mrs. Wallace recalled.

The day had started out dreary and overcast, but not threatening. The weather forecasts had called for winds in the afternoon, but nothing like what the *Claud W. Somers* and her crew were experiencing now. When the skipjack broke loose for the fourth time, Jones couldn't get his workboat around without sinking her. "If we'd tried to turn around, we'd'a capsized," he said.

The two captains were hollering back and forth over the wind and rain. "I'll see you boys," Wallace called to Jones as the boats separated for the last time. "And that was the last time I seen 'em," Jones said.

The fifteen-foot seas were tossing the boats about so badly that when the *Claud W. Somers* came about, "she fell over on the starboard side, and I could see the port side of her [bottom] just as good as I can see this boat now." But she didn't capsize.

When she broke loose the last time, "she was moving away from us so fast, she was flyin' away from us. When she started back to go with the seas, he heisted the jib so he could handle her," Jones said. The wind was blowing from the east, and Wallace and his crew were being carried west toward the Chesapeake Bay. But there was an almost solid line of islands and shoal water between Tangier Sound—where the two boats separated—and the open waters of the Bay. As Jones steered the *Dana Matt* toward Deal Island he held out hope that Wallace would beach the boat on Bloodsworth Island or Sharkfin Shoals, and save himself and his crew.

The trip across Tangier Sound was so rough that, at times, Jones wondered if even he would get back into port. Jones and his crewman, Reggie Morgan, had been tonging for oysters in the Honga River that day and had about fifty bushels on deck. Now they shoveled many of the oysters overboard to keep from sinking. "We couldn't see Deal Island . . . the seas, the spray and the rain were so bad. We had to steer by compass. It looked like a real downpour, so thick you couldn't see."

When they reached the harbor, there were at least a hundred people waiting on shore to see who had made it in. The Department of Natural Resources Police boat was also there at the dock, and Jones went over to tell the officer about the plight of the *Claud W. Somers*.

"We offered to go back out with them," said Jones who believed that quick response could have saved the crew.

When the high winds subsided, the police boat did go out, but it was too late. All six men died when the *Claud W. Somers* sunk in fifteen feet of water in Hooper Strait.

"From where she sunk, I think he was trying to get to shore with her. I think he was trying to go somewhere near Hooper Strait," Jones guesses. "When you do all you can do, sometimes you can't do no more," said Jones who, fifteen years later, is still haunted by the memory of that awful day.

*Fourteen*

# WATCH OUT FOR NOR'WESTERS

*My wife says my personality and all changes when I get ahold o' that wheel. Somethin' about when you get ahold o' that wheel. I start giving orders. Somebody's gotta be the boss.*
—Captain Stan Daniels about the power of sailing

WHEN THE weather's good, it's beautiful. When the weather's bad, it's awful," said Captain Jack Parkinson, summing up the life of a dredger. "What I hate worst about working on the water is a rainy nor'easter," said Parkinson, who lives in Chance, near Deal Island, and owns the *Helen Virginia*. "I done told my wife, if it's a rainy nor'easter, don't bury me when I die. Hold me up. You can't do nothin' with a rainy nor'easter. The fish won't bite. The crabs stop biting. You can't work your boat right in a nor'easter. I just hate nor'easters, but I go out, anyway," says Parkinson, who acknowledges that dredgers will work in harsh conditions—almost anything but a bad blow—as long

as there are oysters to catch. "You go out in sleet, when you got your nose runnin' and freezin' and you gotta break it off like an iceberg."

For the men who work by the wind, weather is of primary importance, second only to the availability of oysters. The weather dictates if they work and make money, or stay in port and spend it; whether they'll be happy or miserable over the oyster bars. Heavy winds can sand and hide oysters from the dredge, while freezing and thawing seems to draw them out of the bottom. Most important, weather determines if they'll make it home at the end of a long day. Consequently, most longtime dredgers are better weather forecasters

A crewman reefs the mainsail as the *Rebecca T. Ruark* runs back to port before a storm.

than the men on TV and, not surprisingly, myths and superstitions have built up around the weather.

"Watch out for Friday; watch out for a northwester," said Captain Pete Sweitzer. "It's the worst time of the week to be hit by a northwester. It's always strongest on Friday, and that's usually true, too, in the winter."

Captain Darryl Larrimore already had too much bad luck going against him when an unlucky northwester hit him off Cook Point in the Choptank River one day. Larrimore was dredging in the *Claud W. Somers,* which had only recently drowned six men in Hooper Strait; he was shorthanded, with only three men aboard; and it was St. Patrick's Day. "That's a bad luck day to dredge," Larrimore explained.

On top of all this bad luck, he made what would later prove to be a bad decision. "Instead of putting any oysters back [aft], we put 'em all forward, so when we come in, we wouldn't have to move the boat," said Larrimore, referring to when they put out their oysters at a packinghouse. Normally, if there are piles of oysters both fore and aft in the skipjack, the boat is better balanced for plowing through the seas, but when it gets into port, the boat has to be moved once so that the other pile of oysters is near the packer's equipment, a process that only takes about two minutes. So, with the hope of saving a couple of minutes' work, the men in the *Claud Somers* headed for port that day with a bow-heavy skipjack.

"That little boat had a hundred bushel of oysters up on her bow, and here come all this wind," Larrimore said. "Christ, the water was just coming over, going through the piles, down through her hatch."

Larrimore had an electric bilge pump, but so much water had come aboard, it wouldn't work. His only hope for saving the boat from sinking was two hand pumps. Two of the three crewmen started pumping the water by hand as fast as they could. One of the crew "wouldn't let anyone else pump, he was that scared."

To add to his troubles, Larrimore had in his push boat a little six-cylinder Chevrolet motor that was losing oil, and he had only six gallons of fuel left to get him back across the Choptank.

The wind was still blowing fifty miles an hour when they crossed the channel and got into four feet of water. "One boy had two life jackets on," recalled Larrimore. "He said, 'We're gone, we're gone.' I said, 'For Christ's sake. Will you shut up. We can walk ashore from here.'"

Larrimore's luck began to improve as he guided the *Claud Somers,* with her oysters now "spread from the bow to the wheel," into Knapps Narrows, toward the packinghouse at Tilghman Island. "We were working on mud that day, and most times you work on mud, you'll get like two dollars less for your oysters. So much water run through them," said Larrimore, referring to the big seas breaking over the bow and sides, "it looked like they come off a stone pile. I got two dollars more for them, so it worked out all right."

Captain Bobby Marshall barely made it across the Chesapeake in a northwester one cold night in February of 1989. "We were over at Old Rock [on the western shore], Gene Tyler and me. It was blowing nor'west, twenty-five–thirty knots. Finally, about the edge of dark, Gene said he wasn't going across the Bay." Tyler, a longtime Tilghman Island dredger, evidently understood the reputation of a northwester for being a long, hard blow. He decided to spend the night holed up in Chesapeake Beach while the gale blew itself out.

But Marshall wanted to get home. "We pulled the [push] boat up, and hoisted sails: a three-reef mainsail and no jib. It was blowin' harder," Marshall said. "Finally, it was blowin' so hard, green water was coming over the high side. Oysters were washin' over the boat. A third of the boom was draggin' in the water."

Marshall thought about turning back to the western shore, which was still closer than Tilghman Island to the east, but he "was scared to go about. If she had miss stayed—didn't go about—I don't know what would have happened."

For an hour and a half, Marshall and his crew struggled across the Bay in a fifty-knot wind which was now blowing out of the north. It was bitter cold and dark. Marshall wasn't worried about capsizing. The *Virginia W,* though small, could handle the weather, but on these old wooden workboats, there was always the worry that something would break. "I was afraid something else would happen to the boat: something coming loose or, say, if somebody slipped overboard, how would you get 'em." They finally reached home, cold and wet, but safer and, perhaps, a little wiser.

As in any field of work, age brings experience. Captain Art Daniels was in his second year as a dredge boat captain, working the *Mollie E. Leonard,* a fifty-foot sloop, when he got caught in a bad northwester on Tangier Sound between Deal Island and Crisfield. His situation may not have been so dangerous had he not been working along a lee shore. As the wind picked up,

Green water spills over the windward rail of the *Nellie L. Byrd* as Captain Darryl Larrimore dredges through heavy seas.

Daniels not only had to deal with the sheer velocity of the wind, but he also had to keep the big dredge boat off the nearby shoals.

"We went down to lu'ward. While we were working, the wind come out to the north, northwest. Got so it was blowing the water up. Blew so hard, we couldn't put the little [push] boat down. The sea got so choppy we were afraid to put it down because we'd lose it, so I had to depend on that sail to get her up there [back to harbor]."

Daniels had a double reef in the mainsail, but there was still too much canvas up for a fifty-knot gale. However, it was too late now to take in more sail. "It was blowin' so hard, we were afraid to try to reef it down more because the sea was getting so bad. I had water all up around her. The seas were ten feet. A man was standing up by the rigging and a sea struck him and he had to grab that rigging. That sea just swept him back.

"We got in the channel, and I had to tack, with the wind blowing forty-fifty. I was concentrating on making it up there, doing what I could to get the boat home safe. It took a couple hours to get up in the

smooth water." After that, "We listen to weather reports and watch the barometer and we don't go to lu'ward. I lived and learned. I could have lost the boat," said Daniels, who at seventy was the oldest captain on the Bay in 1991.

While a northwester packs a lot of wind, it blows in days of crystal clear skies and low humidity. Easterly winds, on the other hand, blow in wet, cold storms off the northern Atlantic and, occasionally, a hurricane or tropical storm.

It was the first week of the dredging season in the late eighties, and most of the Tilghman Island fleet was working on the Diamonds, an oyster bar up the Choptank River, when an easterly breeze turned into a gale. It was about a week after a hurricane had hit the southern states, and the Eastern Shore was now getting the aftermath of the big storm.

"It was blowin' east, harder and harder," said Captain Bobby Marshall. "Everybody started quittin'. Some of them went on up Trappe Creek," which was near the Diamonds. "I was the last one to quit." By the time he hauled in his dredges, the wind was blowing so hard that Marshall tied in all but a few square feet of his mainsail and started scudding home before a fair wind. "I had three hoops in my mainsail up, that's all," said Marshall, referring to the big rings on which the sail rides up the mast. "We were doing 9.8 knots on the loran. She'd get surfin' down waves, big seas."

Surfing on the waves can be exhilarating when a sailor has open waters before him, but Bobby Marshall and the other captains were aiming for the narrow channel of Knapps Narrows, which was bordered by shoals and islands, and in which the current often ran fast—too fast. A big wave could easily throw them off course, and cause them to run aground on a shoal and damage the boat. If that had happened, "the boat wouldn't have lived," Marshall said. "We were either gonna hit the narrows and make it in, or we weren't gonna make it."

Ahead of him, Marshall saw the *Lady Katie*, with Captain Stanley Larrimore at the helm, suddenly slew around in the heavy winds and big seas, losing headway, before the captain brought her back under control just in time to make the channel. "Stanley Larrimore, he almost didn't make it in the eastward side of the Knapps Narrows," Marshall said.

When Captain Billy Bradshaw in the *Maggie Lee* saw what had happened to Larrimore, he turned north and sailed up Harris Creek. Marshall, who was moving fast in the *Virginia W,* however, aimed for the channel.

"We sailed in the narrows, still doing 9.8 knots. I called the bridge tender. He raised the bridge and we went under the bridge, sailed out the other side of the narrows, come about, put the sails down and come back in. That was the most wind I've ever been in. It was clocked at eighty-nine, with sustained fifty knots."

The storm brought an unusually high tide. "The next morning, we had to get somebody with a workboat to get us to this boat. It was knee-deep at the dock."

Even with bigger and bigger engines in their push boats, dredgers sometimes still fall back on that sail to bring them into a safe harbor. Captain Wade Murphy, Jr., remembers sailing to safety when a squall blew out of the southwest: "We were dredging on Clay Banks, six or eight boats, way down below Sharps Island in the middle of the Bay. I could see the wind pops, the wind clouds, come up over the western shore. You could see the wind comin', but before it got across the Bay, to the ship channel, it would drop out. It started about ten o'clock that morning. This hap-

pened several times." It was Tuesday and they were power dredging.

Finally, Murphy relates, one of the boys said, "We pretty well got our limit," so the crew of the *Sigsbee* prepared to go home. It was about one o'clock, and the wind was still moderate, about ten or twelve knots out of the southwest, but Murphy felt it was going to blow. "This damn wind, it's gonna get rough before we get home," he told his crew. "Tell you what, when I get up head to the wind, we'll put this yawl boat up to the davits and we'll scud home . . . sail home, fair wind. If it gets rough, you're liable to sink the yawl boat," he explained.

"We finished the last dip, headed her up into the wind, laid to, and pulled the yawl boat," Murphy recalled. In the few minutes it took them to raise the yawl boat, the wind increased to twenty miles an hour.

"We finally got her squared off and were scudding for the end of Blackwalnut Point [off Tilghman Island], and it blowed twenty-five–thirty," said Murphy. As he sailed home, another dredger, working the *Ralph T. Webster* for Tilghman Island packer Buck Garvin, who owned several skipjacks, pushed by the *Sigsbee.* "He was pushing, with his sails rolled up. He pushed right by me, wide open, pushing that boat to get up the river," said Murphy. By then it was getting rough, and both captains were headed up the Choptank River, trying to get into port before the squall hit. Murphy dropped his sails as he came around the southern point of Tilghman Island.

"Finally when I got around the point, the wind struck; it blowed eighty miles an hour. It blowed so hard that it rolled my boat down to the rollers with no sails up, just the bare poles. I had pulled my sails down, and was layin' to, underneath the shore. I thought it started raining," said Murphy, who asked one of the crew to give him his oilskins. Later, he realized it never rained, but the wind was blowing so much spray off the waves, it felt like rain. "I got one arm in my jacket. I was gettin' my other arm in when the wind got caught in it, and knocked me down by the rail, like to broke my ribs. I was on my knees, trying to get my wind back."

Murphy had tucked the *Sigsbee* in close to land for shelter, but the *Ralph T. Webster* was out in the middle of the river with no bank or trees to protect her from the high winds. It was blowing so hard, Murphy couldn't see the boat, but he heard the captain calling on the radio for help. "He said, 'Mayday, mayday. This god-damn boat is sinking; this god-

A crewman checks the mainsail, lashed to the boom, as Captain Wade Murphy, Jr., steers the *Rebecca T. Ruark* home before a storm.

damn pump won't run, and I'm a scared son-of-a-bitch,'" Murphy recalled.

Buck Garvin heard the mayday, got on the radio, and told the captain of the *Ralph Webster* to beach the boat. The wind was west by then, and beginning to moderate, though it was still blowing fifty knots. The captain, however, didn't know where he was and wasn't close enough to land to run the boat ashore. Finally Garvin, who owned a big buyboat, went out and towed in the *Ralph Webster.* When they got her into port, the skipjack had no water in her. The bilge pump was working fine. She had evidently never come close to sinking. The storm was so quick and violent that the captain had simply become frightened and disoriented in the squall.

"That's the worst I've seen it, but we weren't in danger," said Murphy, who had sailed his way out of danger.

Captain Russell Dize also remembers a time he used sail to reach a safe harbor. It was the mideighties, and Dize, in the *Kathryn,* and Captain Robbie Wilson,

in the *Elsworth,* had left the oyster rocks off Solomons at sunset and started pushing north, home to Tilghman Island. "It was just slick ca'm. Coming up the Bay, the stars were out and it was a beautiful night to be pushing up the Bay," remembers Dize. Both captains had two days' worth of dredging on board—about three hundred bushels.

During the daytime, captains can watch the water for signs of shifts in the wind. They literally read the water to figure the velocity of the wind. On a windless day, a breeze will ruffle the water's surface. Whitecaps begin to show at about twelve knots. A gale, packing forty knots or more, will look like a big, white wall of churning water marching across the sea. At night, however, captains can't see the water to judge the wind.

So, when a northeaster blew across the Bay, with winds up to fifty knots, the two men had little warning. When it hit the *Elsworth,* it washed a big gasoline drum against the wheel, and for a few minutes, as he wrestled the drum away from the huge wheel, Captain Robbie Wilson couldn't turn or control the boat.

"It hit us right off James Point," near the Little Choptank River, Dize said. "I couldn't push her forward into the seas any longer and in ten minutes, you couldn't push her at all. What happened is we can't drive her any further into the sea, and she starts falling back on the yawl boat. As long as you're going ahead, it's pretty safe. Once you stop, it becomes dangerous because then she [the push boat] will fill up with water and sink."

Unable to push into the wind, Dize decided to sail. "When they hoisted the mainsail, the sea just broke over their heads," he said of his crew. "Once it becomes apparent you can't push forward, you have to get the sail on her and tack, or else you gotta go back where you come from. Once you put the sail up, it relieves the pressure on the yawl boat."

If they could get above James Island, at the mouth of the Little Choptank River, the captains knew they could turn east into the river and find refuge from the storm. "Our problem is we didn't know if we were above James Point," said Dize, who also had another problem to deal with. "Most of the oysters were forward. She was bow heavy," Dize said of the *Kathryn*. Once the sail was up, Dize tacked out into the Bay, then tacked back into the Little Choptank River to safety.

"If it hadn't been for sail, it would have been pretty tough," Dize said. "Once you can't push, you've got to sail."

The two boats anchored in the river until the wind subsided, about five A.M. the next morning.

Most captains agree that having their auxiliary motor in a push boat, rather than in the skipjack, is what makes the dredge boat a dangerous vessel to be in when a squall hits. So many things can go wrong with the push boat, which is exposed to the weather. Sometimes a man has to get down in the yawl boat to maneuver it. In big seas, the little boats can easily get swamped. "I've seen them sink a yawl boat before, and if it's blowin' and rough and you sink a yawl boat, you better damn sake get rid of her," said Captain Wade Murphy. "I mean, put a buoy on her and cut her loose. She'll act like a damn ram; if things are right, she'll bang and bang and bang, and knock your rudder off. Now, if it's not too rough, you can get her back on the davits and get her up."

"It would be a lot safer with an engine in the hole," said Dize. However, having an engine in the hole or hull of a working dredge boat is illegal. Maryland outlawed it because law enforcers knew dredgers could easily break the law and power dredge if the engine was stowed in the boat. With its auxiliary power in a separate push boat, law enforcers can easily tell when dredgers are violating the law by simply noting whether the dredge is overboard at the same time that the push boat is in the water.

If the push boat has one redeeming factor it is that it eases the workload on the dredgers. Over the years, dredgers competed to find bigger and bigger engines for their push boats, remembers Captain Clyde Evans. "The first engines, you could near about crawl as fast as they'd go. Then somebody'd put in a bigger engine, a car engine. It got so you'd see how fast they'd go," said Evans, who started dredging with his father on the *Virginia W* in 1926.

Today, most push boats have big enough engines in them that they can push a skipjack through ice. Being able to push through ice that is a half-inch thick or more, or to push through ice floes, allows dredgers to work today, while dredgers at the turn of the century would have been forced to lose days, if not weeks, to icy weather. As Murphy noted, "You can't row through ice."

But working in ice has its drawbacks. In the age of the push boat, ice has replaced squalls as the most dangerous weather a dredger faces.

Several dredge boats were up the Magothy River in the late eighties, blocked in by ice, when the *Sandusky*, a state ice cutter, "came in and broke it all up so we could get out," said Captain Marshall. The skipjacks spent the day working off Sandy Point, near the Bay Bridge, then returned to the Magothy in the afternoon.

"Coming back in the Magothy, there was just a track" through the ice, remembers Marshall. As they started up the track, "a big bunch of ice from upriver got loose and started closin' the track up." Unable to back up, Marshall pushed on through the ice floes. The boat was sheathed in metal along her waterline, like most of the dredge boats, and Marshall hoped this would keep her from being damaged.

"That night, we were staying on the boat, me and Eddie Greenwood. He slept in a bunk with his head forward, a couple feet from the [bilge] pump. I slept in the other bunk with my head aft," Marshall said. Greenwood kept complaining that the pump was turning on. Finally, they went down in the hole to check.

"God-dern, water was pouring in 'from both sides," Marshall said. A few days earlier, they had pushed through thin, windowpane glass, notorious for slicing boats like a knife slices butter. This windowpane ice had not cut any wood on the *Virginia W,* but it had cut the metal sheathing along the skipjack's sides. Then when the crew pushed through the ice that evening, the heavy ice floes had "stove in both sides" of the *Virginia W* at her waterline, cracking the side planks for about twelve feet. The cracks were so bad, "I could see light coming through," said Marshall, who was seeing the floodlights of the marina.

They kept the boat afloat through the night using pumps. The next morning, Marshall pushed the boom to the side and heeled the boat over so that one of the damaged sides was out of the water. He caulked the holes and nailed plywood over the cracked planks from the inside, then did the same to the other side for a makeshift repair. It lasted through the rest of the season, and the next summer Marshall put the *Virginia W* on the railway and replaced the cracked wood.

Whether pushing through ice or sailing into a gale-force wind, it's all done in the pursuit of the oyster. But of all the oysters bars that have ever been dredged, there is at least one out in the Bay that proved mysteriously elusive.

One day in 1982, Marshall and his crew hit a good lick of oysters off Love Point. It was Monday, a push day, and they easily caught 130 bushels before dark. The next day, they returned and gathered 140 bushels. "It was a great big area. Clear oysters. Nothing but oysters. You could make a whole big circle and just stay on 'em," said Marshall, who got marks on the oyster rock before leaving.

Dredgers "mark" an oyster bar by lining up landmarks, or by determining their angle to three landmarks, a mathematical process called triangulation, which boaters commonly use to find their location on water, especially before the advent of loran.

Six days later, on the next push day, the crew of the *Virginia W* returned to the great oyster rock off Love Point. Marshall lined up his marks, but when they hauled in their dredges, the bags were virtually empty. Marshall dragged around, but the dredges kept coming up with nothing in them but shell and mud. He couldn't find the oysters that had been so plentiful just the week before.

Since oysters don't move laterally, Marshall's only explanation for where the oysters went is under a layer of mud or dirt: "Oysters can work in and out of the bottom. They can sand over. We had had a lot of wind later that Tuesday night and maybe they sanded over. You can work a place, a hard bottom," and not find many oysters, Marshall said. "After a freeze, the bottom will loosen up and you can catch oysters."

Believing the elusive oyster bar had simply been sanded by the windstorm, Marshall kept returning to the spot, trying to find oysters. "I've gone over there a lot of times since, looking for that Lost Colony," which is what Marshall and his crew labeled the mysteriously disappearing oyster bar. He always hoped it would mysteriously resurface, and yield a few more good harvests, but in ten years, Marshall and the crew of the *Virginia W* have never again found the Lost Colony.

A crewman hauls the dredge aboard in a heavy sea.

At the end of a long day, crew tackle the tedious job of tying reef points in the jib of the *Rebecca T. Ruark*. Dredgers always reef, or shorten, their sails in order to be prepared if they should face heavy weather the next morning.

# Fifteen

# THE BOOM YEARS

*One time I come home and my wife was in bed. I had a roll of money in my pocket. I threw it in the bed. She said, "What in the world have you done? Stuck somebody up?"*
—Captain Ellis Berridge about hitting a good lick

WHEN HE finished the season working the middle deck of his father's skipjack in the 1960s, Russell Dize swore he'd never get on another dredge boat. As a child, Dize had tagged along with his father, Captain Dan Dize, helping to take care of the family's two skipjacks, the *Fannie L. Daugherty* and the *Annie Lee*, and sailing with his father on Saturdays and vacations. But after spending a whole season dredging aboard the *Fannie L. Daugherty*, Russell Dize had had enough of the old skipjacks. At least, he thought he had.

"I worked on them so much, I swore when I got on my own, I'd never work on one or own one because it was so much work when I was a kid," said Dize.

But in 1980, Dize wanted a skipjack bad, bad enough to travel all the way to Nantucket to look at the *Sallie Bramble*, a one-masted bugeye, sold out of the oyster trade. He wanted a dredge boat bad enough, even, to offer $10,000 more than the asking price of the *Kathryn*, the skipjack he finally bought.

If he hadn't offered the extra cash, Dize may never have acquired the *Kathryn*, one of only two skipjacks left with a round chine to her hull, which made her an especially able sailor. "Five head wanted this boat, then," Dize said. "Johnny Parkinson was talking about $30,000 for the boat. My dad said, 'If you want it, buy it.' So I offered him $40,000."

It was more than the *Kathryn*'s hull construction or her exceptionally good condition that drew so much attention when she was offered for sale. For several years oysters had reproduced exceptionally well in the Chesapeake and the tributaries. These good spat sets, combined with phenomenal increases in the price of oysters, made dredging more attractive than it had been since 1912, when Virginia took its first big cut of the Maryland oyster market. Not only were dredgers making a very good income through the 1970s—better than any other occupation on the water—but they were also catching their limit early.

In the midseventies, Maryland watermen were harvesting 2.5 million bushels from the Chesapeake and the tidewaters annually, and making about $5 per bushel, all before lunch. "In those days, we were back in port by ten," remembers Captain Stanley Larrimore, whose personal records show that even on the last days of the season in March 1975, he was catching his limit of 150 bushels, which was rare. Historically, oyster rocks worked by dredgers were depleted by the last months of the season.

For watermen willing to learn how to sail dredge, the race was on to find a skipjack, go drudgin', bring in the cash, and still have plenty of time to while away the afternoons. It was a high-paying part-time job, and everybody wanted in on it.

The boom years of the seventies not only attracted new, young men into the dredging business, which meant the dying art of sail dredging would be handed down to another generation of skipjack captains, but it also pumped new life into the aging, dying dredge fleet. The size of the fleet had slipped from more than eighty boats in the 1950s, to forty-seven boats in 1962, and down to only thirty in 1977. Skipjacks were reconverted from pleasure to work again, hauled back home from where they had last worked in the Carolinas, returned from museums, and taken off mud flats.

And, for the first time since Bronza Parks built three skipjacks simultaneously in the summer of 1955, three new skipjacks were under construction in the late 1970s and 1980s. Melbourne Smith rebuilt the *Minnie V* for the City of Baltimore which operated her as a charter boat in the summer and a working dredge boat in the winter. At the same time, he built the *Anna McGarvey* on speculation, and sold it to Mike Ashford, owner of McGarvey's Bar and Restaurant in Annapolis. These boats were completed in 1981.

Meanwhile, a longtime waterman/boatbuilder in St. Mary's County had just finished building his first skipjack for a friend in 1980, and was planning to build his own. "Jackie [Russell] and I had been talking about it for some time," said Francis Goddard who built the *Dee of St. Mary's* for Captain Russell and the *Connie Francis* for himself.

Goddard was no novice to boatbuilding or to dredging. For years he had worked by day as a boatbuilder, constructing over two hundred wooden boats, and by night as a waterman, dredging illegally with a powerboat on the Potomac River.

When Goddard started dredging illegally in the forties, there were few oysters anywhere but in the Potomac River. "Everywhere else had died. It was hard times, but there were always a'plenty in the Potomac."

At age twelve, Goddard went power dredging with his uncle. At age fifteen, he had his own powerboat, and continued to dredge through 1975, with the exception of a few violent years in the sixties. "They started shooting at us in the sixties," Goddard said. "They had machine guns on their police boats. Three or four fellows got killed in Virginia. Some of them fellows had shot police officers."

One bullet missed Goddard by just a foot in the early sixties, he said. The violence and deaths convinced most of the oyster pirates to give it up for a

Dredgers talk to the next generation of captains during Tilghman Island Days, where the long heritage of the dredge boat is celebrated with skipjack races before a big crowd of visitors.

Captain Darryl Larrimore, who
rebuilt the *Nellie L. Byrd.*

while, but in a few years, they were back dredging
illegally again, said Goddard. A drastic increase in the
price of oysters encouraged them to continue. "Oysters
had gone from $1.90 to $7 or $8 a bushel," recalled
Goddard, who would dredge fifteen to twenty bushels,
take them into port, then go out again to harvest
another twenty or so bushels.

Goddard quit his illegal activity as oysters became
more scarce in the Potomac and the law cracked down
on the offenders. That's when he thought about dredging legally. Skipjack captains were making a lot of
money, enough to pay for a brand-new dredge boat.
Jackie Russell and Goddard went to look at many of
the skipjacks and took off lines. He built the *Dee of St.
Mary's* in seven months, finishing her in 1980. The
skipjack was "easy to build, just more time and money"
than other workboats, he said. Goddard used spruce
in the boat, which was fifty-six foot on deck, eighty-five
foot overall, and cost $90,000.

After he finished the *Dee of St. Mary's,* Goddard
had to stop work for six months, under his doctor's
orders. To pass the time, he made himself a model of
the skipjack he'd like to have, if he could only afford
the material to build one. "I always wanted one. Never
had the money to build one," he said. After he got well,
he went to a bank and financed the boat. However, he
didn't count on the cost of material increasing so
quickly. In the next three years, as he worked on the
*Connie Francis,* the cost of lumber sometimes increased
by a third.

Goddard had found a stand of virgin pine, and
worked out a deal with the landowner to cut some of
the timber to use in the *Connie Francis* and other boats
he was building. It was native heart pine, old ripe
longleaf pines that were "four foot on the stump," said
Goddard. It was perfect for boatbuilding, and exactly
what the old boatbuilders had used. Heart pine is
harder and denser than younger trees and, consequently, is less likely to rot.

Goddard made the *Connie Francis* the same
length as the *Dee,* but beamier by about two feet and
with a deeper draft. While he worked on her, the
disease, MSX, was already becoming a problem again
in the lower Bay, and Goddard foresaw the day when
dredging wouldn't pay.

"I realized I probably couldn't pay for her [by
dredging], so I built her really big-sided for seed . . . so
I could take the rig off and seed with her. I can carry
fifteen to eighteen hundred," said Goddard, referring
to hauling bushels of seed oysters. He also built her
bigger with the idea that he could run charters. If it
hadn't been for the disease, "I probably would have
built her smaller. She sails wonderful, but she comes
about slow," because of her big size, he said.

By the time he finished the skipjack in 1984, it
had cost him $160,000. And he had only one year
of good dredging to help pay for her before MSX
marched up the Bay and claimed the oysters.

Besides new construction, a number of individuals helped expand the fleet by restoring boats in the

The restored *Nellie L. Byrd* in Knapps Narrows.

seventies and early eighties, but no one did any more than one young man who wasn't supposed to be here.

Darryl Larrimore had grown up in a dredging family and as a teenager worked on many of the dredge boats harbored near his home in Tilghman Island, but in 1971, he had other things on his mind. At the age of eighteen, Larrimore was dying.

Working as a merchant seaman, Larrimore had returned from a twenty-eight-day run on a ship with his neck so swollen that he couldn't raise his head off his shoulder. Doctors diagnosed the problem as Hodgkin's disease, a cancer of the lymph glands. Doctors removed the malignant tumor from his neck, took out his spleen, and started giving him radiation, but they were so pessimistic about this new kind of cancer treatment that they gave him only three months to live. Larrimore refused to let the death sentence interfere with his natural good humor and enjoyment of life.

"I never did get down. I knew I was gonna make it. I just wasn't gonna give up," Larrimore said, twenty years later. "I never gave it [dying] a second thought.

I mean, I did pray and I promised a whole lot of stuff. I'll probably pay for it in the end, for not keeping my promises," he added with a laugh.

Larrimore's father and uncles all had skipjacks, so he often dredged while he was a teenager growing up on Tilghman Island. At one time or another, he worked for almost all the Tilghman captains. At age twenty-two, after his successful bout with cancer, he dredged the *Elsworth* for another man, and planned to buy the skipjack, but the price tag kept increasing, and he could not afford her.

After two years at the helm of a skipjack, "I was without a boat for a year," Larrimore said. He knew the upcoming years were going to be big ones for dredgers; he had seen the little oysters coming up in the dredges when he worked the *Elsworth*. So Larrimore started hunting for a skipjack. In 1979, he went to Broomes Island, above Solomons on the western shore, and brought home the *Claud W. Somers*. "She was in rough shape," he said of the boat that had sunk in Hooper Strait, drowning Captain Thompson Wallace and his crew two years earlier.

"When I got her, it was a lot of things wrong, but she had a good set of Dacron sails. Brought her home, put her on the railway, pumped her out, and she stayed up," said Larrimore, who renailed the boat and went to work dredging her. "She didn't sail well. She'd go sideways faster than she would ahead."

Larrimore had learned a little about working on boats by converting an old yacht into a workboat prior to dredging the *Elsworth*. "To me, the *Claud Somers* wasn't worth rebuilding because she was too small, about forty feet, but she was something to work."

The same summer he acquired the *Claud Somers,* Larrimore got a call from the Calvert Marine Museum in Calvert County, which had been offered the skipjack, the *Geneva May*. A museum in Wilmington, North Carolina, was trying to find a home for the skipjack. The Calvert Marine Museum offered to sell it to Larrimore for a dollar, and they gave him $1,000 to go get her and sail her north. The museum hoped to see the boat work again.

"She looked all right," said Larrimore, who went down to North Carolina to look at the old dredge boat that had once worked on the Bay, and had been sold down south. "Her shape had fell on the back end, but she seemed to be as good as could be."

Larrimore brought her home and tore off her deck, which clearly needed to be replaced. "I thought that was all she needed. Then I started down through her sides. She had dry-rotted from the inside. There was a hard crust on the outside, quarter-inch thick, and everything inside was dust. She was so hogged [her hull had fallen and lost its original shape], I didn't think it was worth going to the trouble to rebuild her. I give up. Stripped everything off her. I kept the bowsprit," which he put on the *Claud Somers*. Too far gone, the *Geneva May* went up a mud bank to die.

Around 1984, Larrimore bought the *Nellie L. Byrd* for $800. It was another wreck. "You could take a good pair of Nike shoes and kick her apart," but she was still in better shape than the *Geneva May*.

Over the years, Larrimore had made friends with businessmen who liked to race aboard the old skipjacks. One of them, Herb Cardin, had told him, "If you need any lumber, just call me up." So, when Larrimore started rebuilding the *Nellie Byrd,* he contacted his friend, who sent him three truckloads of lumber.

Originally, he planned to patch up the *Nellie Byrd,* but "I couldn't find a place to stop. I was just going to

fix the sides up, but there were no sides left to attach to it. I kept tearing them out and tearing them out. I found out her timbers were bad. I had to tear the chine stringers out—the 4 × 6 pieces that run up and down her sides. I had to tear the bottom off. She had a rotten stern." By the time he finished, five months later, almost the only things original on the 1911 *Nellie Byrd* were the keelson, skeg, deck, and mast.

"I put her on the railway in July and I missed the first two weeks of dredging by the time I got the mast back in and all the rigging up. I had one good year before oysters died," Larrimore added, referring to the massive die-off of oysters caused by MSX in 1986-87.

That summer, Larrimore spent all his time working on the *Nellie Byrd,* so he wasn't making any income. While he worked, *National Geographic* came down to shoot some film with plans to do a television special on the skipjacks. Larrimore made an effort to accommodate them by not working on certain areas of the boat

Captain Bobby Marshall, who owns the *Virginia W.*

until their film crew could be there to tape it. He had almost run out of funds by the end of the project, and thought maybe they would make a donation. "You don't think you can talk your people out of a thousand dollars to help me finish up this boat?" Larrimore asked the film crew one day. "That's the last time I saw them."

Some of the captains who bought skipjacks during the oyster boom of the seventies and eighties were familiar with the skipjacks, like Dize and Larrimore. Others were watermen who got in it solely for the money.

Captain Robbie Wilson was twenty-five years old and a fourth-generation waterman when he decided to buy the *Elsworth* in 1978. "I didn't know the mainsail from the jib," Wilson said. "I was soft-shell clamming and the market got bad," he said. "I'd patent tonged and hand tonged." He decided to try dredging partly because of the money that was being made in oysters, and partly because "it's quieter and less physical strain on the captain." In the late eighties, he sold the *Elsworth* and bought the *Wilma Lee,* a much easier boat to sail.

On a good day, Wilson likes to sail with the toe of his boot on the steering wheel and the radio mike in his hand. The captains keep up a constant banter on the air waves, kidding each other and telling stories. For the captains who stand back aft of the cabin, away from their crew, the radio helps fill in the long days of isolation on the water. "We don't make much money, but we have a good time," Wilson said about radio conversations. "I'm hooked on it now. I like sailing. If I hit the lottery, I'd still drudge, but I wouldn't work no rainy no'easter."

For a few owners like Tim Stearns and Kathleen Poole, who owned the *Virginia W,* the job of restoring a skipjack was more a personal challenge than a money-making venture. Stearns did the work himself on the *Virginia W* while crewing on the *Lorraine Rose.*

"I don't think he had any plans to make a career out of it. He was a free spirit. He took this on as a challenge and a project," said Bobby Marshall, who later bought the *Virginia W.* After partially rebuilding the skipjack, Stearns, who wasn't a waterman, tried dredging her, but didn't have much luck catching oysters. "Tim was having terrible days," said Marshall, who would buy his meager catch at the end of the day.

"The others would have a hundred bushels; he would have twenty."

One day, Marshall agreed to go dredging with Stearns and help him out. Marshall had only dredged twice in his life. However, he knew how to sail, having grown up sailing his father's log canoe, *Rover.* And he knew the oyster bottom. "I didn't want to work inside, anyway," said Marshall, who ran fishing parties in the summer and owned a packinghouse. After working the boat with Stearns, Marshall decided he liked it, and bought the skipjack.

The skipjacks that survived forty, fifty, eighty, in some cases, a hundred years, weren't always the best or the biggest. If they had one common thread that helped them survive it was that "they happened to get a captain who cared for them," said Russell Dize. When he bought the *Kathryn,* his father, who knew the boat well, told him, "She always had a captain that would care for her."

"It's the luck of the draw," said Dize. "We've had some great boats go by the wayside."

Captain Robbie Wilson at the helm of the *Wilma Lee.*

# Sixteen

# THE SINKING OF THE *CLARENCE CROCKETT*

*When I was younger it used to be fun. No more fun now; not at my age. When the money's gone, I'm gone. I just do it because I've been doing it so long. Just like these old horses that used to haul the fire engines. Every damn time the bell ring, the horses run around the field.*

—Captain Pete Sweitzer, at age seventy, one of the oldest captains on the Bay

CAPTAIN PAUL HOLLAND and his two-man crew awoke at dawn to a gentle northwesterly breeze, perfect for sailing down the Bay. Aside from the chill in the air, there was nothing on the horizon to indicate a hard passage home.

Normally, Holland enjoyed dredging, but the winter of 1987-88 had been particularly tough on him and his men. Oysters had been scarce in the waters of Tangier Sound, so they had spent most of the season working out of Deep Creek on the Magothy River in Anne Arundel County. The two-and-a-half-hour commute was hard enough on the captain and the men, who spent several days a week living aboard the boat, but the scarcity of oysters turned a job Holland normally relished into drudgery.

"Just surviving was all we were doing, working Mondays and Tuesdays [power dredging]. Often it was blowing a gale and we weren't able to work at all," said Holland. Now, after a long disappointing season dredging the overworked oyster rocks of the upper Bay, it was finally time to go home.

The *Clarence Crockett* had about eighty nautical miles to cover to reach home on Deal Island. It was a long trip, particularly in a sailboat that could only make about eight or nine knots, but with the breeze out of the northwest to help push her along, Holland expected to make the trip in ten or twelve hours and be home that evening.

Since it was the last day of the season, March 15, Holland thought maybe he would spend a few hours dredging under sail before heading home. But as the

*Clarence Crockett* crossed the oyster rocks above the Bay Bridge, the wind freshened, and Holland changed his mind.

Ever since he'd quit school at age fifteen to work the middle deck of a skipjack, Holland had loved sailing and working on the water. A few times he had tried to settle into a land job, only to be lured back to the life of a waterman. For Holland, who had been raised on Deal Island where most men were watermen, the vast open waters represented a kind of freedom he couldn't find on land, not even on the scarcely populated lower Eastern Shore. "There's no congestion; no cars and people bothering you. You've got the magnificent sunrises and sunsets to look out and see God's hand and how he's creating. It's indescribable.

"When I slack my skipjack up, all she's got to do is move three inches away from that dock and I leave everything ashore: bills, house, jobs; it's totally left behind, and I come into another world. You know that you're the captain and you're in complete control . . . outside Father above."

Buying the *Clarence Crockett* in August 1984 was the culmination of a dream for Holland. As a kid, he had listened to his mother tell stories about how his grandfather had traveled from island to island in a sailboat—much like the famed "Parson of the Islands," Joshua Thomas—preaching to the watermen. He got his first feel for the work aboard a skipjack when, at age fourteen, he was roused out of bed by his father one Saturday morning before dawn. Captain Junior Benton, who owned the *Geneva May*, was short of crew, and

Paul's father wanted him to help out. Young Holland got dressed and joined the older crew at the dock. He continued to fill in whenever he was needed that winter.

Then his father hurt his arm in an accident aboard a sea clamming boat in New Jersey the following spring. "I came head of the family as far as making ends meet," Paul said. That winter, he quit school at age fifteen and went to work full-time on a skipjack to help support the family.

While in his twenties, Holland bought a workboat and went patent tonging for oysters, "but I always had that desire to own a skipjack," he said.

For three years he haggled back and forth with Captain Lowery Horner, trying to buy the *Clarence Crockett,* until finally, in the summer of 1984, the older captain agreed to sell the dredge boat for $25,000. "I mortgaged everything I owned and had to get my father to co-sign with me," Holland said.

If the boom years of the early eighties had continued, it wouldn't have been too long before the *Clarence Crockett* would have paid for herself, but as it turned out, Holland couldn't have picked a worse time in history to buy a skipjack.

"Oysters died really bad that summer," victim of an unknown parasite dubbed MSX. Hardest hit were the oysters in salty waters. The bars around Deal Island were virtually dead, but there were still oysters alive up

Skipjack captains headed north of the Bay Bridge to find oysters in the 1980s as parasites contributed to a massive die-off of shellfish in saltier waters south of the Bridge.

north where fresh water from the Susquehanna River kept the Bay less saline. So, for the next few years, Holland joined other Deal Islanders in the exodus north to Cambridge, Rock Hall, and the upper Bay, where oysters could still be found alive. Patent tongers from the lower and mid-Bay region also joined the exodus, which meant that what oysters were left above the Bay Bridge had to be divided among a large number of oystermen.

Now, as Holland approached the Bay Bridge, he didn't have time to think about the bad luck he had experienced since buying the *Clarence Crockett*. The wind was beginning to blow harder, about twenty-five knots. "It wasn't too bad to go with the wind, but past Annapolis it really breezed up, to thirty-forty miles per hour," he said.

They had already passed the rivers south of Annapolis and ahead of them were ten miles of unbroken coast without a deepwater harbor. "We were stuck with it," said Holland, who steered his boat along the western shore in shallow water, in case the weather got worse. "The Bay was completely whitecaps. It was really cold," he recalled. Finally, they reached Chesapeake Beach, where they stayed for the night.

It blew hard for the rest of the day. The next morning, the weather was squally, but the men were anxious to get home. Holland, believing the weather wasn't as bad as the day before, decided to leave port. Out in the Bay, however, he discovered that the seas were big and the wind was blowing twenty-five knots. Holland pushed on south, hoping the weather would moderate, but instead, the wind increased to thirty knots, so Holland again started looking for a harbor of refuge, though the prospect of finding one was bleak. Below Chesapeake Beach, the western shore was relatively unbroken—except for several very shallow creeks—down to the Patuxent River, more than twenty miles south. About ten miles south, however, Holland came across buoys marking the entrance to Long Point, which offered a marina with slips and fuel, but the entrance was tricky and shallow.

Since the *Clarence Crockett* drew only three feet with her centerboard up, Holland decided to try it. The skipjack hit bottom several times. "I about sank my boat at the mouth of that harbor going in. It was real shallow," but he made it in.

Holland stayed in port until about three o'clock that afternoon when the weather improved considerably. "It really got pretty late that day," Holland recalled. "The wind had moderated. It was down to ten knots. The seas weren't as bad. It was fair wind." There was still enough daylight left for the *Clarence Crockett* to reach the familiar waters of Hooper Strait, twenty miles away, by nightfall.

"Once we get into the strait, everything is real familiar to me," thought Holland, who had grown up in these waters and knew them like the back of his hand. So even if nightfall overtook them before they reached Deal, he felt there would be no problem. Anyway, after two days, the crew was anxious to get home. So, they slipped the lines, headed out of the harbor, and set their sails for home.

The passage across the Bay was so pleasant and warm that the men stripped down to their shirtsleeves. After two days of heavy wind, the warmth felt great.

The sun was setting as they approached the strait, so Holland had his men drop the sails, a precaution they always took at night. They proceeded through the familiar waters under just the power of the yawl boat.

"As we got through the strait and through Tangier Sound, I said, 'Boys let's go down to Wenona, then we don't have to worry about gettin' up tomorrow.'"

Wenona was the harbor at the southern tip of Deal, just three miles farther south, where Holland normally kept his boat. Heading there now would save them from moving the *Clarence Crockett* the next day. The only obstacle between them and the port was the county boundary marker between Dorchester and Somerset. Several years earlier, the line had been marked by a simple buoy, but recently the state had replaced the buoys with a big steel fixture, shaped like a tripod. Years ago, the county markers were necessary because watermen had to work within their own county lines. But that restriction had been ruled unconstitutional in 1971, so county markers no longer served any purpose.

Nevertheless, the tripod stood, a giant nuisance to navigation. Worse, it was badly marked, with only two reflectors, one facing due north, the other due south. The *Clarence Crockett* was approaching from the northwest.

"I told the men to get up by the port and starboard sides and watch for the tripod. I was watching my depth-finder. We were down in ten feet of water. I had cut across this shoal all my life," said Holland, who was just inching the boat along. "I was gettin' edgy and nervous because the water hadn't dropped off," Holland said. Only when the depth-sounder indicated they were in deeper water would he feel sure they had safely passed over the shoal and by the tripod.

With no moon to cast some light on the waters, the men were left with only a set of flashlights to help them spot the tripod. Suddenly, Gordon Wallace, on the port side, shouted, "Here it is." The words were hardly out of his mouth when the *Clarence Crockett* struck the fixture.

"If I'd hit the plastic buoy [that used to mark the county boundary lines], she would have bounced off," said Holland later. But there was no give to the steel pole. Holland didn't realize it then, but the *Clarence Crockett* had struck at one of her weakest points, a place where she had been repaired years ago. Holland later counted nineteen boards, shorter than two feet, that had been used in the makeshift repair. Rot had set in where the repair had been made, so the boards easily cracked away, leaving a gaping three-foot hole in her side. She quickly began to fill with seawater.

"I heard the crunch. I could hear the gushing of water. I could tell without even knowing that she was going down toward the front, headfirst," Holland said.

The skipjack had moved ahead several feet. Before leaving the helm to check the damage and while the boat still had some buoyancy, Holland backed her up against the steel marker that had caused the calamity. "I don't know why I did it. Just instinct. I just done it," Holland said later. It would be their salvation.

But for the moment, Holland turned his attention to saving the boat. "I ran up and told the guys, 'Get the hatch up and see how bad the hole is.' I thought I'd take one of the bunks and rip it up and chink it into the hole. When I looked below, there was a foot and a half of water." And only fifteen seconds had passed since the crash.

"All right, let's get back here and get off on this tripod," said Holland, trying to remain calm. "She was filling up with water real fast. I didn't know how much of her would stick up. When she finally went down, she buried the cabin," Holland said.

He helped the two men climb out on the yawl boat and up on the steel structure. Then he returned to the cabin and grabbed his marine radio. "I put two maydays out and all the sudden I heard a noise. I was afraid she was going to suck me down into the cabin and I dropped the radio mike into the water and held onto the side of the cabin."

As the last bit of air bubbled out of the cabin, Holland felt a powerful tug at his body as water gushed past him, into the hull of the skipjack. He held onto the cabin top with all his might as the rush of water sucked at him, trying to pull him under. Finally, the boat settled against the bottom, moving ahead about three feet. Holland found himself immersed up to his waist in water.

Shaking with cold, Holland turned to get off the sunken boat. It was almost too late. The yawl boat, tied fast to the skipjack, had also sunk. His only hope of reaching the tripod was to step out onto the narrow metal davits that held the yawl boat out of the water when it wasn't in use, and try to jump to the tripod.

One side of the davits was just barely above water. Holland climbed out on it, then jumped for the bottom angle iron on the tripod.

"I jumped and grabbed hold of the pole and then I fell back into the water. If it hadn't been for those two guys, I think I would have drowned. They reached down and got a hold of me."

Holland, weighing over two hundred pounds, was much bigger than the other two men, but they managed to hold onto him, pulling at his upper body and his clothes until Holland was able to get a knee up on the flat angle iron they were standing on. Finally, he got both feet up on the metal surface and sat down, facing the pole.

Holland caught his breath, then looked back at what was left of the *Clarence Crockett:* only the boom and mast were visible above water. "Every now and then, a wave would break over the cabin and you could see an inch or two of the cabin or a ledge."

It had taken only fifteen minutes for the *Clarence Crockett* to sink.

The three men realized immediately they would probably be spending the night on the tripod. There wasn't much boat traffic around Deal Island after dark, especially this time of year. Yet an hour or two after the sinking, they spotted the lights of a boat coming out of the Nanticoke River north of them.

None of the three men remembered carrying anything off the boat with him, yet there was a flashlight and a piece of rope lying on the tripod. Now one of them grabbed the flashlight, turned it on, and started waving it at the boat, trying to get the captain's attention. The boat was coming directly toward them. For a moment, a powerful beam of a light fell on them. Rescue appeared imminent and the spirits of the three haggard men soared. Then, suddenly, the vessel turned west, toward Hooper Strait, and they could see the shadow of a tugboat, heading out toward the Bay.

Captain Paul Holland stands on the deck of the *Clarence Crockett,* which he had for sale in 1993, following her collision with a tripod in Tangier Sound, off Deal Island, in 1988.

From their perch on the tripod, just a mile or so offshore, the men could clearly see the lights of their homes on Deal Island.

"Five minutes and I could have been in Deal Island Harbor," Holland mused. "All night long we kept watching these lights goin' across the bridge . . . homes where they were setting up watching TV. We'd watch as they'd turn their lights off and go to bed. It was the loneliest feeling that you'd ever have in your life."

Among the lights crossing the Deal Island Bridge were those of Paul's wife. "I kept riding along the shore at night, looking for a light," Mrs. Holland remembers. She figured that if she spotted a vessel's light, she could be sure it was Paul in the *Clarence Crockett* and she would go down to the wharf to meet him. "Nobody else is going be out there," she reasoned, not knowing that the whole time she searched for his lights, "he was sitting out there."

None of the men were dressed for the near-freezing night that lay ahead of them. When Holland had urgently ordered them from the shelter of the cabin to search for the tripod, Billy Watters hadn't bothered to put on a coat. He was wearing only a thin shirt. Gordon "Bobo" Wallace had at least grabbed a jacket and was the warmest of the three. Holland, who had been leaning over the cabin hatch, warming himself in the heat rising from the cabin stove, had on only a shirt and a light hooded sweatshirt. Worse, he was soaked up to his waist, and as the night progressed, he got colder and colder. Around one o'clock in the morning, Holland began to lose feeling in his lower body.

"I told them boys, I was numb from the waist on down. I can't feel nothin'. At 2:30-3 o'clock, several times I almost fell off of there. All I wanted to do was go to sleep. Several times, I fell asleep. The boys would smack me on the face, pound me on the back, anything to keep me awake. I hadn't smoked for years, but I smoked cigarettes to stay awake."

The temperature had dropped below freezing. The beautiful afternoon that had enticed them out of a safe harbor had turned deadly cold. A northwester was blowing twenty to twenty-five knots. Holland's wet clothes were covered with a thick layer of frost. He could feel himself slowly freezing to death.

"I lost all consciousness of the frozen part of my body," he said. Between two and three o'clock, Holland became so weak and numb, he was certain he was dying. He later learned that his body temperature had fallen to fifty-nine degrees, far below the eighty degrees which is considered life-threatening by medical experts. He had one last request of his two companions on the pole: he wanted to be tied to the tripod. "Boys," he said, "I think I'm gonna die and if I do, I don't want them to have to come draggin' and have my family identify me." Holland was sitting down, his frozen legs jammed down between the pole and the flat piece of angle iron he sat on. Using the rope that had mysteriously appeared on the steel structure, the two men complied with his wish, tying the rope around his wrists and around his body, and then around the pole.

"You ain't gonna die, Captain. We ain't gonna let you die," Gordon Wallace kept telling him, but Holland was overwhelmed with a desire to sleep. "I'd be talking and going to sleep at the same time."

If Gordon and Billy were suffering, they kept it to themselves. "They knew I was wet and I was cold. Maybe the Good Lord let them not give in [because it would have] caused me to be weaker. Their concern was keeping me awake, especially after I told them I was so cold, I didn't think I would make it."

In the middle of the night, the weather began to moderate. "It got clear toward about three o'clock. The stars came out and all," Holland remembered.

Suddenly, Billy Watters started singing an old, familiar hymn they all knew: "Blessed assurance, Jesus is mine."

"All the sudden, I started singing, too," said Holland. They all sang the hymn, over and over, for almost an hour, until they were too tired to sing any longer.

When they finally lapsed into silence, "I felt a warmth come over me," said Holland, who had recently regained his faith in God after a long lapse away from religion. "I just felt the closeness of the Lord; his sheltered hand around me.

"I told the boys, 'Neither of us is gonna die. We'll be all right.'" Holland felt so certain he would survive, he had the men untie the ropes that bound him to the tripod. "I never felt the cold again. That was the last time I got weak," Holland related. But by then, Billy was cold and losing strength. Holland took off his sweatshirt and gave it to him.

When dawn arrived, Holland felt the warmth of the sun as he had never felt it before. "With every rising moment of the sun, it was steady warmth: it just felt like Palm Springs. Someone commented that we had made it through the night and somebody would come along through here soon. Somebody would see us."

Sure enough, about a half hour after sunrise, they spotted two small motorboats roaring out of the Wicomico River, heading south toward them.

Billy stripped off the hooded sweatshirt Holland had lent him during the night. "We shoved Gordon Wallace clear up on the tip-top of this here piece of plywood, and he started waving that hood."

Holland feared that if the boats got down to Deal Island without spotting them south of the channel, they might turn into the harbor and never see them. "Whatever you do, don't stop waving," Holland chided Gordon.

Just as the boats, which happened to be marine police Whalers, were off Haines Point on the mainland, Gordon stopped waving for a brief moment. Holland hollered at him and Gordon renewed his waving.

"All the sudden we seen the one boat turn off toward us, the outboard flippin' a lot of spray. They couldn't see the mast of the skipjack. They couldn't see us. But one guy thought he saw something. He beared off and slowed down and picked up his binoculars. That's when he saw Gordon on top of the pole. In two or three minutes he was here."

With just a narrow width of wood for a seat and the chain bobstay under their feet to steady them, crewmen slide out on the bowsprit of a skipjack to reef the jib as the river churns beneath them.

A crewman hauls aboard a bucketful of seawater to swab the deck of the *Rebecca T. Ruark* as the dredge boat heads home.

# Seventeen

# SAVE THOSE SKIPJACKS!

*"The boat owns you"—now, you been talking to my wife. That's what she says. I had the boat before I had my wife, and I keep telling her that, too.*

—Captain Pete Sweitzer

O VER THE past century, dozens of skipjacks have sunk, but none sparked public interest and concern for the preservation of the country's last remaining commercial fleet working under sail as did the sinking of the *Clarence Crockett* on March 17, 1988.

Perhaps it was the shrinking size of the fleet that sparked the interest; perhaps the harsh conditions under which the men fought for their lives through the long cold night; but the sinking of the *Clarence Crockett* ushered in a new era for the skipjacks: an era of preservation.

The idea of using public funds to repair, maintain, or somehow financially support the privately owned skipjacks had surfaced now and then over the years, particularly after MSX ravaged the oyster bars in the mid-1980s and a fleet of thirty-two active skipjacks dwindled down to twenty-one in 1988, then fifteen in 1991. But it was a difficult concept to fund, even if the monies could be found in the state coffers.

Even among skipjack captains, public financing of the private boats was a highly charged issue that sharply divided the men who so often worked side by side over the oyster rocks. Watermen, by nature, are fiercely independent and suspicious of the state. Many of them worried that state funds would come with strings attached. They feared they might ultimately sacrifice control of their boats in return for a few dollars, or they worried that the funds would be divided unevenly, mainly helping those captains who had failed over the years to reinvest their profits in their boats when repairs were needed.

It took several days for the news of the sinking of the *Clarence Crockett* to trickle north to Baltimore. When it hit the front page of the Baltimore *Sun,* public interest in the fleet heightened, and over the next two weeks, as wind, weather, and lack of funds hindered the job of raising the *Clarence Crockett,* public interest continued to mount.

After all, the *Clarence Crockett* was more than just another skipjack. A painting of her working under sail graced a commemorative stamp and was etched onto state collectibles like coffee mugs, glasses, and plates. She had become an emblem of Maryland's fascinating maritime heritage.

But for the moment, the job of getting the *Clarence Crockett* afloat would prove a long, frustrating one for Paul Holland. Heavy winds and big seas hindered the salvage operation, hampering volunteer divers who heard of the plight of the *Clarence Crockett* and showed up on Holland's doorstep to help. For seventeen days weather battered the boat, which lay in ten feet of water. The wind and seas were churning the bottom of the sound, creating a strong undertow that further ripped open the hole in her side and filled the vessel with sand. The men would dig sand out of the *Crockett*'s hull, only to have her fill up again. The weather "ripped the sails to pieces. The waves were beatin' her," said Holland, who should have been home recovering from his ordeal.

When Holland finally got the skipjack to a railway, "we probably had about five ton of sand in her. The hole went from three foot to eighteen or nineteen foot in diameter by the time we got her to Crisfield," he said.

Holland was already heavily in debt from having purchased the *Clarence Crockett*, so when a Snow Hill businessman offered to help finance the repair of the skipjack, it looked like his problems were solved. Paul Jones, of Paul M. Jones Lumber Company in Snow Hill, donated eighty percent of the lumber and cash for rebuilding the boat. Three other people also donated large sums to the project. However, when the work on the boat was completed by the boatyard in Crisfield, the *Clarence Crockett* would not float. "We had such common work done at the railway," Holland complained, "seventy to eighty percent had to be redone."

Holland eventually trucked the skipjack home and finished the restoration himself in his backyard, with some help from friends. While the *Clarence Crockett* was once again afloat, Holland was not able to dredge her after the accident. All her sails and dredging equipment were lost in the wreck, and he didn't have money to replace them, so he put the vessel up for sale.

Even before the 1990-91 season opened, tragedy hit the fleet again. As the skipjacks were assembling to begin races as part of Chesapeake Appreciation Days, a two-day festival designed to promote the skipjacks with various events, including racing off Sandy Point, one of the skipjacks started taking on water and sank.

Captain Doug West, at age twenty-nine the youngest captain in the fleet, was sailing the *Sigsbee* across the Chesapeake Bay from his home waters in the Chester River, preparing to join the race. As the skipjack approached the shipping channel, the deepest portion of the Bay, West's crewman noticed water in the boat. They immediately started the bilge pump, but it couldn't keep up with the water. West thought about dropping his push boat and trying to push the skipjack to shallow water, but the boat was sinking too fast. He quickly issued a mayday over the marine radio, then the *Sigsbee* heeled on her side, sinking two miles north of Sandy Point Lighthouse in more than fifty feet of water.

It took only two or three minutes for the *Sigsbee* to sink. Fortunately, there were rescue boats already patrolling the waters around the race course, and West and his crew, John Leader, were quickly retrieved. But it took the rest of the day for a salvage crew to tow the *Sigsbee* to shallower waters.

West believed a seam had opened up in the *Sigsbee*, but by the time she was hauled to shore, she was in terrible shape from having been dragged through the water. Over the next few days, the Lady Maryland Foundation intervened, sending a barge and crane to Sandy Point to load the *Sigsbee* and move the skipjack to Baltimore, where she was to undergo repairs at the Lady Maryland's shipyard.

But over the next few months, it became clear that the *Sigsbee*'s damage was far greater than her captain could afford to repair. West also owned the *Flora A. Price*, a big skipjack which had been transformed into an educational boat. It needed a lot of restoration work to make it a working vessel again. Now with the *Sigsbee* in such bad shape, West decided to refurbish the second skipjack, leaving the *Sigsbee*'s future in question.

Two more skipjacks sunk as the season progressed. Captain Stan Daniels found the *Howard* sitting on the bottom of Cambridge Creek on December 20, 1990. Soon afterward, in January 1991, Captain Walton Benton's *Somerset* sunk in the Magothy River, where he left it tied up overnight. Both skipjacks were raised and finished out the season dredging. But the multiple sinkings were a clear sign that at least some of the fleet was in bad shape.

Maryland officials considered a plan to help the captains, but the plan died when the state ran out of funds in the early 1990s. However, a new idea was blossoming in Baltimore, where the *Sigsbee* had been taken for repairs. Dennis O'Brien, head of the Lady Maryland Foundation, an organization that educates children about the Chesapeake Bay and ecology, usually from on deck an old-time working vessel, thought that perhaps troubled youths could be put to work, helping to rebuild the fleet.

Consequently, O'Brien created the "Save Our Skipjacks" program, a plan to raise up to a million dollars to refurbish the fleet. He planned to hold big-ticket fund-raisers that would be attended by Maryland's well-to-do, as well as people interested in the preservation of the old boats. He also planned to tap local businessmen for donations and to use troubled youths to assist shipwrights in rebuilding the boats. The program had a twofold benefit. Youths identified as being "at risk" because of antisocial or violent behavior, or who had already experienced run-ins with the law, would assist with the work on the skipjacks. Teenagers from the Hickey School for juvenile delinquents or from foster homes, or who were otherwise involved in social programs, would attend a "living classroom" at the foundation, where they would receive classroom instruction, as well as

More than twenty patches hold together the sails of the *Howard*. Hard pressed to find the money for new sails during the late 1980s, captains often resorted to makeshift repairs on their old sails.

learn how to work with tools and wood. While rebuilding the skipjacks, they would also learn how to apply themselves to a task and feel the satisfaction of seeing a job completed. "It gives them a sense of accomplishment not found in their everyday life," said shipwright John Kellet. Meanwhile, the captains would get a refurbished boat.

Again, the captains were sharply divided over the merits of the program. Captains who had refurbished or maintained their boats over the years, saving and scrimping in order to keep a boat in good working condition, were dismayed that the monies would go to captains who had let their boats fail.

"That program is fine for the ones who drank beer and gambled their money away and ran women, and their skipjacks went down," said Captain Pete Sweitzer, whose skipjack, the *Hilda M. Willing*, was described by one boat surveyor as being as clean and well kept as a yacht. "The ones who worked and kept their boats up don't need their money. This program's going to help the ones that wasted their money."

"That's my biggest grief," agreed Captain Darryl Larrimore of Tilghman Island. "Here I spent all this money to rebuild this boat and [other people] have let their boats go, and now [the SOS fund] is gonna give them money to repair their boats." Larrimore spent one summer completely rebuilding the *Nellie L. Byrd*, which he later sold to Captain Bart Murphy.

Tilghman Islanders were particularly critical of the program since most of the boats in poor shape belonged to Deal Islanders. "Those people at Deal Island would never take care of their skipjacks. I don't know whether it's the way they were raised, but I've seen perfectly good skipjacks sold to Deal Island and in three years, you wouldn't recognize them. They look like a damn floatin' junk heap," Sweitzer said. "They ride around in big Cadillacs. They'll spend it on a house or a car, but they won't spend neither penny on them skipjacks. That's absolutely crazy. You spend it back on your business first if you expect to keep it going, and a skipjack's a business."

Deal Island captain Jack Parkinson admitted that he and other Deal Islanders had not maintained their boats, but he also noted that Deal Islanders face different economic problems than the captains at Tilghman.

Parkinson bought the *Helen Virginia* from a Tilghman Island family. "When I bought her, she was in good shape." But as she needed repairs, "I kept puttin' it off," he said. "When you buy them, you finance them; you make payments and do upkeep" which doesn't leave much cash for major overhauls. Then bad times hit Deal Island. "Ten years ago, the economic situation started getting so bad, we couldn't keep the boats up. Now, she needs a lot."

How their captains were raised may have something to do with the fact that Deal Island skipjacks are in poorer shape than those at Tilghman Island. Over the last hundred years, most captains in Dorchester and Talbot County owned their own dredge boats. Sometimes packinghouses would finance the boats and some packinghouse operators owned a small fleet of three or four vessels, but for the most part, Tilghman Island captains came from a long line of boatowners who understood the business end, as well as the dredging end, of a skipjack.

By contrast, few Deal Islanders owned their own skipjacks prior to the Great Depression. Many of the dredge boats were owned by companies, like ship chandleries or packinghouses that might own dozens of vessels, or by individual men, like William L. Jones and Elbert Gladden, Sr., who both amassed fairly large fleets of ten or more boats. Consequently, not many Deal Islanders were raised by fathers and grandfathers who had long years of experience handling the business end of dredging.

Other economic factors, however, have affected the ability of Deal Islanders to maintain their boats. At the turn of the century, Deal Island was a hub of activity and Somerset County thrived on the oyster industry. But when oyster rocks died in Tangier Sound and the state closed the Potomac River to dredging, not only did dredgers suffer financially, but the entire region collapsed into poverty. The post–World War II Deal Island was a faraway place with little hope of offering a future to its youth. Even summertime industries like crabbing and fishing were adversely affected by the collapse of the oyster industry. Tilghman Islanders, on the other hand, who sit in the midst of a thriving tourist county, can sometimes command a dollar or two more per bushel of crabs than Deal Islanders, who must

The *Caleb Jones*, which sank in 1992 while loading seed oysters, was the first skipjack to participate in the "Save Our Skipjacks" program sponsored by the Lady Maryland Foundation, which engaged troubled youth to rebuild the vessels.

truck their crop to distant towns and cities. Since dredgers rely more on crabbing than oystering to support themselves today, the difference in price for crabs may help to account for Deal Islanders having to struggle to maintain their skipjacks, while Tilghman Islanders have always seemed to find a few extra dollars.

The first SOS fund-raiser was a much-touted dinner held at Stouffer's Hotel at the Inner Harbor on November 2, 1991. A guest list of six hundred included celebrities, preservationists, historians, environmentalists, and educators, as well as watermen. A ticket cost $125 per couple, and skipjack captains were encouraged to buy a ticket, too, if they wanted to be part of the program. The program never raised the million dollars that O'Brien had hoped it would. In fact, it raised so little money that the captains and the foundation decided to fund only $10,000 per boat, per restoration. Even then, only a handful of boats would get funding in the first few years. Since most of the boats needed over $20,000 worth of work, the captain whose boat has been rebuilt had to come up with the remaining funds, either through his own fund-raiser or out of his own pocket.

Captain Dickie Webster was on vacation, playing golf, when he got news that his skipjack, the *Caleb Jones,* had sunk while planting seed oysters for the state. His brother, Ted, was captaining the boat for him at the time.

The *Caleb Jones* was refloated and sailed to Baltimore, where she became the first to participate in the "Save Our Skipjacks" program. Webster staged a crab feast and other fund-raisers to help raise an additional $13,000 to repair his boat.

The *Caleb Jones,* which had been built at Reedville, Virginia, in 1953, had rot in her planking and frames, said shipwright Jamie Burman, who worked on her, replacing almost everything except the keelson and deck. The *Caleb Jones* was completed in time for the 1992-93 dredging season.

The second skipjack to be part of the restoration program was Captain Stan Daniels's *Howard* which had a broken keelson and had leaked badly since her struggle in the ice back in 1970. Three times in recent years she had sunk and Daniels had little hope of her surviving another season.

The *Howard* was in such poor condition that the foundation decided to start from scratch, essentially creating a new *Howard* from a mold of the old one, and salvaging what they could from the original boat. The shipwrights took the lines off the *Howard,* created a mold, and salvaged a few parts of the boat, like the bowsprit, rudder, and centerboard.

But even as the foundation began work on its second boat, the *Howard,* in the fall of 1992, there were renewed fears that dredging for oysters under sail might soon become obsolete, despite their efforts. For out on the oyster bars, watermen were uncovering their worst nightmares: Chesapeake Bay oysters, which had just begun to recover from the devastation of MSX in the mideighties, suffered a double blow in the fall of 1992: two parasites—MSX and Dermo—had combined to cause a massive die-off. Biologists who sampled the oyster bars prior to the start of the season found at least half the Choptank River oysters dead. Mortality rates were fifty to one hundred percent below the Bay Bridge.

"We can tweak this and tweak that, but we're still at the mercy of these diseases," said William Outten, program administrator for the Maryland Department of Natural Resources, Shellfish Administration.

Meanwhile, Captain Stan Daniels, told by the Lady Maryland Foundation that his share of the cost of rebuilding his skipjack was $18,000, wondered if he would ever sail the *Howard* again.

Old-fashioned wooden blocks are still part of the rigging on a skipjack.

A meager harvest was all dredgers had to look forward to when diseases ravaged the oyster bars of the Chesapeake during the mideighties. A crewman reefs the jib as the skipjack takes her small harvest to market.

*Eighteen*

# LOADED TO HER GUNWALES

*They used to die and come back every seven years. I don't believe they have any more disease now than before.*
—Captain Norman Benton about parasites and oyster die-offs in Tangier Sound

F OR THREE weeks in the spring of 1992 skipjacks joined patent tong boats and buyboats hauling seed oysters from one area of the Chesapeake Bay to another as part of Maryland's yearly effort to reseed and replenish the state's public oyster bars. Up until now, the runs had been short. The boats had worked out of the Little Choptank River, south of Tilghman Island, then had gone down the Bay to the mouth of the Potomac River, where they made local runs up the Potomac River with seed oysters. Now, they were embarking on the longest runs, from the Potomac River up Chesapeake Bay to the Chester River. The big buyboats and patent tongers could make the run fairly quickly, compared with the skipjacks which, whether under sail or pushing, could only make about eight knots. The run would take the skipjacks at least ten hours, if not longer, and the men would have to sail all night back to the Potomac if they hoped to get another load the next day.

For the skipjack captains and their crews, it was a grueling schedule, made all the more treacherous by the fact that they would be loaded to their gunwales with some eight hundred to a thousand bushels of seed oysters. The skipjacks were loaded from their bow to the end of their cabin near the stern of the boat and piled almost as tall as a man stands on deck. When they were fully loaded, there was just enough room for the boom to swing above the huge pile of shells. Some of the boats were so laden with seed oysters that they had only a few inches of freeboard, or clearance, between the water and the

deck. With such a load, the boats were clumsy and difficult to steer, and pounded in the seas.

While most of the big dredge boats were built to haul these large loads, they also were now forty to a hundred years old. Consequently, it was not uncommon for seams to open up when the old boats were put under the stress of carrying so much shell. Few of them carried more than their harvest limit of 150 bushels at any time, other than during "spattin'," as the watermen called it. Spatting put the old dredge boats under more stress than they would have at any other time during the year.

Spatting followed the end of the oyster season in March, and lasted about a month in April, sometimes on into early May. It gave work to the watermen who otherwise had no income as they waited for the crabs to start biting later in the spring to begin their summertime employment working trotlines, crab scrapes, or crab pots.

Almost every spring since the forties when Maryland started its program, watermen contracted with the state to haul the seed-laden shell from areas reserved for seed oysters to bars that had become exhausted over the past seasons. It could be a well-paying job, even with a short haul, but since the state paid according to the length of the run, the long hauls were particularly lucrative. One skipjack captain said he paid for his newly acquired vessel during only one spatting season. With so much money to be made, captains were hard-pressed to turn down the long runs, even though they knew the trips could become dangerous if the weather took a turn for the worse and the seas became rough.

Captain Wade Murphy, who had bought and rebuilt the *Rebecca T. Ruark,* the oldest dredge boat in the fleet, generally moved seed oysters, but he declined to join the others on the long runs in the spring of 1992. "When you run ten hours in a loaded boat, it's not safe. It's a good way to get drowned," Murphy said.

Four of the six skipjacks making the first long hauls from Point Lookout, above the Potomac River, to the Chester River, were already loaded and heading north. There was a steady twenty-knot breeze out of the east, perfect for sailing north on a broad reach, so all of captains had raised their mainsails. They were several miles north of Point Lookout when Captain Ed Farley, who was still loading the *H. M. Krentz,* called on the radio to tell them the wind had shifted from east to west.

"He no sooner said that than sixty seconds later it hit," said Captain Bunky Chance, who owned the *Maggie Lee.* The wind fell out, then suddenly "the wind hauled around westerly," blowing twenty knots, said Chance.

Captain Bart Murphy, at the helm of the *Nellie L. Byrd,* headed the boat into wind. Captain Russell Dize's crew was able to drop the big mainsail. But when the wind shift hit the *Wilma Lee,* it jibed the boom, knocking down Captain Robbie Wilson. The *Wilma Lee* heeled so far leeward that for a moment it appeared she would capsize before the captain could get her back under control.

Likewise, the *Maggie Lee* jibed and heeled, sinking her leeward deck into the sea. "When it hit, half my deck went under water. I had water over my winders. One of my side boards broke, and I lost three hundred bushels right quick," Chance said. "I cut her into the wind to try and right her, get her back on her feet. She must have taken on a thousand gallons . . . maybe ten thousand."

Without so much shell on deck, the *Maggie Lee* straightened, but the near knockdown was just the beginning of trouble for the skipjack. She had taken on so much water that it was knee-deep in her hull. As she recovered from the blow and started to straighten up, thousands of gallons of seawater sloshed to the other side of her hull, causing the boat to roll violently in the seas and the boom to jibe once again.

Meanwhile, "the yawl boat had come out of the chock. I couldn't keep the yawl boat straight behind me," Chance said. Without the yawl boat positioned correctly, Chance couldn't steer. "After I jibed, I was all over the place. I tried to hold her into the wind, but the yawl boat was jammed on an angle, so when I moved the wheel to go straight, she turned."

Before the wind shift, the *Maggie Lee* was so loaded under the weight of a thousand bushels of oysters, that her deck was only two inches off the water. Then Chance's boat swung "like a pendulum," rolling sixty degrees one way, then sixty degrees the other. "The boom jibed at least four times. How that boom never broke, I don't know," he wonders.

Crew aboard the *Wilma Lee* shovel the seed oysters brought up in the dredge. "Spattin'," which is what dredgers call the work of moving seed oysters for the state of Maryland, is a labor-intensive job that requires strong men to shovel as many as a thousand bushels of oysters up on the deck of a skipjack.

The other dredge boat captains stayed nearby in case they were needed to rescue the crew from a sinking vessel, but there was little they could do, only watch and hope that Chance could get the boat under control.

The crew was able to lower the mainsail, but for almost a half hour the boat rolled violently back and forth as the boom jibed repeatedly, out of control.

"She was level with the water, and all her seams that normally were above the waterline were leaking. The sea was going through the deck boards and through the hatch," slowing filling the boat. Chance

had three bilge pumps running, but was losing ground to the incoming seawater. *Maggie Lee* was slowly, steadily sinking.

At this point, Chance realized, "She's got about ten minutes and that's all she's got" before she would be completely submerged. It was an utterly miserable moment for a man who had invested his time, money, and energy in trying to save a dying boat.

The year before, the *Maggie Lee* had been abandoned as a dredge boat, doomed to end her days as a tourist sight. Tilghman Island restaurateur Buddy Harrison had bought the skipjack a few years earlier and

pulled it up on the riverbank for his customers to look at through the window as they dined at Chesapeake House. It was a better fate than most skipjacks that died out of sight, out of mind, on the mud flats, with no one to care but the children who played on their decks as they rotted away.

Bunky Chance had crabbed and hand tonged for oysters since he was a teenager, but had no experience as a dredger. He had gotten the itch to own a skipjack while a guest aboard Captain Wade Murphy's *Rebecca T. Ruark.*

In the next few years, he looked everywhere for a skipjack, before locating the *Maggie Lee* on the beach. She was one of the last of the "Pocomoke round bottoms," which featured an unusual hull style, characteristic of skipjacks built in Pocomoke City.

"One thing that kinda played in my mind is, I knew if someone didn't do something with the *Maggie Lee,* she was going to be done for. I thought it was a good thing to do what I wanted to do and save her, too."

Chance was only twenty-nine, with no practical experience as a sailor. The son of a farmer, he had taught himself to be a waterman, and he felt that by studying books on sailing and listening to the other captains, and through trial and error, he could learn to dredge.

"I worked out a deal with Buddy: 'I'll take her off the beach and fix her up so she's workable for a season.

I might not be successful. If I don't want her, I'll bring her back in better shape,'" he suggested. Harrison agreed.

"She was just about shot when I bought her. She was hogging," the back end of the boat sagging from a crack in her bottom that started at the end of the keelson, or main timber in the hull, several feet from the stern. "She looked like somebody had took her over their knee and snapped her," Chance said.

That first season in 1990-91, he worked the boat with only makeshift repairs to the broken bottom. It was an uneasy feeling when the seas were even a little rough. "Standing by the wheel, it felt like you were standing on the end of a diving board," her stern flexed so much in the waves, Chance said. "I was concerned she would break in two."

By the end of the season, he had made up his mind to keep her, so he bought her from Harrison for $8,000. Then he went about fixing her hull. "I jacked her up sixteen inches at the stern, and pulled her sides and her bottom off."

Rebuilding the bottom of the *Maggie Lee* was more difficult than it would have been for most skipjacks because of her unusual hull design. Unlike the typical skipjack, whose sides butt up against the bottom boards like the corner of a box, the *Maggie Lee* had a rounded chine, created by three boards that were put on at an angle. Her hull was basically a compromise

The *Kathryn,* loaded to her gunwales, transports seed oysters in the Chesapeake Bay.

The *Maggie Lee*, restored by Captain Bunky Chance, was loaded almost to her waterline with seed oysters when a wind shift caused her to jibe violently and almost capsize north of the Potomac River in 1992.

between a sloop and a bateau, or skipjack. Her bottom had just a little deadrise, like a skipjack, but she was built with frames and planked fore and aft like a sloop.

Chance took the boat to Cambridge and quit crabbing early almost every day during the summer of 1991 to work on the skipjack in the afternoons. "Anything we thought we could salvage, we did," he said. When he finished planking her sides and bottom, Chance applied Seaflex, a form of fiberglass, to her sides from the rollers at the middle of the boat, back to the stern, wrapping the Seaflex under the bottom about eighteen inches. It was a tremendous undertaking, but when the 1991-92 dredging season opened, the *Maggie Lee* looked like a brand-new boat.

Now it appeared that all of his efforts to save the eighty-one-year-old vessel would be in vain.

Chance knew he had to stop the boom from swinging and throwing the boat out of control, but the boom swept across the deck so fast, "we couldn't turn the sheet in quick enough," he said. Finally, Chance rigged a four-foot line with a clip on the end, and tied it to the wheel shaft. When the boom jibed, they threw the line over it. It took several tries, but they finally caught the boom and hooked the clip, so the boom couldn't budge beyond the center of the boat.

With the boat stabilized, the men turned their attention to the water in the hull. Chance had a big Briggs & Stratton gasoline engine on board as a backup for the bilge pumps. They had trouble getting the big engine started, but when it finally fired up, it emptied the boat in five minutes.

The *Maggie Lee*, leaking badly, unloaded what remained of the oyster spat at the mouth of the Patuxent River and headed on to Tilghman Island. The skipjack had survived a nearly catastrophic bout with nature. Little did her captain know, though, as he limped his boat home, that something even worse lay ahead. It wouldn't come in the raging form of wind, or rough seas, or dangerous ice. Instead, it would sneak in quietly, almost unnoticed, until the moment came to work the oyster bars again in the fall. Then, even the best dredge boat with the best captain at her helm could not struggle their way out of this worst of natural disasters: disease.

By the fall of 1992, more than half the oysters below the Chesapeake Bay Bridge would be dead.

The fate of the *Lorraine Rose* and the *Ralph T. Webster,* tied in Knapps Narrows at Tilghman Island, was still uncertain in the late 1980s when owner Buck Garvin had them both for sale.

# Nineteen

# FOR THE LOVE OF A BOAT

*If the law don't get rid of us, they'll always be one dredge boat as long as I live, because I'm going to keep one.*

—Captain Bart Murphy

OR FIVE days a northeaster had howled over Deal Island, blowing the water out of Scott's Cove where the *Ida May* lay nestled on a boat lift at Scott's Cove Marina. All week long, the skipjack had been unable to budge from side to side because she fit so tightly inside the lift, and unable to float because there was so little water under her keel.

Twice a day for five days the man in the wheelchair made the short but laborious trip two miles down the road to the marina, his nurse always at his side to help him in and out of the car. And each time he left without the satisfaction of seeing his boat set afloat. But on this Friday in late October 1991, it would be different.

Elbert Gladden, Sr., couldn't contain his joy at seeing the old, wide-beamed skipjack, rebuilt and looking like a whole new boat, lowered into the water at last. Tears welled up in his eyes as he sat in the car, watching as the man on the boat lift lowered his dredge boat into the water.

Elbert Gladden was no newcomer to boat launchings. In the course of a half-century, he had supervised hundreds of launchings. After all, he had owned more dredge boats than any other man from Deal Island or Chance during the post–World War II years. He had owned twelve in his lifetime, and as many as nine at one time back in the forties and fifties.

But the launching of *Ida May* in October 1991— exactly fifty years after he purchased his first skipjack, *Dewey,* for $100 in 1941—was far more important to him than any that had preceded it. Not only was it to be the last time the old man would launch a boat, but

it was also Gladden's opportunity to give back to the vessels that had filled his life and earned him a good living, something he could not give himself: life.

Having had a stroke and now using a wheelchair, Gladden, with the support of his two sons, had chosen to dedicate part of his life's savings—and the remainder of his own life—to the restoration of the *Ida May.* In October 1990, his son Gordon had hauled the *Ida May* off the upper reaches of Scott's Cove, where she had sat for three long years, destined for the same fate that now faced the elder Gladden.

"We knew if she stayed there any longer, she would die. We didn't want her to die," said Gordon, who originally planned just to patch her up and put her on display in Salisbury, where he lived.

They took the old skipjack to Crisfield, where she was fitted with twelve new boards in her bottom, enough to keep her from leaking. Then Gordon towed the boat up the Wicomico River to Salisbury, where they ran lights along her rigging and put her on display in the city's new harbor.

They never thought about dredging her again until spring. Then, Elbert Gladden suggested he might spend some money on her and have her almost completely rebuilt. So the skipjack was trucked to Gladden's home in Chance. For the next six months, Elbert Gladden oversaw her restoration by shipwright Tommy Daniels, board by board, in his backyard.

The project proved much more costly than they expected. Oysters had to be plentiful for a dredge boat to be worth the $60,000 Gladden poured into her, and in 1991 the shellfish were not that plentiful. The restoration was purely an act of love. It was also, for Gladden, a form of therapy. "He was enjoying it so much," said Gordon Gladden, who hoped the work would help restore his father's failing health.

Surprisingly, Elbert Gladden's original experiences on skipjacks were somewhat painful memories of a child doing a man's job, in the hard cold environment of life aboard his father's dredge boat. Born two years after the *Ida May* first set sail in 1906, Gladden, like most boys who grew up on the Eastern Shore in the early part of this century, didn't have the chance to pursue much formal education. Boys were encouraged to earn their keep, so he quit school at age twelve and joined his father on the water. Yet even at twelve, he was no novice waterman. At the tender age of five, he had spent the summer with his father, grandmother, and grandfather on isolated Bloodsworth Island in the Chesapeake where they shedded crabs, worked fish floats, and picked crabs. For the family, it was a means of making a living, but for young Elbert it was fun.

Dredging, however, turned out to be difficult. "It was cold. I didn't realize how hard work it was," Elbert later told his son Gordon. After just one day aboard the boat, Gladden went to his father, Monie Gladden, and begged to go home. "I think I've made a mistake," he told his father, as he asked if he could go home and back to school.

"It's too late now," his father told him frankly. The skipjack was already way up the Bay, far from home. In the early part of the twentieth century, dredgers who sailed up the Bay often anchored out in a cove or creek, and seldom went to shore unless they rowed ashore in a skiff or went into Baltimore to sell oysters and restock their supplies. There would be little chance of getting into any port, and no chance of going home until Christmas, which was two months away. Meanwhile, the dredge boat tied up in the Magothy River, north of Sandy Point, dredging in the Chesapeake by day and selling its harvest to big buyboats.

Even if his father could have taken young Elbert home, he may have chosen not to do so. Monie Gladden, like most watermen of his era, had few financial resources, and if his own son could do a man's job, no matter how young and small he was, it was one less man he had to pay. Elbert faced a hard winter down on his knees on the deck of a boat, culling oysters.

In later life, Gladden would recall "being cold; living in the little cabin where it was always wet; and eating beans." Yet he spent eighteen years on dredge boats, working aboard his father's vessel for six or seven years before he found work on a larger dredge boat, the *Mattie F. Dean.*

"When you lived in Chance, you either worked on the water or you didn't work," Gordon Gladden explained. Chance, located on the mainland across the Upper Thorofare from Deal Island, was something of an island itself. Situated on a few acres of fast land at Haines Point, the watermen's enclave could only be reached by driving miles across marshland. Today the road through the marsh is built up, with deep ditches to carry water away from the blacktop, but back in 1920, it was far easier to sail a boat to Chance and Deal Island than to travel the muddy road.

Elbert Gladden married and in 1938 Elbert, Jr., was born. By then, Gladden was working on the Victor Lynn Line traveling between Salisbury and Baltimore. When his wages were cut from $13.50 a week to $11.50, Gladden realized, "I can make more money crabbing," so he quit.

Gladden did well crabbing through the summer, but the oyster industry was not doing very well in 1938. Consequently, that fall, Gladden made the difficult decision to leave his hometown and take his family to Baltimore where he found a job bending steel at Bethlehem Steel as the country prepared for war.

During his seven years in Baltimore, he missed the Eastern Shore "tremendously," said his son Gordon. He never lost his love for the boats he had worked aboard as a youth, despite the hardships he endured on them. Every Sunday he would walk down to the wharves at Baltimore Harbor and talk to the Eastern Shore captains who had sailed into the city to unload their catch of oysters.

One day in 1941, as he walked near the Hanover Street bridge, he spotted an old flat-bottomed skipjack tied to the pier. Owned by the Sea Scouts, who had used the boat to teach sailing skills to boys, it now had a "For Sale" sign on it. The vessel, named the *Dewey,* was in terrible shape, but at $100, the price was right.

Perhaps Gladden had learned something from his youth, for he decided to keep his job at the steel mill and hire a captain to operate the *Dewey.* Within a few years, Gladden had made enough profit from the *Dewey* to purchase a bigger, better skipjack. He paid $2,500 for the *Mamie Mister.* When he had a free day, he would go out on one of his skipjacks.

In 1945, he returned home, opened Gladden's General Store at Chance and began to amass a fleet of dredge boats.

By 1992, little remained of the *Lorraine Rose*, built for Captain Clyde Evans in 1949. One of the youngest skipjacks on the Bay, she was left to rot after parasites killed oysters in the lower- and mid-Chesapeake Bay region in the 1980s.

"Wherever he went, he looked at boats," said Gordon. "He always carried a big amount of money in his pocket—maybe $4,000." Besides skipjacks, Gladden also bought other types of workboats and, at one time, owned seven or eight tonging boats, as well as the dredge boats.

"When you have that many boats, always one would have a leak," said Gordon, who would accompany his father on his evening walks down to the docks to check the boats.

Deal Island was still a busy place. "The crab houses and oyster houses were bustling. There were lots of boats. Ships were loaded and unloaded. Steamboats came in there every day," said Gordon Gladden, who remembers the size of the dredge fleet at Deal in the late forties. "When I was going to school on the bus, I used to look out the window and see a hundred of them dredging. You could walk across Deal Island Harbor, there were so many of them."

In 1949, Gladden was doing well enough that he had Ira Todd in Reedville, Virginia, build him the *Somerset,* which was almost forty-five feet in length.

Gladden took the dredging equipment off the *Hattie Lloyd,* which was in poor shape, and put it on the *Somerset.*

Gordon was with his father when they laid the *Hattie Lloyd* to rest. "I remember the day on the way to Crisfield. It was a high tide, and we turned the wheel and went up a gut. They took the plug out of her and there she died." She was just one of many skipjacks that died as disease struck Tangier Sound, killing off the oysters.

"Every time the oysters got scarce, he'd just down-size" his fleet, said Gordon. "Most of the skipjacks just died. When MSX hit Tangier Sound, my father just put them on the bank and they just died. *Virgil G. Dean,* a two-masted skipjack, and the *Dewey* died that way.

"It was not the first time the oysters died. I remember as a kid being able to walk across a body of water on the decks of boats that had died," said Gordon, who believes that creek near Deal Island held the hulls of at least ten old, rotten dredge boats.

"Each time you go through one of these periods, people decide they're not going to sit and wait," and

Shipwright Tommy Daniels, *right*, makes a new centerboard for the *Ida May*.

good captains would get out of the business, Gordon Gladden said.

When the ram *Levin J. Marvel* sank on August 12, 1955, killing fourteen people, Gladden bought two of the masts out of the sunken boat. One went in the *Ida May* and the other in the *Mamie Mister*, his son said.

In 1952, Gladden sold the fifty-six-foot *Harry F. Albaugh* as a pleasure boat. Her new owners loaded a Volkswagen on her wide deck and set sail up the Bay. A few hours later, she sank in a storm.

During the fifties, Gladden sold several skipjacks to businesses. The *Myrtle* was sold to The Wharf, a restaurant in Ocean City. The *Myrtle Virginia* was sold to Ocean Pines to be used in their playground equipment. By the late fifties, there were fewer than forty skipjacks on Deal Island, where once hundreds had anchored.

Gladden had owned twelve skipjacks during his lifetime, keeping up to nine dredge boats at one time. *Ida May* was his last. Gladden was in his late seventies when he raced *Ida May* during the Deal Island Labor Day races. When he returned from the race, the old

man refused to put down the push boat, and instead sailed into the harbor under full sail. At the dock he ordered his crew to lower the sails, "and she fit in the slip just like a tugboat," said his son Gordon, who was on the skipjack that day. "I think the pleasure of the sail kept those fellows out there," Gordon reminisced.

By the mideighties, Gladden's health was failing, and the captain of the *Ida May*, who was also in his seventies, had also become too sick to dredge.

"My father just didn't want the boat to die," said Gordon, but for a few years, it appeared that she would just lie in the gut and rot. MSX was again ravaging the oyster bars in the lower Bay, and the old man could not find a captain for her. Gordon and his brother, Elbert, Jr., "decided the boat was such an intricate part of him and his life, we should have it rebuilt."

The rebuilding was done in his backyard, so Gladden could go out daily to talk with the workers. "That was part of the therapy," recalled Gordon, who hoped the reconstruction of the *Ida May* would somehow improve his father's health. By 1991, the senior Gladden was a very sick man. At age eighty-four, he had had a stroke; he had arthritis and eye problems; and he wore a pacemaker to keep his old heart beating steadily.

The estimate on rebuilding the *Ida May* had been $25,000, but before she was completed in October 1991, the cost had mounted to $60,000. As always in these old skipjacks built at the turn of the century, there was more rotten wood than anyone had expected.

Elbert Gladden lived to see his last skipjack sail again over the oyster bars—or at least, he heard about her work from his sickbed at his home in Chance. He did not live long enough to see her start a second season with the new life he had given her.

Perhaps it is just as well that he missed some of the events to come. The 1992-93 season would be remembered as the worst in the history of the Bay as two diseases, Dermo and MSX, took a devastating toll on the oysters of the Chesapeake, leaving most beds south of the Bay Bridge with a mortality rate of fifty to one hundred percent.

The *Ida May*, along with the other nineteen skipjacks still working the Bay, had to sail north above the Bay Bridge to find any harvest at all. Even then, the skipjack crews felt lucky to dredge up thirty bushels on power days. Many of them quit at Christmas. The *Ida May* "didn't dredge ten days," Gordon Gladden said.

By Christmas, the harvest was so poor that most captains were down to a two-man crew, usually men so hard up for cash that even a remote hope of making $50 in a day was worth the fourteen hours it would take them to drive to Tolchester, work for ten hours, and come home late at night.

By February, many of the boats were straggling home, disgusted with the five- to thirty-bushel harvests they could make only on power days. Captain Wade Murphy brought the *Rebecca T. Ruark* home, hoping to find a few good licks to finish off the season.

On Monday, February 8, Murphy headed *Rebecca* out into the Choptank at sunrise, confident he could find some live oysters. His most likely chance, he believed, was in deep water where oysters seldom grow. But he knew of one deep place that always sustained oysters.

"I went to Castle Haven in sixty-seventy feet of water off Chlora Point. The hearts were still in them. They were dead only a month," said Murphy. "Then I went to the mouth of LaTrappe Creek." Dead again.

"Then I went to the mouth of Le Compte Bay." Dead again. Murphy tried The Diamonds in the middle of the Choptank, then he went to the lighthouse off the Tred Avon. All dead. Finally, he tried Todds Point, where he again found recently dead oysters, with the hearts, or dead meat, still in the boxes. Murphy continued south to Cook Point near the mouth of the Choptank. Nothing there. Then to Dawson's Bar. Finally, he went out into the Bay where he tried Sharps Island Narrows and Black Walnut Sands. No live oysters, anywhere.

Murphy had scraped up only a bushel of oysters from the ten bars he had dredged.

Unwilling to give up, Murphy and his two-man crew decided to get up early and leave port at four in the morning to head up the Bay to Love Point, where they hoped the oyster bars had not been killed by the diseases. For the first hour, it looked good. Then, the oysters became scarcer and scarcer.

The harvest in Maryland would barely top 160,000 bushels in 1992. But while many people believed they were seeing the end of oysters and dredging on the Chesapeake Bay, Gordon Gladden and other dredgers held out hope.

"They'll be back," Gladden said of the oysters. And when they do, the *Ida May* will be back, too, he said. "She's been rebuilt. If we keep her painted and the water out of her, she'll be around for another forty years."

Gladden's not alone in his belief that the oyster bars will recover as they have before, and that the skipjacks, perhaps fewer in number than the twenty that made up the fleet in the season of 1992-93, will continue to sail over them.

Whether or not the story of dredge boats and the men who worked them on the Chesapeake Bay is at its end, for an old man who put his heart into saving a skipjack, there could have been no more perfect time to set down the book than on August 24, 1992, when dredgers believed they were on the threshold of their best season in half a dozen years. Elbert Gladden died that day, still holding onto the hope and promise of a new dredging season.

Three skipjacks tied up at Tilghman Island.

Dusk settles over Tilghman Island as the skipjacks return from another day of dredging.

*Appendix*

# VESSEL LIST

*When we moved to Tilghman, the largest fleet was at Cambridge. Cambridge was unbelievable when I was a kid. You could walk near about across Cambridge harbor on the skipjacks, bugeyes, and sloops. Cambridge probably had the biggest fleet. Now they don't have a boat.*
—Captain Russell Dize about Cambridge in the 1950s

THE FOLLOWING list of commercial skipjacks was compiled from these sources: the late John Earle's Maryland Vessel Files at the Maryland Historical Society; various books of history, including the works of Howard Chapelle, Robert H. Burgess, and Marion V. Brewington; and volumes of the *Merchant Vessels of the United States,* published by the Bureau of Navigation of the U.S. Treasury Department.

More than half the list— nearly 300 names—was gathered from *Merchant Vessels of the United States* (*MVUS*). Since the vessels were not specifically listed as "skipjacks," but instead were classified under the broader category, "sloops," vessels meeting certain requirements were assumed to be skipjacks employed in the oyster trade. The author judged, for example, that any sloop built in Somerset, Dorchester, or Talbot County after about 1896 and falling within the general dimensions of a dredge boat was a skipjack. When possible, vessel names were checked against lists of vessels that were issued dredging licenses. Since many dredge boats were quickly sold to buyers in other regions, including Delaware, New Jersey, and the Carolinas, early volumes of *Merchant Vessels of the United States* were consulted to confirm that the vessel in question worked on the Chesapeake. In many cases, captains and former captains were able to verify that a vessel was, indeed, a skipjack. However, many of these boats disappeared too early for these men to recall them.

Due to these necessary assumptions, some boats may be misclassified as skipjacks; many others were simply left off the list because their date of construction, their dimensions, or the places they worked on the Chesapeake Bay made it difficult to label them as skipjacks.

In some cases the dimensions listed in *Merchant Vessels of the United States* appear to be incorrect. Inaccuracies inevitably occurred when the boats were measured, and boat measurements may have been purposely distorted so that the vessel could work in waters restricted to smaller boats. In a few cases, skipjacks were altered and lengthened, and these changes were not reflected in the federal lists.

The description of a skipjack, or "bateau" as most Eastern Shoremen called it, varied widely. In some places, a boat that carried a skipjack rig was considered a skipjack; in other regions of the Shore, the description applied only to the hull of the boat. For the sake of authenticity, vessels originally built as sloops or bugeyes and later converted to the skipjack rig were not listed.

Included here are more than five hundred vessels believed to have been skipjacks. The author surmises that as many as six hundred to seven hundred skipjacks over five tons were built—well below the figure of one thousand often quoted, perhaps because many people use the term "skipjack" interchangeably with "dredge boat." Many other types of vessels were used to dredge, including bugeyes, sloops, and schooners; and around the turn of the century hundreds of boats under five tons were built that pulled a smaller dredge called a hand scrape. These small hand scrapers were the original skipjacks, according to dredgers in Somerset County, who can remember scraping for crabs with these little vessels, which were also used to scrape oysters during the late 1800s and the early 1900s.

### Key to Abbreviations

| | | | |
|---|---|---|---|
| *GT*—*Gross tonnage* | | *B*—*Beam* | |
| *NT*—*Net tonnage* | | *D*—*Depth* | |
| *L*—*Length* | | *DB*—*Date built* | |

| Boat Name | GT | NT | L | B | D | DB | Place Built | Builder |
|---|---|---|---|---|---|---|---|---|
| A. Phillips | 7 | 7 | 37.5 | 14.4 | 2.6 | 1899 | Fishing Creek, Md. | |
| A. Wesley | 5 | 5 | 36.0 | 13.0 | 3.0 | 1896 | Fairmount, Md. | |
| A. C. Marshall | 5 | 5 | 39.0 | 13.7 | 2.8 | 1896 | James, Md. | |
| A. E. Andrews | 10 | 5 | 41.7 | 14.8 | 3.2 | 1889 | Cambridge, Md. | |
| Home port Bridgeton, New Jersey, by 1911. | | | | | | | | |
| A. M. Townsend | 7 | 7 | 41.7 | 13.5 | 3.2 | 1894 | Fairmount, Md. | |
| Ada | 8 | 6 | 41.0 | 13.5 | 3.5 | 1901 | Exmore, Va. | |
| Ada Bozman | 6 | 6 | 38.5 | 14.5 | 3.0 | 1901 | Oriole, Md. | |
| Ada Mae | 9 | 9 | 32.6 | 12.0 | 2.3 | 1915 | Rose Bay, N.C. | |
| Cross-planked, renamed *Chester Peake* by National Brewing Company. | | | | | | | | |
| Ada May | 8 | 8 | 42.0 | 14.0 | 3.2 | 1897 | Pocomoke, Md. | |
| Addie Branford | 7 | 7 | 42.1 | 14.2 | 3.4 | 1898 | Inverness, Md. | John Branford |
| Addranet | 6 | 6 | 40.0 | 12.8 | 3.0 | 1899 | Oriole, Md. | |
| Adell Phoebus | 9 | 8 | 43.0 | 14.2 | 3.0 | 1908 | Oriole, Md. | |
| Adith | 6 | 6 | 37.3 | 13.6 | 2.7 | 1901 | Crapo, Md. | |
| Formerly bugeye *Willie H. White.* | | | | | | | | |
| Admiral Dewey | 8 | 8 | 41.2 | 14.3 | 3.5 | 1898 | Crisfield, Md. | |
| Alabama | 6 | 6 | 39.0 | 13.7 | 3.0 | 1904 | Hunting Creek, Va. | |
| Albatross | 10 | 10 | 40.0 | 15.8 | 2.7 | 1899 | Cambridge, Md. | George E. Leach |
| Dimensions in Carpenter's Certificate 45 × 16 × 3.5. | | | | | | | | |
| Albert Parks | 6 | 6 | 40.0 | 13.7 | 3.0 | 1897 | Wingate, Md. | |
| Aldeen | 5 | 5 | 35.0 | 12.0 | 3.4 | 1899 | Crisfield, Md. | |
| Aleta | 7 | 5 | 39.5 | 13.0 | 3.3 | 1898 | Pocomoke, Md. | |
| Alex | 10 | 10 | 45.7 | 15.2 | 2.9 | 1900 | Winchester, Md. | Martin W. Thomas |
| Built it for himself. | | | | | | | | |
| Alfred J. Lewis | 7 | 5 | 41.5 | 13.5 | 2.5 | 1905 | Hopkins, Va. | |
| Alice V. Tawes | 6 | 6 | 39.4 | 13.9 | 3.4 | 1897 | Crisfield, Md. | |
| Allen | 8 | 8 | 41.0 | 14.2 | 3.4 | 1900 | Baltimore, Md. | William Allen |
| Alma | 6 | 6 | 38.3 | 14.3 | 2.8 | 1898 | Fishing Creek, Md. | |
| America | 9 | 7 | 39.1 | 14.1 | 3.3 | 1921 | Crisfield, Md. | |
| Had windmill pieces instead of chunk in forefoot in 1936. | | | | | | | | |
| Amy Goldstrom | 8 | 8 | 43.0 | 14.5 | 3.2 | 1901 | Deal Island, Md. | |
| Amy Mister | 30 | 25 | 57.0 | 19.7 | 5.6 | 1914 | Oriole, Md. | |
| Raced at Sandy Point in 1966; now hulk at Whitehaven, Md. | | | | | | | | |
| Andrews Brother | 9 | 9 | 45.0 | 15.3 | 3.3 | 1897 | Crapo, Md. | |
| Anna May Rich | 15 | 11 | 50.8 | 16.1 | 4.0 | 1908 | Oriole, Md. | |
| Annette | 6 | 6 | 34.2 | 12.6 | 2.7 | 1902 | Golden Hill, Md. | |
| Annie | 7 | 7 | 38.3 | 13.2 | 3.2 | 1897 | Whitehaven, Md. | |
| Annie Bennett | 10 | 10 | 46.6 | 15.8 | 3.6 | 1898 | Inverness, Md. | J. Branford |
| Annie F | 7 | 7 | 36.0 | 14.1 | 3.6 | 1902 | Ewell, Md. | |
| Annie Gertrude | 11 | 11 | 42.0 | 16.4 | 4.1 | 1902 | Hopkins, Va. | |
| Annie James | 6 | 5 | 37.3 | 11.9 | 3.1 | 1894 | Crisfield, Md. | |
| Annie Lee | 13 | 7 | 43.0 | 15.4 | 3.5 | 1912 | Youngs Creek, Va. | |
| Inboard rudder, fore and aft planking at stern. | | | | | | | | |
| Annie M | 10 | 7 | 46.0 | 15.0 | 3.7 | 1903 | Messongo, Va. | |
| Annie W | 8 | 8 | 42.4 | 14.6 | 3.0 | 1906 | Deep Creek, Va. | |
| Ex-*Mary Sue.* | | | | | | | | |
| Annie White | 5 | 5 | 38.7 | 12.9 | 3.0 | 1901 | Oriole, Md. | |
| Annie E. Todd | 6 | 6 | 41.7 | 13.9 | 2.9 | 1897 | Bishops Head, Md. | |
| Apollo | 34 | 23 | 55.8 | 19.8 | 5.5 | 1914 | Solomons, Md. | J. Henry |
| Inboard rudder, fore and aft planked at stern. | | | | | | | | |
| Arlington | 9 | 7 | 45.6 | 14.7 | 2.8 | 1901 | Hopkins, Va. | |
| Arneta S. Robinson | 6 | 5 | 36.2 | 11.8 | 2.9 | 1905 | Oriole, Md. | |
| Augusta | 7 | 6 | 39.0 | 13.0 | 2.9 | 1904 | Hopkins, Va. | |
| Avery Gordon | 11 | 8 | 49.0 | 16.0 | 3.9 | 1900 | Hopkins, Va. | |
| B. Phillips | 7 | 7 | 39.0 | 14.5 | 2.8 | 1899 | Fishing Creek, Md. | |
| B. F. Sulender | 8 | 8 | 44.3 | 14.5 | 3.0 | 1897 | Bishops Head, Md. | |

| Boat Name | GT | NT | L | B | D | DB | Place Built | Builder |
|---|---|---|---|---|---|---|---|---|
| Bena | 10 | 10 | 44.0 | 15.1 | 3.6 | 1897 | Wittman, Md. | John T. Landon |

Built for Captain Charles Jones.

| Boat Name | GT | NT | L | B | D | DB | Place Built | Builder |
|---|---|---|---|---|---|---|---|---|
| Ben Hur | 10 | 8 | 48.5 | 15.9 | 3.3 | 1906 | Champ, Md. | |
| Benjamin F | 5 | 5 | 35.0 | 12.7 | 3.0 | 1899 | Fairmount, Md. | |
| Bernice J | 8 | 8 | 40.6 | 14.5 | 3.3 | 1904 | Accomack Co., Va. | |

Owned by Echo Hill Outdoor School; rotting in swamp near Betterton in 1993.

| Boat Name | GT | NT | L | B | D | DB | Place Built | Builder |
|---|---|---|---|---|---|---|---|---|
| Bertha M. Dean | 5 | 5 | 36.0 | 13.5 | 2.6 | 1897 | Fishing Creek, Md. | |
| Bessie & Loleta | 7 | 6 | 40.3 | 14.1 | 3.6 | 1905 | Crisfield, Md. | |
| Bessie May | 9 | 6 | 41.3 | 14.4 | 3.3 | 1896 | Sharptown, Md. | |
| Betty A | 9 | 7 | 44.6 | 15.0 | 3.1 | 1901 | Marsh Market, Va. | |
| Betty Smith | 6 | 6 | 37.0 | 12.6 | 3.2 | 1904 | Oriole, Md. | |
| Black Hawk | 8 | 8 | 40.0 | 13.9 | 2.7 | 1908 | Hudson, Md. | |
| Bray | 7 | 6 | 41.9 | 14.4 | 2.9 | 1906 | Deep Creek, Va. | |
| Bye | 8 | 8 | 45.0 | 13.3 | 2.8 | 1901 | Rock Hall, Md. | Elmer Leary |

Built for himself.

| Boat Name | GT | NT | L | B | D | DB | Place Built | Builder |
|---|---|---|---|---|---|---|---|---|
| C. Corbin | 6 | 5 | 40.0 | 12.3 | 3.0 | 1904 | Sanford, Va. | |
| C. A. Parks | 5 | 5 | 36.9 | 12.6 | 3.0 | 1904 | Fairmount, Md. | |

In 1962, she was on the bottom of the shoal Back Creek at west end of Knapps Narrows.

| Boat Name | GT | NT | L | B | D | DB | Place Built | Builder |
|---|---|---|---|---|---|---|---|---|
| C. E. Spencer | 6 | 6 | 40.0 | 13.6 | 2.8 | 1898 | Oriole, Md. | |
| C. F. Bosman | 9 | 9 | 43.9 | 15.4 | 3.7 | 1901 | Pocomoke, Md. | |
| C. F. Richardson | 9 | 9 | 43.0 | 15.4 | 3.5 | 1900 | Pocomoke, Md. | |
| C. L. Marie | 7 | 7 | 40.0 | 15.1 | 2.9 | 1902 | Wittman, Md. | J. H. Harrison |
| C. W. Crockett | 9 | 9 | 45.0 | 15.8 | 3.9 | 1902 | Pocomoke, Md. | |
| C. W. Roamer | 7 | 5 | 44.0 | 12.0 | 3.0 | 1902 | Dreka, Va. | |
| Caleb Jones | | | 44.1 | 16.5 | 2.5 | 1953 | Reedville, Va. | C. H. Rice |

Owned in 1993 by Captain Dickie Webster; rebuilt by Lady Maryland Foundation in 1992 for Webster.

| Boat Name | GT | NT | L | B | D | DB | Place Built | Builder |
|---|---|---|---|---|---|---|---|---|
| Calvert | 7 | 7 | 36.0 | 14.5 | 2.6 | 1901 | Cambridge, Md. | Henry E. Bennett |
| Cannon | 5 | 5 | 35.6 | 12.9 | 2.3 | 1900 | Cambridge, Md. | George E. Leach |

Inboard rudder.

| Boat Name | GT | NT | L | B | D | DB | Place Built | Builder |
|---|---|---|---|---|---|---|---|---|
| Carrie Marie | 8 | 8 | 39.6 | 14.3 | 3.1 | 1896 | Wittman, Md. | John T. Landon |

Built for William Caldwell; foundered in Choptank River, April 1918.

| Boat Name | GT | NT | L | B | D | DB | Place Built | Builder |
|---|---|---|---|---|---|---|---|---|
| Carrie Price | 7 | 7 | 39.5 | 14.3 | 3.5 | 1897 | Holland Island, Md. | |

Cabin forward; bulged amidship.

| Boat Name | GT | NT | L | B | D | DB | Place Built | Builder |
|---|---|---|---|---|---|---|---|---|
| Carroll T | 7 | 7 | 37.5 | 14.5 | 3.6 | 1897 | Fairmount, Md. | |
| Carroll Todd | 6 | 6 | 39.7 | 12.9 | 3.0 | 1897 | Holland Island, Md. | |
| Catharine Bundy | 13 | 12 | 38.0 | 12.0 | 3.2 | 1898 | Urbanna, Va. | |
| Catharine E. Shores | 10 | 9 | 52.5 | 14.2 | 3.2 | 1892 | Oriole, Md. | |
| Catherine | 12 | 12 | 49.5 | 15.5 | 4.2 | 1901 | Pocomoke, Md. | |
| Cecrops | 7 | 7 | 36.5 | 13.6 | 2.7 | 1900 | Hooper Island, Md. | Wilfred Tyler |

Built for John H. Cannon of Golden Hill.

| Boat Name | GT | NT | L | B | D | DB | Place Built | Builder |
|---|---|---|---|---|---|---|---|---|
| Celia | 7 | 7 | 33.5 | 12.8 | 3.4 | 1899 | Claiborne, Md. | Greenbury M. Coffin |
| Charlotte | 7 | 7 | 42.0 | 13.7 | 2.9 | 1901 | Hudson, Md. | Samuel E. Marshall |

Built for himself.

| Boat Name | GT | NT | L | B | D | DB | Place Built | Builder |
|---|---|---|---|---|---|---|---|---|
| Charles B. Mason | 8 | 6 | 40.0 | 14.0 | 3.0 | 1900 | Hopkins, Va. | |
| City of Crisfield | 10 | 10 | 44.7 | 15.8 | 3.7 | 1949 | Reedville, Va. | C. H. Rice |

Still working in 1993; owned by Captain Art Daniels of Deal Island.

| Boat Name | GT | NT | L | B | D | DB | Place Built | Builder |
|---|---|---|---|---|---|---|---|---|
| Clara Dunnock | 11 | 10 | 44.3 | 14.5 | 4.0 | 1901 | Golden Hill, Md. | |

1911 MVUS has 6, 6; 37.8 × 14.4 × 3.6.

| Boat Name | GT | NT | L | B | D | DB | Place Built | Builder |
|---|---|---|---|---|---|---|---|---|
| Clarence Crockett | 9 | 7 | 44.6 | 14.7 | 3.0 | 1908 | Deep Creek, Va. | |

Struck pole in Tangier Sound in 1988 and sunk; raised and repaired but hasn't worked since. Captain Paul Holland had the boat for sale in 1993.

| Boat Name | GT | NT | L | B | D | DB | Place Built | Builder |
|---|---|---|---|---|---|---|---|---|
| Claudia | 5 | 5 | 36.0 | 11.6 | 2.7 | 1900 | Wittman, Md. | John H. Harrison |

Built for $600.

| Boat Name | GT | NT | L | B | D | DB | Place Built | Builder |
|---|---|---|---|---|---|---|---|---|
| Claud W. Somers | 8 | 6 | 42.6 | 14.0 | 3.0 | 1911 | Young's Creek, Va. | |

Being restored by private owner at Tilghman Island in 1992.

| Boat Name | GT | NT | L | B | D | DB | Place Built | Builder |
|---|---|---|---|---|---|---|---|---|
| Clifford Oscar | 15 | 12 | 49.8 | 16.7 | 4.0 | 1908 | Deal Island, Md. | |
| Columbia | 7 | 7 | 49.5 | 14.5 | 3.4 | 1899 | Fairmount, Md. | |

| Boat Name | GT | NT | L | B | D | DB | Place Built | Builder |
|---|---|---|---|---|---|---|---|---|
| Columbia | 9 | 6 | 45.0 | 15.0 | 3.0 | 1900 | Pocomoke, Md. | |
| Columbia | 6 | 6 | 39.3 | 13.9 | 3.7 | 1901 | Hunting Creek, Va. | |
| Connie Francis | 45 | 45 | 56.0 | 21.0 | 4.3 | 1984 | Piney Point, Md. | Francis Goddard |
| Built for himself; working in 1993, but Goddard had the boat up for sale. | | | | | | | | |
| Cordie S | 7 | 6 | 43.0 | 14.0 | 3.0 | 1908 | Cashville, Va. | |
| Creston W. Ford | 6 | 6 | 38.0 | 14.0 | 3.3 | 1904 | Fairmount, Md. | |
| D. W. White | 6 | 6 | 38.4 | 12.3 | 3.2 | 1898 | Deal Island, Md. | |
| Daisy M. Tall | 10 | 9 | 42.2 | 15.3 | 3.3 | 1889 | Madison, Md. | |
| Danville | 7 | 7 | 38.1 | 13.7 | 2.9 | 1901 | Hudson, Md. | Robert H. Thomas |
| Built for himself and Oliver M. Seward. | | | | | | | | |
| Dee of St. Mary's | 25 | 25 | 55.0 | 18.5 | 3.9 | 1979 | Piney Point, Md. | Francis Goddard |
| Owned and dredged by Jackie Russell in 1990s. | | | | | | | | |
| Defender | 6 | 6 | 35.4 | 13.4 | 3.0 | 1895 | Poplar Island, Md. | Charles W. Landon |
| Built for himself; in 1905 owned in Elizabeth City, North Carolina. | | | | | | | | |
| Defiance | 7 | 7 | 40.0 | 12.6 | 2.6 | 1908 | Fairbank, Md. | |
| Della Griffin | 5 | 5 | 37.5 | 12.8 | 3.0 | 1899 | Holland Island, Md. | |
| Della May | 7 | 6 | 37.3 | 13.7 | 3.0 | 1894 | Fairmount, Md. | |
| Vessel reported sunk in collision with schooner *Allrevoir* in Baltimore Harbor, November 11, 1911. | | | | | | | | |
| Delma W | 6 | 6 | 39.8 | 13.3 | 2.8 | 1904 | Oriole, Md. | |
| Dewey | 6 | 6 | 42.8 | 13.7 | 2.8 | 1898 | Deal Island, Md. | |
| Left to die near Deal Island Bridge. | | | | | | | | |
| Donna Forester | 24 | 18 | 55.0 | 18.3 | 5.2 | 1911 | Oriole, Md. | |
| Dora Hall | 7 | 5 | 39.0 | 13.3 | 3.1 | 1896 | Fairmount, Md. | |
| Dorothy | 10 | 8 | 47.8 | 15.7 | 3.6 | 1905 | Deal Island, Md. | |
| Steered with tiller; owned in 1948 by Leslie Pope of Oxford. | | | | | | | | |
| Dunnock | 7 | 7 | 41.8 | 14.9 | 3.0 | 1898 | Hooper Island, Md. | |
| E. C. Collier | 19 | 14 | 52.0 | 17.9 | 4.3 | 1910 | Deal Island, Md. | G. W. Horseman |
| Went to rescue of crew of *Gladys Melba* on December 31, 1952; owned by Chesapeake Bay Maritime Museum in St. Michaels and used in a land exhibit. | | | | | | | | |
| E. C. Lily | 9 | 6 | 44.6 | 14.8 | 3.0 | 1900 | Marsh Market, Va. | |
| E. M. Hubbard | 8 | 8 | 41.0 | 13.5 | 2.9 | 1898 | Hudson, Md. | |
| Seen at Oxford in 1936 on railway. | | | | | | | | |
| E. S. Croswell | 10 | 10 | 41.7 | 14.8 | 3.8 | 1898 | Fairmount, Md. | |
| E. T. Riggin | 6 | 6 | 38.0 | 13.5 | 2.8 | 1898 | Crisfield, Md. | |
| Eagle | 9 | 9 | 38.6 | 14.8 | 3.4 | 1924 | Crisfield, Md. | |
| Earl | 5 | 5 | 36.1 | 13.5 | 2.3 | 1899 | Cambridge, Md. | George E. Leach |
| Said to be first skipjack with inboard rudder. | | | | | | | | |
| Earl | 7 | 6 | 41.8 | 14.0 | 3.0 | 1906 | Deep Creek, Va. | |
| Eben | 27 | 21 | 54.3 | 18.7 | 5.2 | 1911 | Oriole, Md. | |
| Abandoned at Deal Island by 1948. | | | | | | | | |
| Eddie Collier | 9 | 9 | 46.4 | 15.2 | 3.6 | 1902 | Deal Island, Md. | G. W. Horseman |
| Eddie Lee | 8 | 6 | 44.0 | 13.0 | 3.4 | 1902 | Dreka, Va. | |
| Edgar W | 6 | 5 | 34.5 | 12.1 | 2.6 | 1908 | Saxis, Va. | |
| Edith C | 6 | 6 | 39.6 | 13.5 | 2.8 | 1906 | Deep Creek, Va. | |
| Edith Bozman | 6 | 6 | 41.0 | 13.6 | 3.5 | 1901 | Oriole, Md. | |
| Edith C | 6 | 6 | 39.6 | 13.5 | 2.8 | 1906 | Deep Creek, Va. | |
| Edith Creighton | 6 | 6 | 39.0 | 13.7 | 2.8 | 1897 | Fishing Creek, Md. | |
| Edith L. Leonard | 10 | 9 | 42.5 | 14.8 | 3.3 | 1889 | Cambridge, Md. | |
| Edith M. Clarke | 14 | 14 | 53.0 | 16.5 | 4.2 | 1898 | Inverness, Md. | John Branford |
| Edna G. Croswell | 6 | 5 | 37.5 | 13.4 | 3.2 | 1904 | Oriole, Md. | |
| Edna J | 6 | 6 | 37.0 | 13.6 | 3.2 | 1899 | Fairmount, Md. | |
| Edna J. Cox | 6 | 6 | 37.4 | 13.7 | 2.8 | 1897 | Fairmount, Md. | |
| Edward McDaniel | 7 | 7 | 38.9 | 14.8 | 3.7 | 1901 | Oriole, Md. | |
| Effie B | 7 | 7 | 40.3 | 13.5 | 3.4 | 1900 | Oriole, Md. | |
| Effie K | 9 | 7 | 40.3 | 14.5 | 3.0 | 1896 | Fairmount, Md. | |
| Effie May | 7 | 5 | 41.0 | 14.0 | 3.0 | 1900 | Chesconnessex, Va. | |

| Boat Name | GT | NT | L | B | D | DB | Place Built | Builder |
|---|---|---|---|---|---|---|---|---|
| Elbert | 6 | 6 | 34.6 | 13.1 | 3.0 | 1901 | Oxford, Md. | John E. Gibson |
| Built for Nancy J. Gibson. | | | | | | | | |
| Eldora | 8 | 7 | 42.3 | 14.4 | 2.9 | 1906 | Deep Creek, Va. | |
| Eleanor | 6 | 5 | 37.2 | 13.1 | 2.9 | 1901 | Oxford, Md. | Nicholas B. Stevens |
| Eliza T | 7 | 6 | 42.0 | 13.3 | 3.0 | 1902 | Justisville, Va. | |
| Ella Frances | 8 | 6 | 43.0 | 14.0 | 3.5 | | Hopkins, Va. | |
| Ella M. Todd | 6 | 6 | 39.5 | 13.0 | 3.3 | 1900 | Oriole, Md. | |
| Ella Wilson | 7 | 7 | 41.0 | 14.1 | 3.8 | 1901 | Oriole, Md. | |
| Elmer C | 6 | 6 | 35.0 | 12.2 | 2.8 | 1902 | Oxford, Md. | John Loscumb |
| Built for himself and Collie Hubbard. | | | | | | | | |
| Elmer W. Somers | 25 | 18 | 48.3 | 16.9 | 5.2 | 1920 | Honga, Md. | |
| May have been spelled *Sommers* in *MVUS*. | | | | | | | | |
| Eloise | 24 | 20 | 54.0 | 18.8 | 4.9 | 1911 | Oriole, Md. | |
| Seen at Salisbury in 1940. | | | | | | | | |
| Elsie | 8 | 8 | 40.3 | 14.4 | 3.6 | 1901 | Wittman, Md. | John T. Landon |
| Built for George K. Harrison of Wittman. | | | | | | | | |
| Elsie E | 8 | 8 | 41.0 | 14.5 | 4.0 | 1900 | Hopewell, Md. | |
| Elsie May | 6 | 6 | 35.8 | 12.6 | 3.0 | 1910 | Oriole, Md. | |
| Elsworth | 8 | 8 | 39.9 | 14.3 | 3.1 | 1901 | Hudson, Md. | Robert H. Thomas |
| Owned by Echo Hill Outdoor School in Kent County, Maryland, in 1993; used for teaching in the summer and dredging in the winter. | | | | | | | | |
| Elvira C | 7 | 7 | 41.3 | 14.1 | 3.0 | 1906 | Deep Creek, Va. | |
| Emerson | 11 | 8 | 42.6 | 14.2 | 3.4 | 1902 | Broomes Island, Md. | |
| Emily | 8 | 5 | 42.9 | 14.2 | 2.7 | 1896 | Royal Oak, Md. | Oliver Duke |
| Built for William B. Adams. Baltimore Carpenter's Certificate describes the boat as having a figurehead and elliptic stern. | | | | | | | | |
| Emily | 6 | 6 | 36.5 | 12.8 | 2.5 | 1901 | Tilghman Island, Md. | John B. Harrison |
| Built for himself and Maurice A. Cummings. | | | | | | | | |
| Emma | | | 38.0 | 12.5 | 3.0 | 1901 | Oriole, Md. | John M. Laird |
| Built for himself. | | | | | | | | |
| Emma B | | | 52.0 | 17.0 | 4.0 | 1901 | Wittman, Md. | John B. Marshall |
| Built for himself. | | | | | | | | |
| Emma Frances | 7 | 7 | 41.0 | 14.0 | 2.8 | 1898 | Hooper Island, Md. | |
| Emma M. Bradshaw | 6 | 6 | 38.0 | 11.6 | 3.3 | 1898 | Crisfield, Md. | |
| Emma May | 7 | 7 | 41.8 | 14.1 | 3.6 | 1901 | Oriole, Md. | |
| Emma Newbill | 9 | 6 | 38.2 | 13.7 | 2.9 | 1900 | Crisfield, Md. | |
| Eretha Jackson | 14 | 14 | 46.4 | 17.5 | 4.1 | 1902 | Whitehaven, Md. | |
| Eretha Murray | 7 | 7 | 44.8 | 14.6 | 3.0 | 1897 | Mount Vernon, Md. | |
| Ernestine | 5 | 5 | 36.0 | 12.6 | 2.9 | 1897 | Hopewell, Md. | |
| Ernie | 6 | 6 | 37.2 | 14.5 | 3.0 | 1901 | Cambridge, Md. | |
| Esther F | 10 | | 39.5 | 13.3 | 3.8 | | Fairmount, Md. | |
| Owned and dredged by Captain Bartlett Murphy in 1992. | | | | | | | | |
| Esther Hur | 10 | 8 | 48.5 | 15.8 | 3.3 | 1906 | Champ, Md. | |
| Esther W | 30 | 25 | 55.6 | 20.1 | 5.5 | 1914 | Oriole, Md. | |
| Hull used to bulkhead private property on Deal Island. | | | | | | | | |
| Ethel | 7 | 7 | 38.5 | 13.4 | 3.6 | 1891 | Pocomoke, Md. | |
| Ethel | | | 45.0 | 14.0 | 3.3 | 1897 | Royal Oak, Md. | Oliver Duke |
| Built for E. B. Walters; oak keel, inboard rudder. | | | | | | | | |
| Ethel and Lydia | 16 | 12 | 40.8 | 14.9 | 4.4 | 1925 | Onancock, Va. | |
| Ethel E | | | 36.2 | 13.7 | 3.0 | 1896 | Oxford, Md. | John H. Towers |
| Ethel Lewis | 8 | 6 | 42.5 | 14.0 | 3.0 | 1906 | Chesconnessex, Va. | |
| Ethelyn Dryden | 9 | 9 | 45.0 | 15.5 | 3.9 | 1901 | Pocomoke, Md. | |
| Advertised for sale in *Star-Democrat,* January 29, 1954. | | | | | | | | |
| Etna | 6 | 6 | 38.0 | 13.7 | 3.0 | 1905 | Crisfield, Md. | |
| Etta | 7 | 7 | 38.5 | 14.0 | 2.7 | 1901 | Cambridge, Md. | George E. Leach |
| Wreck at Shad Point near Salisbury. | | | | | | | | |
| Etta and Acie | 5 | 5 | 37.8 | 13.5 | 3.0 | 1897 | Wingate, Md. | |
| Etta Burdis | 12 | 9 | 42.5 | 14.8 | 3.9 | 1900 | Pocomoke, Md. | |

| Boat Name | GT | NT | L | B | D | DB | Place Built | Builder |
|---|---|---|---|---|---|---|---|---|
| *Etta Lee* | 7 | 5 | 39.5 | 13.0 | 3.0 | 1896 | Crisfield, Md. | |
| *Eunice S* | 5 | 5 | 35.7 | 12.5 | 2.8 | 1897 | Hopewell, Md. | |
| *Eva* | 7 | 7 | 39.1 | 12.9 | 3.1 | 1883 | Cambridge, Md. | |

Built 1883-1888; schooner-rigged; Howard Chapelle refers to it as the first skipjack ever built.

| | | | | | | | | |
|---|---|---|---|---|---|---|---|---|
| *Eva* | 5 | 5 | 37.0 | 13.1 | 2.6 | 1897 | Fairmount, Md. | |
| *Evelyn* | 7 | 7 | 39.2 | 15.2 | 2.8 | 1901 | Wittman, Md. | John H. Harrison |

Built for himself.

| | | | | | | | | |
|---|---|---|---|---|---|---|---|---|
| *Ewell* | 6 | 6 | 40.0 | 13.0 | 2.5 | 1901 | Cambridge, Md. | H.G. Stephens |
| *Ewing Bradshaw* | 7 | 7 | 38.0 | 13.0 | 3.2 | 1897 | Crisfield, Md. | |
| *F. C. Carpenter* | 9 | 9 | 46.0 | 15.9 | 3.9 | 1901 | Deal Island, Md. | |
| *F. C. Lewis, Jr.* | 6 | 6 | 39.0 | 14.6 | 3.0 | 1907 | Hopkins, Va. | |

Under restoration at Knapps Narrows in 1993.

| | | | | | | | | |
|---|---|---|---|---|---|---|---|---|
| *F. F. Carpenter* | 9 | 9 | 46.0 | 15.9 | 3.9 | 1901 | Deal Island, Md. | |
| *Fannie F. Bradshaw* | 6 | 6 | 36.7 | 12.4 | 3.2 | 1898 | Ewell, Md. | |
| *Fannie L. Daugherty* | 8 | 8 | 41.3 | 15.0 | 3.6 | 1904 | Crisfield, Md. | Jim Daugherty |

Rebuilt and dredged by Captain Delmus Benton of Deal Island in 1980s; still dredging in 1990s.

| | | | | | | | | |
|---|---|---|---|---|---|---|---|---|
| *Father and Son* | 7 | 7 | 38.6 | 13.0 | 3.2 | 1897 | Crisfield, Md. | |
| *Father and Son* | 6 | 6 | 38.7 | 13.5 | 2.8 | 1897 | Toddville, Md. | |
| *Fay* | 7 | 6 | 42.0 | 14.0 | 3.0 | 1906 | Deep Creek, Va. | |
| *Fitzhugh Lee* | 5 | 5 | 37.6 | 13.0 | 3.0 | 1898 | Crisfield, Md. | |
| *Fletcher J. Barnes* | 6 | 5 | 41.0 | 13.2 | 2.6 | 1901 | Hopkins, Va. | |
| *Flora A. Price* | 23 | 18 | 56.2 | 18.4 | 4.8 | 1910 | Champ, Md. | |

Owned by Sea Scouts of Wilmington; returned to dredging by Captain Doug West in 1990s.

| | | | | | | | | |
|---|---|---|---|---|---|---|---|---|
| *Flora B* | 7 | 6 | 39.5 | 13.2 | 3.0 | 1904 | Fairmount, Md. | |
| *Flora Ellen* | 10 | 6 | 42.5 | 15.0 | 3.8 | 1899 | Pocomoke, Md. | |
| *Florence* | 8 | 7 | 37.2 | 14.1 | 3.2 | 1914 | Fishing Creek, Md. | |
| *Florence & Julia* | 10 | 6 | 41.7 | 14.4 | 3.5 | 1899 | Churchton, Md. | |
| *Florence Louise* | 40 | 33 | 58.1 | 19.6 | 5.5 | 1924 | Crisfield, Md. | Frank Tull |

Considered by captains to be the biggest skipjack ever built (*Connie Francis*, built in 1984, may be larger).

| | | | | | | | | |
|---|---|---|---|---|---|---|---|---|
| *Florence May* | 8 | 5 | 35.0 | 13.3 | 2.8 | 1898 | Hooper Island, Md. | |

Sold to New Jersey by 1909.

| | | | | | | | | |
|---|---|---|---|---|---|---|---|---|
| *Four Brothers* | 7 | 7 | 41.6 | 14.0 | 3.0 | 1906 | Deep Creek, Md. | |
| *Franklin* | 7 | 7 | 38.7 | 13.4 | 2.7 | 1901 | Hudson, Md. | Robert T. Seward |

Built for Frank Spedden.

| | | | | | | | | |
|---|---|---|---|---|---|---|---|---|
| *Freddie* | 7 | 7 | 38.6 | 13.1 | 2.8 | 1901 | Hudson, Md. | Robert H. Thomas |

Built for Charles H. Beckwith.

| | | | | | | | | |
|---|---|---|---|---|---|---|---|---|
| *Freddie L. Bennett* | 8 | 8 | 42.0 | 14.5 | 3.2 | 1899 | Inverness, Md. | John Branford |
| *Fulton T. Mister* | 20 | | 52.8 | 18.1 | 4.5 | 1910 | Deal Island, Md. | |
| *G. A. Anderson* | 7 | | 43.5 | 14.3 | 2.9 | 1908 | Bishops Head, Md. | |

Three-sail bateau.

| | | | | | | | | |
|---|---|---|---|---|---|---|---|---|
| *G. C. Bradshaw* | 8 | 8 | 42.0 | 13.9 | 3.3 | 1898 | Ewell, Md. | |
| *G. C. Williams* | 8 | 8 | 41.3 | 14.7 | 4.2 | 1901 | Crisfield, Md. | |
| *G. G. Vetra* | 8 | 8 | 39.9 | 13.8 | 3.1 | 1908 | Wenona, Md. | |
| *G. M. K. Meek* | 6 | 6 | 40.5 | 13.4 | 3.2 | 1900 | St. Peters, Md. | |
| *Geneva May* | 15 | 11 | 49.8 | 16.6 | 3.9 | 1908 | Wenona, Md. | |

Brought home from Washington, North Carolina, museum in 1979 by Captain Darryl Larrimore, then abandoned at Tilghman in 1979.

| | | | | | | | | |
|---|---|---|---|---|---|---|---|---|
| *George L. Hardester* | 7 | 7 | 42.6 | 14.7 | 3.6 | 1901 | Oriole, Md. | |
| *George Smith* | 6 | 5 | 39.0 | 12.0 | 3.0 | 1902 | Hopkins, Va. | |
| *George W. Collier* | 9 | 9 | 45.5 | 15.2 | 3.5 | 1900 | Deal Island, Md. | G. W. Horseman |
| *Georgia & Inez* | 6 | 6 | 36.0 | 13.4 | 2.9 | 1897 | Fairmount, Md. | |
| *Georgie* | 7 | 7 | 40.5 | 14.0 | 2.8 | 1901 | Hudson, Md. | Robert H. Thomas |
| *Gertie E. Collier* | 7 | 7 | 38.0 | 13.5 | 3.0 | 1899 | Deal Island, Md. | |
| *Gertrude Wands* | 8 | 8 | 42.6 | 14.3 | 3.4 | 1899 | Inverness, Md. | John Branford |
| *Gladys* | 8 | 8 | 36.8 | 14.0 | 2.7 | 1896 | Royal Oak, Md. | Oliver Duke |

Built for himself; inboard rudder; sold to Wilmington, Delaware, by 1911.

| Boat Name | GT | NT | L | B | D | DB | Place Built | Builder |
|-----------|-----|-----|------|------|-----|------|-------------|---------|
| Gladys | 11 | 7 | 50.0 | 15.6 | 3.6 | 1900 | Pocomoke, Md. | |
| Gladys | 5 | 5 | 36.8 | 13.4 | 2.1 | 1901 | Cambridge, Md. | George E. Leach |
| Gladys | 7 | 5 | 41.5 | 13.3 | 3.1 | 1903 | Justisville, Va. | |
| Gladys Melba | 15 | 10 | 43.4 | 15.6 | 3.7 | 1924 | Crisfield, Md. | |

Struck an obstruction near Sharps Island and was wrecked on December 31, 1952.

| Boat Name | GT | NT | L | B | D | DB | Place Built | Builder |
|-----------|-----|-----|------|------|-----|------|-------------|---------|
| Gladys White | 5 | 5 | 37.8 | 12.0 | 2.7 | 1896 | Deal Island, Md. | |
| Gloucester | 10 | 10 | 42.5 | 14.2 | 3.5 | 1899 | Hudson, Md. | |
| Grace | 14 | 9 | 39.0 | 14.0 | 3.5 | 1903 | Urbanna, Va. | |
| Gracie Leonard | 10 | 6 | 41.7 | 14.8 | 3.2 | 1889 | Cambridge, Md. | |
| Gussie | 6 | 6 | 39.5 | 13.4 | 2.8 | 1899 | Oriole, Md. | |

Recorded in 1922 as converted into a yacht.

| Boat Name | GT | NT | L | B | D | DB | Place Built | Builder |
|-----------|-----|-----|------|------|-----|------|-------------|---------|
| Guy | 5 | 5 | 36.2 | 11.3 | 2.7 | 1894 | Marion, Md. | |
| H. C. Townsend | 5 | 5 | 39.2 | 11.9 | 2.7 | 1898 | Upper Fairmount, Md. | |

Sold to New Bern, North Carolina, by 1903.

| Boat Name | GT | NT | L | B | D | DB | Place Built | Builder |
|-----------|-----|-----|------|------|-----|------|-------------|---------|
| H. G. Alexander | 10 | 8 | 47.5 | 16.0 | 3.6 | 1907 | Wenona, Md. | |
| H. M. Krentz | 9 | | 44.3 | 15.6 | 4.9 | 1955 | Harryhogan, Va. | Herman Krentz |

Owned and dredged by Captain Ed Farley in 1993.

| Boat Name | GT | NT | L | B | D | DB | Place Built | Builder |
|-----------|-----|-----|------|------|-----|------|-------------|---------|
| Hambleton | 7 | 7 | 38.1 | 13.9 | 2.6 | 1901 | St. Michaels, Md. | John P. Jackson |

Built for David A. Shockley.

| Boat Name | GT | NT | L | B | D | DB | Place Built | Builder |
|-----------|-----|-----|------|------|-----|------|-------------|---------|
| Harry Anderson | 8 | 8 | 44.3 | 15.2 | 3.1 | 1899 | Deal Island, Md. | |
| Harry D. Cook | 8 | 8 | 41.4 | 14.7 | 3.4 | 1902 | Oriole, Md. | |
| Harry F. Albaugh | 24 | 19 | 56.4 | 18.4 | 4.8 | 1910 | Champ, Md. | |

Sold as a pleasure boat and sunk in a squall off Smith Point, Virginia, in Bay on November 3, 1952.

| Boat Name | GT | NT | L | B | D | DB | Place Built | Builder |
|-----------|-----|-----|------|------|-----|------|-------------|---------|
| Harry Ford | 9 | 8 | 41.0 | 15.7 | 4.4 | 1901 | Crisfield, Md. | |
| Harvey A. Parks | 8 | 8 | 42.1 | 16.0 | 2.8 | 1899 | Holland Island, Md. | |
| Hattie C. Laird | 13 | 9 | 46.0 | 15.0 | 3.2 | 1905 | Pocomoke, Md. | |
| Hattie E. Travers | 7 | 7 | 41.0 | 14.0 | 2.8 | 1898 | Hooper Island, Md. | |
| Hattie Lloyd | 11 | 11 | 48.0 | 16.0 | 3.5 | 1897 | Whitehaven, Md. | |

Round stern, round bilge; sold to Washington, North Carolina, by 1930; worked on Chesapeake again in 1940s; towed near Crisfield and left to rot by 1950-1960s.

| Boat Name | GT | NT | L | B | D | DB | Place Built | Builder |
|-----------|-----|-----|------|------|-----|------|-------------|---------|
| Helen | | | 41.0 | 13.0 | 3.0 | 1901 | Bellevue, Md. | Levi D. Roe |

Built for himself.

| Boat Name | GT | NT | L | B | D | DB | Place Built | Builder |
|-----------|-----|-----|------|------|-----|------|-------------|---------|
| Helen | 6 | 6 | 38.6 | 13.3 | 2.3 | 1901 | St. Michaels, Md. | Edward S. Harper |

Built for himself.

| Boat Name | GT | NT | L | B | D | DB | Place Built | Builder |
|-----------|-----|-----|------|------|-----|------|-------------|---------|
| Helen Barnes | 8 | 8 | 41.5 | 14.4 | 3.8 | 1900 | Hopewell, Md. | |
| Helen Louise | 7 | 6 | 37.2 | 12.7 | 3.0 | 1910 | Londonville, Md. | |
| Helen Roe | 6 | 6 | 37.0 | 13.0 | 2.8 | 1902 | Bellevue, Md. | |

Sold to New York City by 1911.

| Boat Name | GT | NT | L | B | D | DB | Place Built | Builder |
|-----------|-----|-----|------|------|-----|------|-------------|---------|
| Helen Virginia | 10 | 10 | 43.2 | 15.6 | 2.2 | 1949 | Crisfield, Md. | Gus Forbush |

Owned and dredged by Captain Jack Parkinson in 1993.

| Boat Name | GT | NT | L | B | D | DB | Place Built | Builder |
|-----------|-----|-----|------|------|-----|------|-------------|---------|
| Henry B | 7 | 7 | 36.1 | 14.2 | 2.7 | 1901 | Cambridge, Md. | Henry E. Bennett |
| Hilda | 5 | 5 | 35.3 | 11.9 | 2.8 | 1904 | Crisfield, Md. | |
| Hilda D | 6 | 6 | 38.5 | 13.0 | 3.3 | 1899 | Oriole, Md. | |
| Hilda M. Willing | 8 | 6 | 40.0 | 14.0 | 3.1 | 1905 | Oriole, Md. | |

Owned and dredged by Captain Pete Sweitzer in 1993.

| Boat Name | GT | NT | L | B | D | DB | Place Built | Builder |
|-----------|-----|-----|------|------|-----|------|-------------|---------|
| Hobart | 5 | 5 | 38.7 | 14.4 | 2.6 | 1901 | Fishing Creek, Md. | |

Converted to a yacht in 1935.

| Boat Name | GT | NT | L | B | D | DB | Place Built | Builder |
|-----------|-----|-----|------|------|-----|------|-------------|---------|
| Howard | 10 | 8 | 45.0 | 15.3 | 3.1 | 1909 | Deep Creek, Va. | John D. Allen |

Owned and dredged by Captain Stan Daniels in 1992. Was being rebuilt from molds of original boat in 1993 by Lady Maryland Foundation for Daniels.

| Boat Name | GT | NT | L | B | D | DB | Place Built | Builder |
|-----------|-----|-----|------|------|-----|------|-------------|---------|
| Ida Bedsworth | 7 | 7 | 39.5 | 14.5 | 3.7 | | Oriole, Md. | |
| Ida C | | | 27.1 | 8.8 | 2.6 | 1896 | Oxford, Md. | Charles Mason |

Under five tons.

| Boat Name | GT | NT | L | B | D | DB | Place Built | Builder |
|-----------|-----|-----|------|------|-----|------|-------------|---------|
| Ida May | | | 40.0 | 14.0 | 3.6 | 1896 | Oxford, Md. | William J. Andrews |

Built for Charles E. Stevens; listed in *MVUS* as 36.2 × 14.1 × 3.2; built with elliptic stern.

| Boat Name | GT | NT | L | B | D | DB | Place Built | Builder |
|-----------|-----|-----|------|------|-----|------|-------------|---------|
| Ida May | 10 | 7 | 42.2 | 14.4 | 3.3 | 1906 | Deep Creek, Va. | |
| Ida V. Beauchamp | 7 | 7 | 38.6 | 13.3 | 3.0 | 1899 | Oriole, Md. | |

| Boat Name | GT | NT | L | B | D | DB | Place Built | Builder |
|---|---|---|---|---|---|---|---|---|
| Ira T. Croswell | 10 | 8 | 48.0 | 15.7 | 3.7 | 1907 | Oriole, Md. | |
| Wreck at Shad Point. | | | | | | | | |
| Irene and Ruth | 8 | 8 | 41.0 | 14.7 | 3.4 | 1899 | Fairmount, Md. | |
| Isidore Shores | 7 | 7 | 42.3 | 14.0 | 3.3 | 1897 | Chance, Md. | |
| Iva | 5 | 5 | 35.8 | 12.8 | 2.8 | 1902 | Hunting Creek, Va. | |
| Iva Pearl | 6 | 6 | 38.5 | 14.3 | 3.0 | 1899 | Elliott, Md. | |
| J. B. Vetra | 15 | 12 | 50.0 | 16.6 | 4.0 | 1908 | Wenona, Md. | |
| J. T. Tyler | 7 | 7 | 35.5 | 13.0 | 3.2 | 1898 | Ewell, Md. | |
| J. W. Walker | 7 | 7 | 42.0 | 14.4 | 4.0 | 1901 | Oriole, Md. | |
| Home port Washington, North Carolina, by 1928. | | | | | | | | |
| Jacob T. Bradshaw | 7 | 7 | 36.9 | 13.8 | 3.6 | 1898 | Ewell, Md. | |
| James Edson | 6 | 5 | 39.0 | 13.0 | 2.9 | 1903 | Hopkins, Va. | |
| James H. Cullen | 6 | 6 | 38.6 | 12.6 | 3.4 | 1903 | Crisfield, Md. | |
| Jessie Price | 15 | 12 | 50.9 | 16.3 | 4.3 | 1908 | Oriole, Md. | |
| John F. Mitchell | 8 | 8 | 41.0 | 14.8 | 3.6 | 1898 | Crisfield, Md. | |
| John L. Thomas | 5 | 5 | 37.6 | 12.0 | 3.0 | 1897 | Holland Island, Md. | |
| John S. Harvey | 5 | 5 | 34.5 | 12.9 | 2.9 | 1898 | Guilford, Va. | |
| John W. Dize | 5 | 5 | 48.0 | 12.3 | 2.6 | 1896 | Crisfield, Md. | |
| John W. Parker | 6 | 6 | 38.3 | 14.3 | 3.0 | 1901 | Fishing Creek, Md. | |
| Joy Parks | 17 | | 46.4 | 15.5 | 4.0 | 1936 | Parksley, Va. | |
| Judy | 7 | 5 | 37.7 | 13.1 | 3.0 | 1895 | Hopewell, Md. | |
| Kathleen | 6 | 6 | 37.4 | 14.0 | 3.3 | 1901 | Fishing Creek, Md. | |
| Kathryn | 12 | 12 | 50.0 | 16.8 | 4.2 | 1901 | Crisfield, Md. | |
| Rounded chine; fore and aft planking; owned and dredged by Captain Russell Dize in 1993. | | | | | | | | |
| Katie | 28 | 21 | 56.3 | 18.8 | 5.4 | 1911 | Oriole, Md. | |
| Katie and Edith | 9 | 6 | 46.0 | 15.0 | 3.7 | 1896 | Whitehaven, Md. | |
| Katie Cannon | 6 | 6 | 37.5 | 14.0 | 3.2 | 1901 | Fishing Creek, Md. | |
| Katie May | 6 | 6 | 41.5 | 13.0 | 2.8 | 1900 | Bishops Head, Md. | |
| Three-sail bateau; seen in Cambridge in 1948. | | | | | | | | |
| Katie Rowe | 28 | 21 | 55.3 | 18.8 | 5.4 | 1911 | Oriole, Md. | |
| At Deal Island in 1936. | | | | | | | | |
| Klondike | 7 | 7 | 41.5 | 13.5 | 3.0 | 1897 | Pocomoke, Md. | |
| Lady Eleanor | 27 | 22 | 58.0 | 22.0 | 5.2 | 1915 | Oriole, Md. | |
| Left to die in a cove at Wenona on Deal Island by owner Captain Jesse Thomas. | | | | | | | | |
| Lady Katie | 8 | 8 | 46.2 | 16.7 | 3.3 | 1956 | Wingate, Md. | Bronza Parks |
| Owned and dredged by Captain Stanley Larrimore in 1993. | | | | | | | | |
| Laura J. Barkley | 6 | 6 | 37.0 | 13.9 | 3.0 | | Fishing Creek, Md. | |
| Laura M. Evans | 10 | 8 | 42.7 | 15.3 | 3.6 | 1911 | Crisfield, Md. | |
| Raced at Chesapeake Appreciation Days in 1969. | | | | | | | | |
| Lelia Gunby | 6 | 6 | 39.1 | 13.4 | 2.9 | 1898 | Crisfield, Md. | |
| Lena Louise | 7 | 7 | 39.5 | 13.8 | 4.0 | 1899 | Fairmount, Md. | |
| Lena May | 5 | 5 | 36.0 | 13.4 | 2.6 | 1898 | Hopewell, Md. | |
| Lena Rose | 16 | 10 | 42.8 | 15.1 | 4.2 | 1924 | Parksley, Va. | |
| Inboard rudder; sold off Bay out of oyster trade in 1971 by Captain Bartlett Murphy. | | | | | | | | |
| Lena Schroder | 5 | 5 | 36.8 | 11.8 | 2.8 | 1903 | Oriole, Md. | |
| Lenora | 8 | 6 | 41.3 | 14.3 | 3.0 | 1907 | Deep Creek, Va. | |
| Leonard | 7 | | 38.4 | 12.5 | 3.1 | 1908 | Oriole, Md. | |
| Converted to a powerboat by 1950. | | | | | | | | |
| Lieutenant | 6 | 6 | 35.8 | 12.0 | 2.8 | 1910 | Bedsworth, Md. | |
| Lillian | 7 | 7 | 41.6 | 13.0 | 2.8 | 1898 | Whitehaven, Md. | |
| Lillian | 8 | 8 | 40.1 | 14.5 | 3.1 | 1901 | St. Michaels, Md. | William A. Lambdin |
| Home port Bridgeton, New Jersey, in 1911. | | | | | | | | |
| Lillian & Carrie | 9 | 6 | 39.6 | 15.0 | 3.8 | 1899 | Hopkins, Va. | |
| Lillian & Earl | 10 | 7 | 43.4 | 15.0 | 4.0 | 1911 | Inverness, Md. | John Branford |
| Lillian & Elva | 5 | 5 | 38.3 | 13.2 | 2.5 | 1897 | Crapo, Md. | |

| Boat Name | GT | NT | L | B | D | DB | Place Built | Builder |
|---|---|---|---|---|---|---|---|---|
| *Lillie* | 10 | 9 | 45.2 | 14.2 | 3.7 | 1883 | Tilghman, Md. | J. L. Harrison |

Schooner or bugeye rig on a deadrise hull; perhaps one of the first skipjacks, along with *Yttria,* built same year by same builder.

| Boat Name | GT | NT | L | B | D | DB | Place Built | Builder |
|---|---|---|---|---|---|---|---|---|
| *Lillie E. Shores* | 14 | 10 | 51.8 | 16.6 | 3.3 | 1908 | Oriole, Md. | |
| *Lillie G. Spicer* | 7 | 7 | 38.2 | 15.0 | 3.1 | 1903 | Taylors Island, Md. | Joseph T. Spicer |
| *Lillie Lewis* | 7 | 7 | 41.0 | 13.6 | 3.2 | 1898 | Crisfield, Md. | |
| *Lillie R. Parker* | 7 | 7 | 40.0 | 14.6 | 2.6 | 1898 | Hooper Island, Md. | |
| *Lina* | 7 | 6 | 43.0 | 14.6 | 3.0 | 1910 | Deep Creek, Va. | |
| *Lizzie* | 5 | 5 | 30.5 | 11.8 | 3.0 | 1896 | Cambridge, Md. | |
| *Lizzie B* | 7 | 7 | 37.2 | 14.0 | 3.7 | 1897 | Fairmount, Md. | |
| *Lizzie S. Johnson* | 8 | 6 | 43.2 | 14.0 | 3.4 | 1896 | Pocomoke, Md. | |
| *Lloyd Cox* | 6 | 6 | 37.8 | 13.2 | 2.6 | 1898 | Upper Fairmont, Md. | |
| *Lockwood* | 6 | 6 | 36.7 | 12.4 | 2.9 | 1902 | Oxford, Md. | |

Described in mechanic's lien as skiff.

| Boat Name | GT | NT | L | B | D | DB | Place Built | Builder |
|---|---|---|---|---|---|---|---|---|
| *Lois* | 6 | | 36.6 | 13.4 | 2.6 | 1901 | Oxford, Md. | Joseph McDaniel |

Built for John T. May of Tilghman; disappeared before 1919.

| Boat Name | GT | NT | L | B | D | DB | Place Built | Builder |
|---|---|---|---|---|---|---|---|---|
| *Lois S* | 9 | 6 | 45.8 | 15.3 | 3.2 | 1900 | Pocomoke, Md. | |

Home port Washington, North Carolina, by 1928.

| Boat Name | GT | NT | L | B | D | DB | Place Built | Builder |
|---|---|---|---|---|---|---|---|---|
| *Lola* | 9 | 7 | 42.0 | 14.0 | 3.5 | 1904 | Mearsville, Va. | |
| *Lola* | 8 | 5 | 40.5 | 13.4 | 3.2 | 1896 | Inverness, Md. | John Branford |

Fore and aft planking at stern; inboard rudder; apparently abandoned on marsh near Jim Richardson's yard on Le Compte Creek by 1969.

| Boat Name | GT | NT | L | B | D | DB | Place Built | Builder |
|---|---|---|---|---|---|---|---|---|
| *Lorraine Rose* | 10 | | 44.3 | 15.4 | 3.8 | 1949 | Reedville, Va. | C. H. Rice |

Captain Clyde Evans had it built; sold the boat in 1976; dredged until 1983; left to rot in Knapps Narrows since about 1983.

| Boat Name | GT | NT | L | B | D | DB | Place Built | Builder |
|---|---|---|---|---|---|---|---|---|
| *Lottie* | 8 | 6 | 38.6 | 12.3 | 3.5 | 1899 | Oriole, Md. | |

Home port was Newport News, Virginia, in 1911.

| Boat Name | GT | NT | L | B | D | DB | Place Built | Builder |
|---|---|---|---|---|---|---|---|---|
| *Lottie Bell* | 20 | 14 | 53.0 | 18.0 | 4.8 | 1910 | Deal Island, Md. | |
| *Louise* | 8 | 8 | 41.0 | 14.3 | 4.0 | 1900 | Hopewell, Md. | |
| *Louise Miles* | 6 | | 40.0 | 12.6 | 3.0 | 1899 | Crab Island, Md. | |
| *Lucy* | 8 | | 39.3 | 13.7 | 3.6 | 1901 | Cacaway Point, Md. | Samuel G. Bennett |

Built for Howard W. Haddaway of Lankford; one of the few skipjacks built in Kent County, Maryland.

| Boat Name | GT | NT | L | B | D | DB | Place Built | Builder |
|---|---|---|---|---|---|---|---|---|
| *Lucy M. Tyler* | 7 | 5 | 36.0 | 13.2 | 2.8 | 1906 | Honga, Md. | Wilfred Tyler |

Stern has rounded bilges resembling sloop but hull is chine and cross-planked. Seen at Cambridge in 1952.

| Boat Name | GT | NT | L | B | D | DB | Place Built | Builder |
|---|---|---|---|---|---|---|---|---|
| *Lucy V* | 10 | | 44.0 | 15.1 | 3.9 | 1897 | Wittman, Md. | John T. Landon |

Built for Joseph S. Harrison of Wittman.

| Boat Name | GT | NT | L | B | D | DB | Place Built | Builder |
|---|---|---|---|---|---|---|---|---|
| *Lula and Emma* | 9 | 6 | 44.5 | 15.4 | 3.8 | 1900 | Pocomoke, Md. | |
| *Lula Bell* | 7 | 6 | 40.0 | 13.4 | 3.0 | 1902 | Justisville, Va. | |
| *Lydia Iola* | 9 | 6 | 40.4 | 13.8 | 3.5 | 1905 | Crisfield, Md. | |
| *Mabel* | 6 | 6 | 38.2 | 13.7 | 2.6 | 1900 | Cambridge, Md. | John C. Dailey |

Built for J. W. D. Pryor of Cambridge.

| Boat Name | GT | NT | L | B | D | DB | Place Built | Builder |
|---|---|---|---|---|---|---|---|---|
| *Mabel Somers* | 5 | 5 | 36.5 | 12.0 | 3.0 | 1896 | Crisfield, Md. | |
| *Maggie* | 7 | 6 | 43.0 | 13.5 | 3.0 | 1901 | Hopkins, Va. | |
| *Maggie Florence* | 6 | 6 | 39.5 | 13.3 | 2.9 | 1902 | Hopkins, Va. | |
| *Maggie Lee* | 10 | 8 | 51.0 | 16.0 | 3.8 | 1903 | Pocomoke, Md. | |

Repaired by Captain Bunky Chance in 1990 and returned to dredging; built with a rounded chine, she is the last of the Pocomoke "round bottoms."

| Boat Name | GT | NT | L | B | D | DB | Place Built | Builder |
|---|---|---|---|---|---|---|---|---|
| *Maggie Lee* | 5 | | 36.6 | 11.6 | 2.9 | 1908 | Inverness, Md. | John Branford |

Inboard rudder.

| Boat Name | GT | NT | L | B | D | DB | Place Built | Builder |
|---|---|---|---|---|---|---|---|---|
| *Maggie Ruth* | 7 | 6 | 39.0 | 13.5 | 3.0 | 1903 | Chesconnessex, Va. | |
| *Mamie A. Mister* | 24 | 19 | 56.2 | 18.4 | 4.8 | 1910 | Champ, Md. | |

Rebuilt at Krentz Shipyard in 1955 from keel up; sold to New York and converted to a yacht carrying two masts; returned to the Bay and dredged as a three-sail bateau from 1991 to 1993.

| Boat Name | GT | NT | L | B | D | DB | Place Built | Builder |
|---|---|---|---|---|---|---|---|---|
| *Manie B. Bradshaw* | 9 | 9 | 47.0 | 15.8 | 3.1 | 1897 | Hopewell, Md. | |
| *March Gale* | 6 | 5 | 38.0 | 12.2 | 2.7 | 1906 | Hunting Creek, Va. | |

Seen in Knapps Narrows in 1955; interesting trailboards.

| Boat Name | GT | NT | L | B | D | DB | Place Built | Builder |
|---|---|---|---|---|---|---|---|---|
| *Marcie* | 7 | | 39.6 | 14.0 | 2.8 | 1901 | Oxford, Md. | William T. McAlister |
| Stem head; square stern. | | | | | | | | |
| *Marcus* | 7 | | 42.0 | 14.3 | 3.4 | 1899 | Fairmount, Md. | John Branford |
| *Margarete* | 15 | 15 | 49.6 | 15.8 | 4.6 | 1901 | Pocomoke, Md. | |
| *Margie S* | 6 | | 37.6 | 12.8 | 3.2 | 1902 | Monie, Md. | |
| *Marie* | 8 | 5 | 41.7 | 13.5 | 3.2 | 1896 | Inverness, Md. | John Branford |
| *Marie Somers* | 7 | 7 | 40.1 | 13.7 | 3.0 | 1897 | Crisfield, Md. | |
| *Martha Lewis* | 8 | | 46.2 | 16.7 | 3.3 | 1955 | Wingate, Md. | Bronza Parks |
| Still dredging in 1993. | | | | | | | | |
| *Martha M. Lewis* | 6 | 6 | 38.8 | 14.1 | 2.5 | 1897 | Wingate, Md. | |
| *Mary and Inez* | 11 | 8 | 46.0 | 15.6 | 4.6 | 1899 | Pocomoke, Md. | |
| *Mary and Susan* | 6 | 6 | 40.0 | 14.3 | 2.8 | 1897 | Holland Island, Md. | |
| Wreck seen at Wingate Point in 1948. | | | | | | | | |
| *Mary and Susie* | 8 | 8 | 42.0 | 14.8 | 3.4 | 1896 | Cabin Creek, Md. | |
| *Mary C* | 7 | 6 | 40.3 | 13.2 | 3.4 | 1897 | Crisfield, Md. | |
| *Mary E* | 6 | 5 | 39.0 | 13.0 | 2.6 | 1901 | Hopkins, Va. | |
| *Mary E. Cranston* | 8 | 7 | 43.3 | 14.3 | 3.0 | 1906 | Deep Creek, Va. | |
| *Mary E. Tyler* | 8 | | 42.6 | 14.5 | 2.8 | 1898 | Fishing Creek, Md. | |
| *Mary Elizabeth* | 10 | 10 | 41.9 | 15.6 | 2.8 | 1889 | Cambridge, Md. | |
| *Mary F. Croswell* | 15 | 11 | 51.9 | 16.5 | 3.4 | 1908 | Oriole, Md. | |
| In 1946 the boat was in Washington, North Carolina, and in 1962 on the mud in a cove behind Bellevue, Maryland. | | | | | | | | |
| *Mary Gunby* | 7 | 5 | 38.7 | 13 | 3.2 | 1897 | Crisfield, Md. | |
| *Mary Hazel* | 8 | | 40.0 | 13.7 | 3.1 | 1896 | Wittman, Md. | Joseph Thomas |
| *Mary I. Wroldsen* | 7 | 5 | 38.4 | 14.6 | 3.2 | 1897 | Fairmount, Md. | |
| Home port Elizabeth City, North Carolina, in 1911. | | | | | | | | |
| *Mary M. Clark* | 10 | | 45.5 | 16.5 | 3.9 | 1903 | Whitehaven, Md. | |
| Died near Deal Island Bridge in 1950s. | | | | | | | | |
| *Mary S* | 7 | | 40.0 | 14.1 | 2.7 | 1901 | Wittman, Md. | William Caldwell |
| Built for himself; stem head, square stern. | | | | | | | | |
| *Mary Sue* | 8 | | 42.4 | 14.6 | 3.0 | 1906 | Deep Creek, Va. | |
| Later renamed *Annie W.* | | | | | | | | |
| *Mary V* | 8 | 8 | 40.7 | 14.4 | 3.5 | 1896 | Fairbank, Md. | George A. Cummings |
| *Mary W. Somers* | 9 | | 41.9 | 14.0 | 3.4 | 1904 | Mearsville, Va. | |
| Participated in Chesapeake Appreciation Days in 1966; spelled *Mary W. Sommers* in 1909 and 1911 *MVUS.* | | | | | | | | |
| *Mattie A. Walston* | 7 | 7 | 39.6 | 13.8 | 3.0 | 1897 | Crisfield, Md. | |
| *Mattie Croswell* | 7 | 7 | 42.0 | 13.5 | 3.6 | 1899 | Oriole, Md. | |
| Home port Richmond, Virginia, in 1911. | | | | | | | | |
| *Mattie L. Tyler* | 5 | 5 | 35.5 | 12.6 | 2.6 | 1899 | Pocomoke, Md. | |
| *Maud* | 8 | 8 | 41.0 | 14.4 | 3.7 | 1902 | Monie, Md. | |
| *Maud Bennett* | 10 | 5 | 43.7 | 14.9 | 3.6 | 1896 | Crisfield, Md. | |
| *May Flower* | 6 | 5 | 40.0 | 12.5 | 4.2 | 1897 | Tappahannock, Va. | |
| *Mayflower* | 8 | 7 | 39.5 | 13.2 | 3.1 | | Unknown | |
| Home port Crisfield in 1952. | | | | | | | | |
| *Melissa Lawrence* | 10 | 10 | 48.0 | 15.5 | 4.2 | 1901 | Oriole, Md. | |
| *Melson* | 7 | 7 | 39.0 | 13.4 | 3.2 | 1901 | St. Peters, Md. | |
| *Merl* | 5 | | 35.0 | 12.6 | 3.1 | 1898 | Hopewell, Md. | |
| *Micah A. Parks* | 7 | 7 | 40.0 | 13.7 | 3.0 | 1894 | Fairmount, Md. | |
| Questionable because of early date. | | | | | | | | |
| *Mildred B* | 8 | 8 | 42.5 | 14.4 | 3.9 | 1902 | Oriole, Md. | |
| *Mildred Bennett* | 8 | | 42.2 | 14.2 | 3.3 | 1899 | Fairmount, Md. | John Branford |
| *Millard* | 5 | 5 | 37.0 | 12.4 | 2.8 | 1897 | Crisfield, Md. | |
| *Milton F. Yeakel* | 7 | 7 | 42.0 | 14.2 | 3.3 | 1901 | St. Peters, Md. | |
| *Minnie* | 5 | 5 | 36.5 | 12.9 | 2.1 | 1893 | Crisfield, Md. | |
| Questionable because of early date. | | | | | | | | |
| *Minnie* | 6 | 6 | 36.7 | 11.6 | 3.1 | 1896 | Smith Island, Md. | |

| Boat Name | GT | NT | L | B | D | DB | Place Built | Builder |
|---|---|---|---|---|---|---|---|---|
| Minnie Blanche | 5 | 5 | 38.0 | 13.0 | 2.8 | 1903 | Whitehaven, Md. | |
| Minnie M. Thompson | 8 | 8 | 42.8 | 14.0 | 3.5 | 1900 | Kent Island, Md. | |
| Minnie May | 7 | 6 | 40.6 | 13.3 | 3.3 | 1896 | Oriole, Md. | |
| Minnie V | 10 | 8 | 45.3 | 15.7 | 3.0 | 1906 | Wenona, Md. | John Vetra |
| Rebuilt by City of Baltimore; used to dredge and take passengers in 1993. | | | | | | | | |
| Mollie A | 6 | | 40.0 | 13.6 | 3.0 | 1897 | Holland Island, Md. | |
| Mollie E | 6 | 6 | 41.5 | 14.0 | 2.8 | 1899 | Holland Island, Md. | |
| Montrose | 7 | 7 | 40.0 | 13.5 | 3.0 | 1899 | Oriole, Md. | |
| Morning Herald | 7 | 7 | 39.5 | 14.0 | 3.2 | 1899 | Fairmount, Md. | |
| Morrison C | 7 | | 38.4 | 13.8 | 2.7 | 1908 | Thomas, Md. | |
| Myrtle | 8 | | 40.2 | 14.5 | 2.9 | 1908 | Hudson, Md. | |
| Sold to the Wharf Restaurant in Ocean City. | | | | | | | | |
| Myrtle Virginia | 6 | 5 | 40.0 | 13.0 | 2.8 | 1903 | Chesconnessex, Va. | |
| Sold to Ocean Pines, Maryland, as playground equipment. | | | | | | | | |
| Nellie L. Byrd | 22 | 18 | 53.6 | 16.7 | 4.8 | 1911 | Oriole, Md. | |
| Rebuilt by Darryl Larrimore in 1980s; owned by Captain Bartlett Murphy in 1993. | | | | | | | | |
| Nellie Somers | 8 | 6 | 42.0 | 14.4 | 3.0 | 1911 | Hunting Creek, Va. | |
| Nellie White | 7 | 7 | 40.0 | 14.1 | 3.5 | 1901 | St. Peters, Md. | |
| Nodie North | | | 43.0 | 14.5 | 3.5 | 1896 | Tilghman Island, Md. | John B. Harrison |
| Round stern. | | | | | | | | |
| Nora | 6 | | 36.9 | 13.2 | 3.0 | 1899 | Bozman, Md. | J. N. Larrimore |
| Norma K | 30 | 24 | 58.7 | 19.8 | 5.2 | 1915 | Whitehaven, Md. | |
| Fitted with a U.S. Navy Rhino, a Chrysler 100-horsepower auxiliary engine about 1950 and used to ship watermelons on Bay; abandoned by 1956. | | | | | | | | |
| Oceanic | 6 | | 37.4 | 13.3 | 3.0 | 1897 | Fairmount, Md. | John Branford |
| Oceanic | 6 | | 45.6 | 14.4 | 3.1 | 1897 | Applegarth, Md. | |
| Said to be a sister boat of the Thelma G. Roberts. | | | | | | | | |
| Olive M | 5 | 5 | 37.8 | 11.7 | 2.7 | 1898 | Oriole, Md. | |
| Oliver | 5 | 5 | 36.4 | 12.3 | 2.8 | 1900 | Crisfield, Md. | |
| Sold to Elizabeth City, North Carolina, between 1911 and 1928. | | | | | | | | |
| Omar J. Groswell | 9 | 7 | 44.6 | 14.9 | 3.3 | 1905 | Oriole, Md. | |
| Omoo | | | 46.0 | 16.0 | 2.9 | 1905 | Shadyside, Md. | Charles E. Leatherberry |
| Onward | 9 | 9 | 42.0 | 14.5 | 3.7 | 1896 | Harrison, Md. | |
| Oregon | 10 | | 43.0 | 13.9 | 3.2 | 1898 | Hudson, Md. | |
| Seen on shoal in creek north of Knapps Narrows in 1962. | | | | | | | | |
| P. H. Tawes | 10 | 10 | 44.0 | 15.1 | 3.6 | 1897 | Wittman, Md. | |
| Page & Donald | 7 | 7 | 40.3 | 14.0 | 3.0 | 1897 | Holland Island, Md. | |
| Pauline | 6 | 6 | 40.0 | 13.5 | 2.7 | 1898 | Deal Island, Md. | |
| Pauline | 8 | 8 | 41.9 | 16.0 | 3.5 | 1901 | Crisfield, Md. | |
| Percy E. Shores | 7 | 7 | 45.0 | 15.4 | 3.4 | 1901 | Deal Island, Md. | |
| Sold to Washington, North Carolina, between 1911 and 1928. | | | | | | | | |
| Phyllis | 10 | 8 | 45.6 | 15.5 | 3.4 | 1908 | Oriole, Md. | |
| Quick Time | 5 | 5 | 39.5 | 12.2 | 2.8 | 1907 | Deep Creek, Va. | |
| R. A. Meredith | 10 | 7 | 39.2 | 13.8 | 3.9 | 1911 | Rumbley, Md. | |
| Abandoned in marsh by 1975. | | | | | | | | |
| R. J. Allen | 12 | 12 | 46.0 | 15.8 | 4.6 | 1902 | Oriole, Md. | |
| R. L. Miles | 8 | 5 | 39.9 | 13.1 | 3.3 | 1896 | Oriole, Md. | |
| Ralph T. Webster | | | 47.7 | 15.3 | 3.5 | 1905 | Oriole, Md. | J. T. Muir |
| Worked until early 1980s when it was abandoned in Knapps Narrows. | | | | | | | | |
| Rasa Augusta | 10 | 8 | 47.6 | 15.3 | 3.5 | 1905 | St. Peters, Md. | |
| Raymond C | 5 | | 36.5 | 12.6 | 2.8 | 1899 | Oriole, Md. | |
| Raymond S | 6 | | 40.8 | 13.5 | 2.4 | 1901 | Tilghman, Md. | Joseph L. Harrison |
| Reba May | 6 | 6 | 39.0 | 13.6 | 3.3 | 1899 | Crisfield, Md. | |
| Reliance | 6 | | 38.8 | 13.2 | 3.6 | 1903 | Leemont, Va. | |
| Reliance | 7 | | 41.0 | 14.3 | 2.7 | 1904 | Fishing Creek, Md. | |
| Rena B | 7 | 7 | 38.0 | 14.7 | 3.0 | 1899 | Fairmount, Md. | |
| Reta May | 6 | 6 | 40.0 | 12.7 | 3.2 | 1897 | Deal Island, Md. | |

| Boat Name | GT | NT | L | B | D | DB | Place Built | Builder |
|---|---|---|---|---|---|---|---|---|
| Rew Brothers | 6 | | 41.5 | 14.6 | 3.2 | 1907 | Justisville, Va. | |
| Rhoda M. Parker | 6 | 6 | 37.6 | 14.3 | 2.7 | 1901 | Fishing Creek, Md. | |
| Home port Washington, North Carolina, in 1928. | | | | | | | | |
| Ringgold Brothers | 29 | 22 | 56.0 | 19.2 | 5.3 | 1911 | Oriole, Md. | |
| Seen as a power freighter at Bowers Beach, Delaware, in 1951. | | | | | | | | |
| River View | 6 | 6 | 41.0 | 13.1 | 2.4 | 1897 | Bishops Head, Md. | |
| Roamer | 10 | 6 | 41.7 | 14.1 | 3.7 | 1899 | Churchton, Md. | |
| Robert L. Tawes | 9 | | 45.6 | 15.6 | 4.0 | 1901 | Pocomoke, Md. | |
| Robert L. Webster | 35 | 29 | 60.0 | 20.3 | 5.8 | 1915 | Oriole, Md. | Sylvester Muir |
| Longest skipjack built, but *Florence Louise* could carry more oysters; worked until early 1970s; remains at Janes Island State Park near Crisfield. | | | | | | | | |
| Robert W. Cole | 25 | 20 | 54.7 | 18.3 | 5.1 | 1911 | Oriole, Md. | |
| Roland B. French | 6 | 6 | 35.5 | 12.9 | 3.0 | 1899 | Fairmount, Md. | |
| Rona C. Hammond | 9 | 9 | 40.9 | 15.3 | 4.1 | 1901 | Bedsworth, Md. | |
| Roosevelt | 6 | | 36.0 | 14.0 | 2.5 | 1901 | Cambridge, Md. | Henry E. Bennett |
| Rosa Augusta | 10 | 8 | 47.6 | 15.3 | 3.5 | 1905 | St. Peters, Md. | |
| Rose E. Chelton | 8 | 8 | 42.0 | 14.2 | 3.3 | 1899 | Londonville, Md. | |
| Rosie Parks | 8 | 8 | 46.2 | 16.7 | 3.3 | 1955 | Wingate, Md. | Bronza Parks |
| Owned by Chesapeake Bay Maritime Museum in St. Michaels and used as floating exhibit. | | | | | | | | |
| Rowena | 6 | | 33.6 | 12.2 | 2.5 | 1901 | St. Michaels, Md. | William B. Harper |
| Built for himself; square stern. | | | | | | | | |
| Ruby | 6 | 6 | 37.8 | 12.3 | 2.5 | 1897 | Hudson, Md. | |
| Ruby G. Ford | 9 | 5 | 45.0 | 15.6 | 2.6 | 1891 | Fairmount, Md. | William Smith |
| Considered the first skipjack built in Somerset County. | | | | | | | | |
| Russell & Alice | 16 | 12 | 49.4 | 15.7 | 4.2 | 1908 | Oriole, Md. | |
| Ruth | 8 | | 39.0 | 13.7 | 3.2 | 1896 | Fairbank, Md. | George A. Cumming |
| Ruth | 8 | 8 | 43.2 | 14.5 | 3.7 | 1901 | Oriole, Md. | |
| Ruth | 7 | 5 | 39.0 | 14.0 | 3.0 | 1906 | Deep Creek, Va. | |
| Ruth A. Thomas | 30 | 25 | 56.4 | 19.7 | 5.6 | 1914 | Oriole, Md. | |
| Ruth C | 6 | 6 | 37.0 | 13.6 | 3.2 | 1899 | Fairmount, Md. | |
| S. A. Holland | 10 | 9 | 50.0 | 14.7 | 3.3 | 1893 | Marion, Md. | |
| Three-sail bateau; abandoned in 1941. | | | | | | | | |
| S. Bozman | | | | | | | | |
| Wreck at Irving Cannon's Yard, Fishing Creek, in 1937. | | | | | | | | |
| S. C. Kirk | 10 | 8 | 45.0 | 14.2 | 3.5 | 1901 | Dreka, Va. | |
| S. F. Smith | 6 | 6 | 40.0 | 13.7 | 2.8 | 1897 | Dames Quarter, Md. | |
| S. H. Tolley | 8 | 7 | 42.0 | 15.3 | 2.7 | 1909 | Fishing Creek, Md. | |
| Sunk in shoal water in Knapps Narrows. | | | | | | | | |
| S. J. Bennett | 7 | | 43.0 | 15.3 | 3.2 | 1903 | Inverness, Md. | |
| Last worked in 1965, according to *MVUS*. | | | | | | | | |
| Sadie | | | 40.0 | 11.9 | 3.5 | 1900 | St. Michaels, Md. | John P. Jackson |
| Sadie D | | | | | | | | |
| Sadie Francis | 15 | 12 | 49.8 | 16.6 | 3.9 | 1905 | Deal Island, Md. | |
| Later sold to Washington, North Carolina. | | | | | | | | |
| Saginaw | 7 | 5 | 37.9 | 13.2 | 3.0 | 1896 | Crisfield, Md. | |
| Sallie Mitchell | 5 | 5 | 35.5 | 12.1 | 3.2 | 1898 | Crisfield, Md. | |
| Sarah Taylor | 5 | 5 | 34.0 | 13.4 | 2.7 | 1899 | Dames Quarter, Md. | |
| Schley | 7 | 7 | 36.3 | 14.1 | 2.6 | 1900 | Cambridge, Md. | |
| Seabright | 8 | 6 | 41.3 | 13.6 | 3.2 | 1896 | Oriole, Md. | |
| Seagull | 17 | | 46.6 | 15.9 | 4.3 | 1924 | Crisfield, Md. | C. A. Dana |
| Raced in 1966. | | | | | | | | |
| Sea King | 6 | 6 | 39.5 | 12.5 | 2.8 | 1897 | Hudson, Md. | |
| Sea King | 5 | 5 | 34.7 | 11.5 | 3.0 | 1898 | Crisfield, Md. | |
| Seth T. Bozman | 5 | 5 | 37.0 | 12.7 | 2.9 | 1902 | Monie, Md. | |
| Shamrock | 6 | | 37.5 | 13.8 | 3.0 | 1899 | Fairmount, Md. | George E. Leach |
| Inboard rudder. | | | | | | | | |
| Shamrock | 5 | 5 | 37.5 | 13.3 | 3.0 | 1901 | Hunting Creek, Va. | |

| Boat Name | GT | NT | L | B | D | DB | Place Built | Builder |
|---|---|---|---|---|---|---|---|---|
| *Sigsbee* | 9 | | 47.0 | 15.8 | 3.8 | 1901 | Deal Island, Md. | William A. Noble |

Sunk north of Bay Bridge at Chesapeake Appreciation Days in 1990; raised and sold to Lady Maryland Foundation which had plans to restore the boat in 1993.

| Boat Name | GT | NT | L | B | D | DB | Place Built | Builder |
|---|---|---|---|---|---|---|---|---|
| *Silverine* | 5 | | 38 | 12.6 | 3.2 | 1897 | Solomons, Md. | |

Cabin forward; inboard rudder; home port Bridgeton, New Jersey, in 1911.

| Boat Name | GT | NT | L | B | D | DB | Place Built | Builder |
|---|---|---|---|---|---|---|---|---|
| *Silver Spray* | 9 | 5 | 40.8 | 13.9 | 3.7 | 1896 | Crisfield, Md. | |
| *Somerset* | 9 | | 44.9 | 15.7 | 3.5 | 1949 | Reedville, Va. | C. H. Rice |

Owned and dredged by Captain Walton Benton of Mt. Vernon in 1993.

| Boat Name | GT | NT | L | B | D | DB | Place Built | Builder |
|---|---|---|---|---|---|---|---|---|
| *Stanley Norman* | 10 | | 47.5 | 15.3 | 4.0 | 1902 | Salisbury, Md. | Otis Lloyd |

Owned by the Chesapeake Bay Foundation in 1990s; used in its programs.

| Boat Name | GT | NT | L | B | D | DB | Place Built | Builder |
|---|---|---|---|---|---|---|---|---|
| *Star* | 9 | | 38.4 | 14.4 | 3.2 | 1924 | Crisfield, Md. | |
| *Stella* | 9 | | 40.1 | 13.6 | 3.5 | 1900 | Bellevue, Md. | Charles A. Lee |

Built for himself and Lewis Lee.

| Boat Name | GT | NT | L | B | D | DB | Place Built | Builder |
|---|---|---|---|---|---|---|---|---|
| *Stella* | 7 | 6 | 38.5 | 13.3 | 2.8 | 1906 | Deep Creek, Va. | |
| *Susan May* | 10 | | 46.0 | 15.9 | 3.6 | 1901 | Pocomoke, Md. | |

Left on mud flat at Wenona to die in 1980s; Pocomoke round-bottom; fore and aft planking at bow and stern.

| Boat Name | GT | NT | L | B | D | DB | Place Built | Builder |
|---|---|---|---|---|---|---|---|---|
| *Susie Dryden* | 9 | 9 | 45.3 | 15.9 | 4.0 | 1901 | Pocomoke, Md. | |
| *Susie Lee* | 7 | 7 | 41.5 | 13.8 | 3.0 | 1899 | Holland Island, Md. | |
| *Thelma* | 13 | 8 | 45.5 | 16.1 | 4.1 | 1905 | Fairbank, Md. | |

Home port Bridgeton, New Jersey, by 1911.

| Boat Name | GT | NT | L | B | D | DB | Place Built | Builder |
|---|---|---|---|---|---|---|---|---|
| *Thelma* | 5 | 5 | 35.7 | 12.2 | 2.5 | 1909 | Bedsworth, Md. | |
| *Thelma G. Roberts* | 6 | | 45.3 | 14.0 | 2.7 | 1897 | Applegarth, Md. | |

Three-sail bateau.

| Boat Name | GT | NT | L | B | D | DB | Place Built | Builder |
|---|---|---|---|---|---|---|---|---|
| *Thomas Clyde* | 27 | 21 | 54.5 | 18.2 | 5.3 | 1911 | Oriole, Md. | |

Owned and dredged by Captain Lawrence Murphy in 1992.

| Boat Name | GT | NT | L | B | D | DB | Place Built | Builder |
|---|---|---|---|---|---|---|---|---|
| *Thomas S. Price* | 6 | 6 | 41.5 | 14.0 | 2.8 | 1899 | Holland Island, Md. | |
| *Three Partners* | 7 | 7 | 38.0 | 13.9 | 3.5 | 1899 | Pocomoke, Md. | |
| *Three Sisters* | 7 | 5 | 38.2 | 12.8 | 3.3 | 1896 | Crisfield, Md. | |
| *Triumph* | 7 | | 39.4 | 13.8 | 2.9 | 1901 | Hudson, Md. | Mitchell Hubbard |

Built for Irvin Wingate.

| Boat Name | GT | NT | L | B | D | DB | Place Built | Builder |
|---|---|---|---|---|---|---|---|---|
| *Two Sisters* | 8 | | 43.1 | 14.5 | 3.5 | 1896 | Tilghman, Md. | John B. Harrison |
| *Upshur Q* | 7 | 6 | 38.5 | 13.8 | 3.0 | 1905 | Justisville, Va. | |

Sunk during Hurricane Hazel in 1954; refloated and still afloat in 1972.

| Boat Name | GT | NT | L | B | D | DB | Place Built | Builder |
|---|---|---|---|---|---|---|---|---|
| *Valkyrie* | 7 | | 39.0 | 13.7 | 3.0 | 1896 | Wittman, Md. | John H. Harrison |
| *Vera* | 7 | 5 | 38.5 | 13.1 | 3.1 | 1896 | St. Peters, Md. | |
| *Vera D* | 6 | 6 | 38.2 | 13.4 | 2.7 | 1897 | Hopewell, Md. | |
| *Vernon Daniel* | 23 | 18 | 56.2 | 18.4 | 4.8 | 1910 | Champ, Md. | |
| *Victor* | 9 | 7 | 46.0 | 15.0 | 3.0 | 1901 | Hopkins, Va. | |

Sold to Washington, North Carolina, between 1911 and 1928.

| Boat Name | GT | NT | L | B | D | DB | Place Built | Builder |
|---|---|---|---|---|---|---|---|---|
| *Viola* | 8 | 6 | 39.5 | 12.9 | 3.2 | 1900 | Broomes Island, Md. | |
| *Viola* | 5 | 5 | 36.5 | 12.2 | 2.7 | 1904 | Fairmount, Md. | |
| *Violet E* | 8 | | 39.4 | 13.4 | 3.1 | 1896 | Wittman, Md. | John T. Landon |
| *Violet W* | 5 | 5 | 37.0 | 11.8 | 2.6 | 1899 | Oriole, Md. | |
| *Virell* | 5 | 5 | 35.0 | 12.6 | 2.8 | 1898 | Oriole, Md. | |
| *Virgie* | 9 | 6 | 47.0 | 14.0 | 3.0 | 1899 | Pocomoke, Md. | |
| *Virgil G. Dean* | 6 | | 40.5 | 13.7 | 2.7 | 1897 | Bishops Head, Md. | |

Three-sail bateau; often misspelled *Virgie*; died in Chance before 1972.

| Boat Name | GT | NT | L | B | D | DB | Place Built | Builder |
|---|---|---|---|---|---|---|---|---|
| *Virginia* | 6 | | 36.3 | 13.9 | 2.2 | 1901 | Cambridge, Md. | Edward Pearson |
| *Virginia* | 10 | | 41.7 | 15.7 | 3.5 | 1901 | St.Michaels, Md. | Charles L. Tarr |

Square stern.

| Boat Name | GT | NT | L | B | D | DB | Place Built | Builder |
|---|---|---|---|---|---|---|---|---|
| *Virginia* | 6 | 6 | 39.0 | 13.2 | 2.7 | 1905 | Deep Creek, Va. | |
| *Virginia W* | 8 | | 44.0 | 14.4 | 3.7 | 1902 | Oriole, Md. | Harrison Lewis (?) |
| *Virginia W* | 5 | 5 | 37.5 | 13.5 | 3.3 | 1904 | Guilford, Va. | |
| *W. J. Bradshaw* | 7 | 7 | 39.0 | 13.0 | 3.5 | 1897 | Crisfield, Md. | |
| *W. O. Livingston* | 6 | 6 | 41.0 | 13.9 | 3.2 | 1898 | Deal Island, Md. | |
| *W. S. Schley* | 5 | 5 | 38.2 | 12.7 | 3.0 | 1898 | Capitola, Md. | |

| Boat Name | GT | NT | L | B | D | DB | Place Built | Builder |
|-----------|-----|-----|------|------|-----|------|-------------|---------|
| W. S. Schley | 7 | 6 | 45.0 | 14.0 | 3.0 | 1898 | Pocomoke, Md. | |
| *Perhaps built to carry freight.* | | | | | | | | |
| Wallace S | 6 | 6 | 39.0 | 11.7 | 2.6 | 1890 | Crisfield, Md. | |
| Walter A. Venable | 9 | 9 | 43.0 | 15.0 | 3.5 | 1897 | Harrison, Md. | |
| Walton L. Taylor | 12 | 8 | 55.0 | 16.0 | 3.0 | 1904 | Marsh Market, Va. | |
| *Dredged out of Crisfield in 1928.* | | | | | | | | |
| Wanda | 9 | | 43.8 | 15.2 | 3.6 | 1897 | Wittman, Md. | John T. Landon |
| Water Lily | 6 | 6 | 37.8 | 13.0 | 2.6 | 1897 | Saxis Island, Va. | |
| *Dredged out of Smith Island in 1928.* | | | | | | | | |
| Water Lily | 7 | | 38.8 | 14.7 | 3.1 | 1897 | Crapo, Md. | |
| *Crushed by ice at Tilghman Island, January 22, 1918.* | | | | | | | | |
| Wheatley | 7 | | 41.0 | 13.6 | 2.8 | 1900 | Hudson, Md. | Robert H. Thomas |
| Whites Yacht | 7 | | 40.5 | 13.2 | 3.4 | 1899 | Deal Island, Md. | |
| *Seen at Deal Island in 1936.* | | | | | | | | |
| Wilber | 5 | 5 | 38.0 | 12.4 | 2.9 | 1897 | Ewell, Md. | |
| Willard | 6 | | 36.0 | 12.9 | 2.8 | 1901 | Hudson, Md. | Robert H. Thomas |
| *Dimensions on Carpenter's Certificate: 38 × 13.5 × 3.5; square stern.* | | | | | | | | |
| William E. Earl | 5 | 5 | 37.2 | 13.4 | 2.6 | 1897 | Bishops Head, Md. | |
| William E. Parks | 6 | 6 | 36.6 | 14.0 | 3.5 | 1898 | Fairmount, Md. | |
| William F. King | 7 | 6 | 41.6 | 13.0 | 3.0 | 1902 | Hunting Creek, Va. | |
| William J | 5 | 5 | 40.5 | 12.8 | 3.0 | 1899 | Allen, Md. | |
| William J. Pell | 8 | 5 | 40.0 | 13.0 | 3.6 | 1909 | Crisfield, Md. | |
| William L. Webster | 6 | 6 | 41.5 | 13.4 | 3.0 | 1899 | Deal Island, Md. | |
| William McKinley | 5 | 5 | 35.6 | 12.2 | 2.6 | 1897 | Crisfield, Md. | |
| William R | 8 | 8 | 40.5 | 13.9 | 2.6 | 1896 | Cambridge, Md. | George E. Leach |
| *Dimensions on Carpenter's Certificate: 42 × 14.2 × 2.9; sold to Bridgeton, New Jersey, by 1911.* | | | | | | | | |
| William R | 7 | 7 | 39.5 | 15.0 | 3.0 | 1899 | Holland Island, Md. | |
| William S. White | 8 | | 42.5 | 14.8 | 3.4 | 1901 | Deal Island, Md. | |
| *Trailboards seen nailed on a barn in Leeburg, New Jersey, in 1951.* | | | | | | | | |
| Willie & Edward | 10 | 7 | 35.9 | 13.9 | 2.9 | 1898 | Hampton, Va. | |
| Willie L. Bennett | 8 | | 42.6 | 14.8 | 3.4 | 1899 | Inverness, Md. | John Branford |
| *Later trailboards printed as Wiley Bennett.* | | | | | | | | |
| Wilma A. Florence | 9 | 6 | 45.5 | 14.5 | 3.2 | 1900 | Dreka, Va. | |
| Wilma Lee | 20 | | 46.8 | 16.2 | 4.5 | 1940 | Wingate, Md. | Bronza Parks |
| *Owned and dredged by Captain Robbie Wilson in 1993; at one time the trailboards were accidentally printed Wilmer Lee.* | | | | | | | | |
| Wilmer T | 9 | 7 | 39.0 | 13.7 | 3.5 | 1901 | Kings Point, Va. | |
| Wilton V | 5 | 5 | 35.0 | 12.0 | 2.5 | 1896 | St. Peters, Md. | |
| Wm & Jessie | 6 | 6 | 40.2 | 14.5 | 2.8 | 1898 | Hopeside, Va. | |
| Yttria | 10 | 9 | 45.5 | 14.1 | 3.7 | 1883 | Tilghman, Md. | Joseph L. Harrison |
| *Schooner-rigged deadrise hull; believed to be the first deadrise, along with Lillie, built at the same time, to be used on a dredge boat; not found in the 1911 MVUS.* | | | | | | | | |
| Zella | 13 | 9 | 49.3 | 17.0 | 3.4 | 1908 | Deal Island, Md. | |
| Zola | 7 | 7 | 39.5 | 13.9 | 3.4 | 1899 | Fairmount, Md. | |

The hull of the *Ruby G. Ford,* considered the first skipjack built in Somerset County, rests in a marina at Tilghman Island.

# SOURCES

*"Yeah, I guess I enjoy it. I didn't think I'd ever say that. I worked on them so much when I was a kid, I swore when I got on my own I'd never work on one or own one because it was so much work."*
— Captain Russell Dize

THE FOLLOWING skipjack captains were interviewed between October 1991 and April 1993 to gather oral histories for this book: Delmus Benton, Walt Benton, Bunky Chance, Art Daniels, Stan Daniels, Russell Dize, Ed Farley, Francis Goddard, Darryl Larrimore, Stanley Larrimore, Bobby Marshall, Bart Murphy, Lawrence Murphy, Wade Murphy, Jr., Jack Parkinson, Pete Sweitzer, and Robbie Wilson.

Also interviewed were several retired or former dredge boat captains: Norman Benton, Ellis Berridge, Mervin Christy, Dan Dize, Clyde Evans, Paul Holland, Willie Middleton, Jesse Thomas, Wilson Todd, Eldon Willing, Jr., and Ralph Windsor.

Interviews were also conducted with individuals who had had some association with dredging, boat-building, or the oyster industry: Crisfield resident Edward Milbourne; waterman Buddy Jones; Charles "Chuck" Vane, Baltimore ship chandler; the late Elbert Gladden, Sr., owner of a fleet of skipjacks; Gordon Gladden; George Wheatley, survivor of the storm of 1939; Mrs. Esther Wallace; family members of retired Captain Stanford White; family members of the late Captain Edgar Bradshaw; Tom Daniels, boatbuilder; Jamie Burman and John Kellet, shipwrights with the Lady Maryland Foundation; Chris Judy, biologist with the Maryland Department of Natural Resources; and William Outten, program administrator, Maryland Department of Natural Resources, Shellfish Administration.

## BOOKS

Brewington, M.V. *Chesapeake Bay: A Pictorial Maritime History.* Cambridge, Md.: Cornell Maritime Press, 1953.

Chapelle, Howard I. *National Watercraft Collection.* United States National Museum Bulletin 219. Washington, D.C.: Smithsonian Institution, Government Printing Office, 1960.

————. *Notes on Chesapeake Bay Skipjacks.* St. Michaels, Md.: Chesapeake Bay Maritime Museum.

Dize, Frances. *Smith Island.* Centreville, Md.: Tidewater Publishers, 1990.

Evans, Ben. *Memories of Steamboats, Campmeetings, Skipjacks & Islands of the Chesapeake.* Princess Anne, Md.: Marylander & Herald, Inc., 1977.

Footner, Hulbert. *Rivers of the Eastern Shore.* New York: Farrar & Rinehart, 1944. Reprint. Centreville, Md.: Tidewater Publishers, 1964.

Peffer, Randall S. *Watermen.* Baltimore, Md.: The Johns Hopkins University Press, 1979.

Richardson, James B., with Robert C. Keith, editor. *The Jim Richardson Boat Book, From Interviews with the Late James B. Richardson.* Baltimore, Md.: Ocean World Publishing Co., Inc., 1985.

Tilp, Frederick. *Chesapeake Bay of Yore.* Alexandria, Va.: Chesapeake Bay Foundation, 1982.

Wennersten, John R. *The Oyster Wars of Chesapeake Bay.* Centreville, Md.: Tidewater Publishers, 1981.

Wilson, Woodrow T. *History of Crisfield and Surrounding Areas of Maryland's Eastern Shore.* Baltimore, Md.: Gateway Press, Inc., 1973.

## DOCUMENTS FROM THE FILES OF THE MARYLAND STATE ARCHIVES, ANNAPOLIS

Brooks, W.K., Associate in Biology, Johns Hopkins University. *The Development of the American Oyster,* for the Maryland Commission of Fisheries, 1879.

Dredging licenses: Dorchester County, Somerset County, Talbot County.

Goode, George Brown. *Report to the U.S. Congress on Oyster Industry on the Chesapeake Bay,* 1884.

Haman, B. Howard. *Report on Oyster Culture,* to the Board of Shellfish Commissioners, 1909.

Seth, Joseph B., Commander. *1891 Report of the Commander of Maryland State Fishery Force to the Board of Public Works,* made February 1, 1892.

*Shell Fish Commission Report:* 1907 and 1914-1915.

Timmons, William E., Commissioner of the Fishery Force of Maryland. *Report of the Oyster Fisheries of Maryland,* January 1, 1874.

## NEWSPAPER AND MAGAZINE ARTICLES

"Types of Bay Craft," *Baltimore Sun,* December 8, 1901.

"New Oyster Dredge," *Crisfield Times,* September 21, 1907.

"Favor Shelling Rocks," *Crisfield Times,* September 21, 1907.

"Warning to Oystermen," *Crisfield Times,* October 19, 1907.

"King Winter Still Reigns," *Crisfield Times,* February 3, 1912.

"Hollands Island Alright[*sic*]," *Crisfield Times,* February 10, 1912.

"A Splendid Proposition," *Crisfield Times,* February 10, 1912.

"Oyster Legislation," *Crisfield Times,* February 10, 1912.

"Severe Wind Storm," *Crisfield Times,* February 24, 1912.

"Think It Was Overdone," *Crisfield Times,* February 24, 1912.

"Hands and Feet Were Frozen, He Charges," *Crisfield Times,* February 3, 1917.

"Somerset Sailors Ice-Bound in Bay," *Crisfield Times,* February 3, 1917.

"Shipping Heavy Hit by Terrific Storm," *Crisfield Times,* February 10, 1917.

"Booze Ship Captain Dies of His Wounds," *Crisfield Times,* March 3, 1917.

"Zero Weather," *Star-Democrat,* January 5, 1918.

"Fuel Order Obeyed," *Star-Democrat,* January 19, 1918.

"Abandoned Light House," *Star-Democrat,* January 19, 1918.

"Terrific Wind Storm," *Star-Democrat,* January 19, 1918.

"Oxford," *Star-Democrat,* January 19, 1918.

"Dredgers Foodless & Fireless," *Star-Democrat,* January 26, 1918.

"Benoni Light May Go," *Star-Democrat,* January 26, 1918.

"Tilghman's Island Isolated," *Star-Democrat,* February 2, 1918.

"A Near Blizzard Comes," *Star-Democrat,* February 2, 1918.

"Trouble on River When Ice Moves," *Star-Democrat,* February 16, 1918.

"Benoni's Point Light Falls," *Star-Democrat,* February 23, 1918.

"Motor Boat Hauls Ice Away," *Star-Democrat,* February 23, 1918.

"Ice Floes Thirty Feet High," *Star-Democrat,* February 23, 1918.

"Crisfield and the Entire Eastern Shore Swept by Terrific Storm; Highest Tide in History," *Crisfield Times,* August 25, 1933.

"Estimates of Damage from Storm of Last Week Still Mounting," *Crisfield Times,* September 1, 1933.

"Special Session of State Legislature May Consider Opening the Potomac River," *Crisfield Times,* September 22, 1933.

"Sen. Coad Favors Use of Hand Dredges in the Potomac River," *Crisfield Times,* October 27, 1933.

"Meeting of Dredgers Held Saturday Night at Deals Island Hall," *Crisfield Times,* November 24, 1933.

"Prohibition Ended on Tuesday Evening," *Crisfield Times,* December 8, 1933.

"Bill to Open Potomac River to Hand Scraping Was Defeated Monday," *Crisfield Times,* December 15, 1933.

"Nine Drowned Here Yesterday," *Daily Banner,* February 4, 1939.

"Bodies of Eight Watermen Recovered over Week-End, Captain Bradford Missing," *Daily Banner,* February 6, 1939.

McNamara, Ivy B., "I Remember Dredging Oysters Through the Ice," *Baltimore Sun,* December 26, 1954.

"Boat Traffic Halted Several Days Because of Freeze-Up," *Crisfield Times,* January 16, 1970.

"Warmer Weather Expected to Break Ice-Jammed River, Sound," *Crisfield Times,* January 30, 1970.

Walls, Chuck, "Where Have All the Skipjacks Gone?" *Daily Banner,* November 11, 1970.

"Skipjack Capsizes near Bay Bridges Early Tuesday," *Star-Democrat,* December 8, 1976.

"Skipjack 'Claud W. Somers' Returned Home," *Daily Banner,* March 9, 1977.

Frye, John, "A New Skipjack Heads for Maryland's Oyster Grounds," *National Fisherman,* November 1979.

Jolechek, James, "No More Oysters for the 'Robert L.,'" *Baltimore Sun,* October 19, 1980.

Bowie, Liz, "Skipjacks May Not be Ready to Die Out Yet," *Star-Democrat,* January 16, 1981.

McMartin, Philip, "Baltimore Restores One Skipjack and Builds Another," *National Fisherman,* June 1981.

Evans, Ben, "Survivor Recalls Tragedy on Choptank River," *Daily Times,* July 4, 1982.

Steinberg, Martin, "Garvin Won't Sell to Just Anyone," *Star-Democrat,* October 5, 1983.

"New Grant Could Help Preserve Skipjack Fleet," *Star-Democrat,* July 29, 1988.

Ollove, Michael, "Skipjack Sigsbee Sinks in Bay Before Start of Race," *Baltimore Sun,* October 28, 1990.

Rawlings, Kristen, "Project to Save Skipjacks Planned," *Star-Democrat,* August 8, 1991.

"Skipjack 'Caleb Jones' Sinks in Kedges Straits," *Star-Democrat,* April 2, 1992.

*A special thanks to the individuals and groups listed below who assisted me in locating information.*

Pete Lesher, curator, Chesapeake Bay Maritime Museum

Dr. Mary Ellen Hayward, Maryland Historical Society

Talbot County Free Library, Maryland Room

Maryland State Archives

The Maryland Department of Natural Resources

# INDEX

Page numbers in italics indicate photographs.

# HULL PROFILE

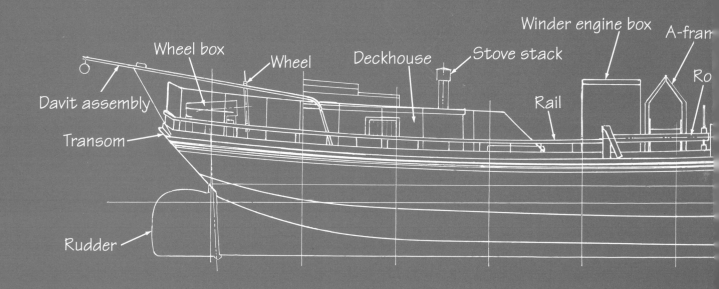

Davit assembly

Wheel box

Wheel

Deckhouse

Stove stack

Winder engine box

A-fram

Ro

Rail

Transom

Rudder

# PLAN VIEW

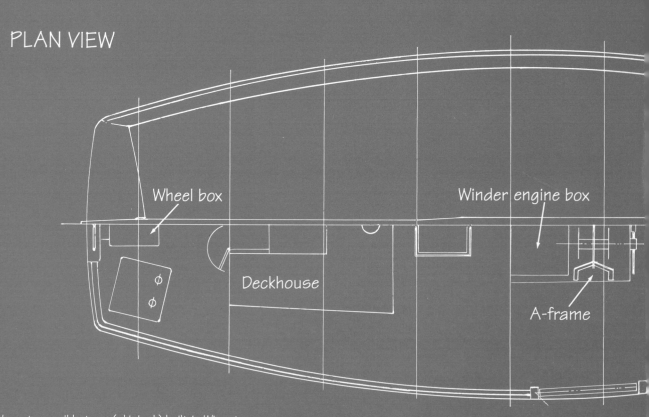

Wheel box

Winder engine box

Deckhouse

A-frame

φ
φ

Rosie Parks, a two-sail bateau (skipjack) built in Wingate,
Maryland, in 1955 by Bronza Parks. Drawing by Leavenworth
Holden based on an earlier drawing by J. G. Lord. (Courtesy
of Chesapeake Bay Maritime Museum)